Divine Fe[minine]

"With breathtaking scope and insight, Lee Irwin ... a powerful spiritual promise within humanity and the world, providing an inspirational roadmap into a positive future."

"In this sensitive, inspiring, and well-informed exploration of divine feminine gnosis, Lee Irwin weaves masculine logos with feminine eros and wisdom to offer us seven pathways to engage in a more Sophianic spirituality: embodied, relational, and relevant to today's changing world, where old paradigms, particularly around the patriarchal masculine, are crumbling. This book is a profound, illuminating, and soulful response to the call of our times. I wholeheartedly recommend it."

"Lee Irwin's brilliant book, *Divine Feminine Gnosis*, unveils a new understanding of Sophia—her wisdom and love—that guides us in our evolution through our lived experiences and intuitions and points the way to a transformed world where all of life is honored and partnerships in relationships of every kind are valued, whether between individuals, the Earth, or our sentient Cosmos and World Soul. His book is both timeless and timely, wisdom so needed now, as we make the journey of transformation."

"How are we to understand the mysterious figure of Sophia in terms of the present age? What is meant today by divine feminine gnosis? In this book, Lee Irwin provides very contemporary answers to these and related questions and reveals an emerging paradigm. Explore new terrains and perspectives—read *Divine Feminine Gnosis*!"

Divine Feminine Gnosis

THE LESSER AND GREATER MYSTERIES OF SOPHIA

Lee Irwin

INNER TRADITIONS
ROCHESTER, VERMONT

Inner Traditions
One Park Street
Rochester, Vermont 05767
www.InnerTraditions.com

Cataloging-in-Publication Data for this title is available from the Library of Congress

ISBN 979-8-88850-253-2 (print)
ISBN 979-8-88850-254-9 (ebook)

Printed and bound in the United States by Lake Book Manufacturing, LLC

10 9 8 7 6 5 4 3 2 1

Text design and layout by Kenleigh Manseau
This book was typeset in Garamond Premier Pro with Fang and Mrs Eaves XL Serif OT used as display typefaces.

To send correspondence to the author of this book, mail a first-class letter to the author c/o Inner Traditions, One Park Street, Rochester, VT 05767, and we will forward the communication, and we will forward the communication, or contact the author directly at **IrwinL@cofc.edu**.

Scan the QR code and save 25% at InnerTraditions.com. Browse over 2,000 titles on spirituality, the occult, ancient mysteries, new science, holistic health, and natural medicine.

Contents

Acknowledgments

This book could not have been written without the support of many women in my life to whom I am truly grateful. First and foremost I thank my wife, Catherine Evans, for her unfailing love, support, and encouragement. Our many conversations help me to clarify my thinking and to engender a lasting appreciation of feminine spirituality and the importance of animal rights. Our dialogues on dreams and the Infinite played an important role in the formation of my dream theories. I also thank my dear beloved sister Lynnea Stadelmann whose busy and dedicated life epitomizes feminine kindness and love; I thank my niece Liana Stadelmann for her brilliant, creative, playful art and her hard work in creating her own path. I also give thanks, with deep appreciation, to the following women: Carolyn Rivers (Sophia Institute), Susan McClure (psychotherapist), Jen Wright (scholar and feminist), Julie Spangler (mother and spiritual leader), Helena Daly (dream expert and psychic adept), Susan Hull (feminist spiritual guide), and Lauren (Chism) Schmidt and Cary Baldwin (inspiring friends and students). I also thank my mother, Jeanne Irwin, and my wife's mother, Anne Evans, whose enduring intelligence, fortitude, and courage taught me about elder wisdom. My many women students also inspired me to engage feminine spiritual as a core topic in teaching and created a lasting respect for the diversity and creativity of feminine thinking. I thank you all, with great warmth, appreciation, and respect!

Preface

A book on Divine Wisdom is a great challenge because the mysteries of wisdom cannot be fully contained in rational words and constructs. This is not because such revelations are ineffable or beyond words in an indescribable, mystical sense. It is because language and thought are inadequate vessels for the full disclosure of these mysteries. It is a profound paradox that these mysteries require words and yet cannot be fully explained by words. For many generations, for thousands of years, revelations of spirit have been epitomized in sacred texts and these texts have become a primary expression of social, spiritual, and ecclesiastical authority. Sacred texts, holy words that represent a medium of revelation from the highest sources of spiritual empowerment, usually received from a masculine God, have become the foundational base of many spiritual traditions. This valuation of sacred writings arises from a masculine attitude that wishes to reify these written texts as the ultimate expressions of truth and revelation. Thus, the "Word of God" has a special sacred authority in the minds of many men the world over, in the Jewish Tanakh, the Christian New Testament, the Holy Qur'an of Islam, also among the Parsees and Sikhs; many of these same reifying tendencies are also found in the Dharma Shāstras and Sūtras of

Hinduism, Buddhism, and Jainism. Far Eastern traditions demonstrate a similar pattern as in the Tao Tsang (Daozang), the collected writings of Daoism, or in the many Confucian and neo-Confucian texts as well as those of Japan (Shinto) and the many Asian Buddhist text traditions.

By *reify*, I refer to the tendency to treat the abstract ideas in these texts as if those ideas are real, material, actual, and unquestionably true expressions of what is and shall be. Often this reification is held with an inflexible commitment to the unchanging, absolute value of the texts, thus closing off dialogical or creative interpretations and often establishing norms for resistance to the formation of new, equally valid texts. It is also true that sacred texts clearly make claims that lend themselves to reification. However, it is usually the absolute nature of the claims within these texts that reinforces the masculine tendency. Not all members of a tradition regard these texts as unquestionably true and this is particularly relevant to a more feminine view of the sacred and its revelations. Revelation is not simply through words or through texts but is also more salient and knowable through direct perception and embodied, mature living. The basis of inspired teachings on Feminine Wisdom cannot be simply reduced to words, thoughts, and texts but more significantly such teachings arise from relationships, loving kindness, moral concerns, and heart-centered, relational values.

In the Western esoteric traditions, the ancient *hieros logos* or sacred teachings attributed to various teachers who articulated a valued way of life was not just through a text or *logion* ("saying") as much as through a quality of knowledge reflected in the daily life of the individual. There is, in fact, a Pythagorean logion concerning this view, "He best honors God who makes the intellect as like God as possible."[1] This kind of knowledge was honored, not simply as text or teaching, but as a special type of knowing (gnosis) whose contents were found in a living heart and mind deeply aligned with the sources of godliness and divinity. And now, in the present, that same possibility remains valid, to know and value in one's own heart-mind, the primary source of sacred perception. In our current era, this knowing is found in the text of a life lived with integrity and dedication to the forthcoming of Feminine Wisdom in the real lives of a multitude of women and men as vessels for that teaching. Surely we should honor the sacred teachings of these actual lives and listen with ears fully open to the diversity and breadth of their teachings. There is no one text or one teacher, no one path, but a multitude of paths, teachers, and voices seeking to articulate this wisdom, each struggling to be born in the receding tides of masculine monologue and didactic authority. Such wisdom requires a virtuous life and a compassionate attitude aligned with deep divinity, a caring kindness, an inner peace that is the true text, where the actualization of that text is the lived life of the embodied individual.

This does not mean that nothing can be written. Indeed, a host of women are engaged in the writing of books, the creation of art, the analysis of social transformation and, in expressive social gatherings, they seek to articulate Feminine Wisdom though direct participant knowing. It is clear that this knowledge is part of a global social process, based in communal efforts among women seeking to express not only a critique of masculine spirituality, but also to give form and content to new spiritualties more suited to a wide variety of feminine (and reformed masculine) perspectives. In this arising, diversity and inclusion hold greater significance than the older patriarchal values of exclusion and convergence. The social transformative basis of this development emphasizes the formation of communal networks and interlinked spiritual communities. It encourages diversity, pluralism, and differences as part of a larger, collective conversation whose subject is the exploration of possibilities in the context of a shared spiritual awakening.[2] In this context, spirituality is no longer controlled by men, nor by masculine institutions whose authority is questionable and often dogmatically assertive.

Such a global movement is certainly a threat to many men and, more particularly, to male-created institutions that claim the highest authority in all things spiritual and religious. The repression of feminine spirituality cannot and will not continue because this movement has tremendous significance for women of all races, nations, ethnicities, ages, and global locations. It is not based in a local political concern simply because women have been mistreated, controlled, or subordinated by men. It arises through a deep aspiration for spiritual identity, a need for a fully authentic expression of genuine spiritual empowerment and authentic creative freedom. And it is rising in the context of partnership, relatedness, community, and shared responsibilities, not through false characterizations of individual superiority or models of dominant control. In this process, Feminine Wisdom seeks to reveal through the social transformative process a new harmonization that does not exclude men nor male spirituality but offers partnership between equals as a lasting and sound basis for a healthy, integrated humanity.

I write this as a man who has spent many years in ongoing creative, exploratory dialogues with women of all ages. The primary consequence of these dialogues has been to foster mutual creative freedom and development, to encourage the exploration of new modes of spiritual expression, and to develop interactive awareness through self-reflection, dream interpretations, co-creative dialogues, and a sincere receptivity to a feminine point of view. Multiple artistic and nonverbal expressions of perception and feeling have resulted in the emergence of a rich cornucopia of possible forms of Feminine Wisdom. Through one-on-one meetings, group work, talks, enduring friendships, and a long successful marriage, I have come to appreciate, most deeply, the wisdom of women and their beauty of soul, heart, and spirit. In many ways, this book is a testimony to their wisdom and spiritual perseverance, their collective determination to articulate their own diverse views of wisdom, Sophia, as manifest in a lucid, personal spirituality open to all. My understanding of this global movement is as a man in the midst of loving women, particularly my wife and female friends and relatives, who have over the years taught me the value of listening, caring, and delving into the feminine mystery with respect and genuine appreciation. It is primarily through these relationships that my understanding of Feminine Wisdom has flourished and been nurtured.

As a lifelong teacher of comparative religions, I have had many inspiring female students whose efforts and enthusiasm have further heightened my appreciation for the multifold interests of women with regard to the sacredness of life, other people and cultures, and the personal transformative process. There are passionate desires in women to explore their inner spiritual potential in forms and manifestations that have yet to be fully revealed as spiritual traditions. The revelations of Feminine Wisdom are not directed toward the creation of spiritual pathways in the context of older, male-constructed spiritual traditions, but in the formation of new pathways and new attitudes of spiritual celebration. In this celebration, the central metaphor of *partnership* is crucial, not simply the male-female erotic partnership, but partnership in the broadest and most inclusive terms with a multitude of other beings—human, animal, plant, elemental, planetary consciousness, spirit relations, mystical harmony with transpersonal entities, imaginal relations with guides, teachers, masters, and Holy Spirituals. There is a vast network of relations between the living and those who have died, with invisible spirits, through the power of dreams, visions, and mystical connections, not only with the living but also with those who have been and passed beyond death or who may yet manifest and communicate.

My own encounter with Feminine Wisdom began many years ago in my mid-twenties through a series of mystical dreams and visionary encounters with feminine guiding spirits. Both feminine guides and Goddess imagery manifested in my life and have continued to appear over many years; what started over fifty years ago continues to this day. Manifestations of the Divine Feminine are not the only contexts of these soulful encounters, but there is a constant inner thematic series, dreams and visions, that has resonance with my lived relationships with embodied women and men disposed positively toward the Divine Feminine. The interplay of relatedness between living human relationships and a series of visionary and mystical encounters has led me to a synthesis of perception and knowledge as reflected in this work. The themes of this volume are centered on what I have called the Mysteries of the Sophianic Wisdom, mysteries that cannot be fully articulated nor recorded in words. I call them "mysteries" because they reflect into our lives a potential for growth and development whose realization must move beyond any text or written work, sacred or secular. A text is a call to action, a sketch of pathways whose walking requires much more than reading or thinking; the call to creative action and to contemplation is a personal challenge, there is no map that can take you there. Every book, however sacred, is only a collection of signs, a basis for development along the way, a possible useful set of guidelines, images, metaphors, values, and teachings whose wisdom must be found in the soul and heart of the reader, found and then personalized.

The mysteries of this work are as I see and know them, not as learned from others nor as a synthesis of study or scholarship, but as direct perception. These perceptions are informed through my relationships with many different women and by the visionary intuitions that have guided my development as a man. Perhaps the best way to think of this work is as an offering, a gift of spirit, respectfully given to the reader by a devotee of Sophia. My intention is to offer a perspective on sacred wisdom, its mysteries as I see them, in order to celebrate the forthcoming of a rich and complex spirituality whose diverse layers will be constructed by many women and partnered, receptive men. The inspiration for this work is, for me, symbolized by the figures of Isis-Sophia, goddesses of classical Mediterranean and Western esoteric traditions, both gnostic and Hermetic. Other feminine images are also resonant with this wisdom Goddess figure—the Regina Angelium or Queen of Angels, usually the Virgin Mary of Christianity; the Shekinah of Jewish Kabbalah; the Prajñāpāramitā or Tārā of Mahayana Buddhism; Quan Yin of Chinese and Japanese tradition; and the feminine "Earth Angel" of Persian Sufism.[3] Together, these and other feminine images reflect the many diverse sources of sacred Feminine Wisdom as it is constituted in the past. However, this is a work about the spirituality of Sophianic Wisdom in the present and future sense, not as images of the past and not as a subordinate image within patriarchal traditions, but as a vital, living presence now manifesting, like a rising full moon, through mysteries of Spirit.

While I do not discuss any specific religious tradition, my own approach is Hermetic, which is a perspective I see in many religious traditions. By *Hermetic* I refer to the "art of spiritual transformation" as a form of knowledge induced by visionary experiences. Most religious traditions have visionary aspects, mystical forms of soul illumination or altered states that result in new insights and knowledge (gnosis). In this work I will explore seven mysteries of gnosis associated with Feminine Wisdom, divided into "lesser" and "greater" mysteries. The lesser mysteries represent the incarnate state of body, soul, and mind, with reference to actual spiritual practices. The greater mysteries reference Hermetic wisdom teachings (Sophiana) of salvation, World Soul, sacred union, and rebirth. Each mystery is described from a contemporary perspective and interpreted in accord with dreams, visions, and reflections of the author.

In a more personal sense, this book is an exploration of perceptions and visionary knowledge as grounded in a developed spirituality centered on what I term *Praxis Sophiana* (the practice of wisdom) but also reaching beyond the veils of those perceptions, into a transfigured cosmos irreducible to a strictly gendered conception. The emphasis on Feminine Wisdom is a guiding motif within a larger musical composition, it sets the tone and stage for the whole musical performance and it comes and goes as a dramatic, recursive motif or theme. However, it is also only a theme within a greater Whole whose scope and content includes all possible genders, compositions, and musical possibilities. It is, nevertheless, a motif of our time, a dramatic, resonant melody whose harmonic signature is being written on the hearts of sensitive women and men as a call to action and spiritual practice. It is not a march, nor does it require a brass band; it is more like a haunting, soulful melody whispered softly in the wind, like an ecstatic breath taken in partnership with another's joy.

We must open our ears and our hearts to breathe in that inspiring melody, to embody its teachings in living human relations for the good of the whole. The Divine Feminine cannot be reduced to issues of gender or simply to "women's spirituality."* Wisdom spreads her wings to guide us on a soulful journey into

---

*For an overview of the Divine Feminine, see Rosemary Ruether, *Goddesses and the Divine Feminine: A Western Religious History*, Susanne Schaup, *Sophia: Aspects of the Divine Feminine Past and Present*, and Thomas Schipflinger, *Sophia-Maria: A Holistic Vision of Creation*.

the darkness and depth of soul's awakening, uniting the above and below, the female and the male, the inner and outer, the earth and the heaven. In the deep core, Wisdom is also transpersonal, beyond form, and holding within that formless potential all possible modalities of spiritual awakening. We are each called to find the path that best expresses our individual capacity and our shared efforts. Only in this way can revelations be fostered and realized as inseparable from a Living Cosmos, as Holy Mother Spirit of all life and awareness, even beyond gender and form. Blessed is that Presence, now and always!

The Feminine Eros

This is a book about wisdom. In it I discuss the cultivation of various practices that can help the reader to develop wisdom in both the theoretical and practice sense. But even more, this is a book about a spiritual revolution and a new cycle of wisdom in the current and future age as grounded in a deep alchemy of a united masculine-feminine trinity. A wisdom saying captures the tripart symbolism of this union: "Where two or three are gathered in my name, there am I in the midst of them" (Matt. 18:20). And what is the name in which we gather? Sophia, Wisdom, the living presence of spirit and life, the third aspect, bringing the gift of communion to those who gather in her name. This is a wisdom that is fully embodied in real human relations, in our relations to the natural world, to other species, to every creature of land and air and sea. It is also about our relationships with the subtle worlds, to the unseen sources of personal, communal, and world empowerment. This is a book about peace and understanding that cannot be contained as a particular system of thought or a rigid structure of ideas or beliefs. This living, subtle Wisdom, as a rebirth of ancient knowledge in contemporary forms, is an uncontainable ocean that cannot be captured by any one human perspective. The glass or cup of containment inevitably overflows, as it should. What is required is a willingness to surrender and to receive, in her name, the gift of inspiration, in partnership with those we love.

This Wisdom, this Sacred Name, this Mystery, is something much more than a concept or idea; it is about living Presence, the deep unitary field that gives coherence and form to each life and living thing. The archetype of this Wisdom is found in multiple goddess forms, in the Sophianic teachings of the Hermetic tradition, in the female-male mysteries of Demeter, Persephone, and Hades. The core archetype spans the bridge between the sacred directions of east, west, north, and south—from the primordial traditions of the East, China (Guanyin as a unitary symbol of male-female) and Japan (Amaterasu and Susanoto, brother-sister), to Egypt and the ancient Middle East (Isis and Osiris, Innana and Dimuzi, Ishtar and Marduk), to the northern Hyperborean traditions of the Nordic and Celtic traditions (Freya and Freyr, Cerridwen and Cernunnos), south to India (Brahma and Sarasvati, Ram and Sita), in Tibetan Buddhism (Jestsun Dolma and Phagme Nyingthig), and in Euro-American West, Sophia and Christ. As a partnered archetype, it is a relational Wisdom, reflecting an intimacy of connection and mutual care. However, these ancient archetypes are not the concern of this work, though I certainly honor them all. What I am offering is not a historical account of traditional relations and influences but a synthesis of how these great archetypal forms have become distilled into the alchemical forms of contemporary spiritual world awakening. In spirit, I honor these ancient archetypes as partnered birth mothers of an ongoing, emergent spirituality.

Today, we stand on the threshold of a transformation that will encompass many generations to come; we hold the possibility of a global consciousness, an awakening to World Soul, that cannot be contained in any particular or explicit image. Like the ocean poured into a cup, the potential for spiritual transformation overflows the limited context of individual conceptualization. We cannot contain the ocean; rather, we must learn the art of merging, of complete saturation and interpenetration, for rebirth as partnered individuals and as diverse collectives that allow for the rediscovery of our hidden potentials. This is a Wisdom process; it is not an explicit teaching, not a framework that wants to contain the possibilities of Wisdom's self-awakening but an *invitation*, a call for *partnership* and *participatory embodiment*, a solicitation for commitment to creative discovery. This call, a call of the heart, of the soul, of the deep desire for meaning and fulfillment, comes not from the mind or emotions, but from inner beingness, from the deepest elements of our aspiration to become, to self-surpass, to go beyond the limits of the known into the unknown, into Wisdom that reveals, uncovers, and makes whole the fractured hearts of our shared humanity.

We are not complete because we have not yet reached the state of inner balance where we can abandon our desire for explicit meanings in order to receive a deeper guidance that does not serve our personal longings for immediate insight or social recognition. What we seek, in terms of Wisdom's gift, is a new attitude toward knowledge. We are challenged to give up our assessment that knowledge is quantifiable, that learning it is a matter of absorbing, assimilating, integrating the many facts, data streams, and possibilities of information. We are asked to take on a new reticence, a genuine humility in the face of possible learning, that accepts limitation and yet accepts the responsibility of staying open to what may become in order to discover new beingness, a realness that cannot be predicted or predetermined. Wisdom, in this sense, is revelatory and spontaneous, an overflowing creativity, a metaphysics of discovery, not a known content, not a plan, a prediction, a cosmic event, or a marked threshold—it is much more than any of these. Such Wisdom, as a forthcoming of the alchemical union, is a *philosophia*, a "shared loving wisdom" that reveals the possible in the creative context of the actual, that shapes our intentions into a leading point; such Wisdom must be trusted, accepted, embodied, and lived to become real.

Wisdom does not abandon her children but nourishes them to grow beyond adolescence and immaturity into a grounded, centered way of life that fully honors the Wisdom teachings of others and that recognizes the many forms and possibilities of Wisdom. The individual challenge is to embody Wisdom as a way of life that is whole and loving, healthy and heart-centered, stable and yet creative. If we debate with one another to sharpen our understanding, to find the limits of our own commitments, to seek insights that are self-surpassing, then we serve Wisdom well. But when we attempt to impose, deny, castigate, and belittle others because they do not think as we think, nor act as we might act, then we rend the fabric of Wisdom's veil, a veil that should not be lifted but revered.

The face of unknown Wisdom is hidden by the veil, in the depths of an infinite potential that no series of images can exhaust; yet, the face of Wisdom is our own face, the face of a beloved other, a child, an animal, a friend. Every face is a face of Wisdom that beckons us to recognize that hidden face, the veiled potential, the face infused by Wisdom in each person, often hidden beneath pain, sorrow, and regret. What Wisdom encourages in us is something more than tolerance or patience; our task is to make peace, all the way down to the roots, to disentangle the origins of bias, hatred, racism, bigotry, arrogance, and violent actions meant to oppress, terrify, and control the lives of others. We are called to this task of disentanglement first within our own lives, then with family and friends, with community and motivated others, then with those willing to listen and to act; to model within the emerging World Soul a truly liberated, luminous face.

The *practice* of Wisdom is not easy, but not impossible either; it is within reach of every person who can find a way to live that does not impose on others a controlling or blind will, however well-intentioned. Practice is born out of discovery, not through the mere repetition of form, but out of a living intensity of insights that leads to reformation and reconstruction. For this Wisdom to be sustained, it must find roots, clear and disentangled, in the soil of each place, in the world, in the human heart, in a lived context of trust and collaboration. The embodiment of Wisdom is inseparable from the health and well-being of the world, from the preservation of species, lands, climates, ecological zones, and the full honoring of diversity and difference that does no harm. Wisdom begins where you are right now—your home, family, friends, work or local environment—and it grows where you plant your roots, in the things you cultivate as prime importance. The fruit of Wisdom is not forbidden, it is a free and accessible knowledge, but it has roots and a reach that far exceeds any one vision.

Wisdom is not a single tree but a world of trees in every variety; it is the shape of every unique leaf, the smell of a specific place, locale, or habitat. It produces every good fruit, extracting from the soil just those elements necessary for true ripening. And the light that brings this ripening shines on all trees and all souls, on the inscribed leaf where a sacred Name is written that is engraved on the heart as an indication of its call. To know this inscribed Name, to taste its sweetness, to bathe in the purity of its celestial emanations, is to discover Wisdom—and it is found through practice, discipline, and inner purification. The Name calls us, can we hear its song and feel the rhythm of its repetition? Can we embody its potential in real action?

Wisdom is a source of beauty and love—not a pale detached love, but a passionate Eros, a deep longing of soul for ecstasy, a poetic desire for song, dance, music, ritual, and art. Overflowing Wisdom, though uncontainable, is rendered visible through forms, ideas, institutions, and the architecture of constructive imagination, through visionary knowledge crafted into harmonies of form and feeling. Just as there is no one standard for beauty, there is no one perfection or ideal Wisdom, but a multitude of ideals, forms, varieties, and expressions. Like the flowers of the field, they do not contend but harmonize—each in its own place and in its own time. As the path of Wisdom is a winding way, straight but then curved, flat but then hilly, mountainous and then a valley fed by mountain water, so too the practice of Wisdom is not a single discipline, but a series of diverse pearls on a unitary strand; the strand is world peace, shared harmony, mature caring relations that do not result in conflict or violence.

The very heart of the discipline is to find the way to no contestation and with skilled abilities, to demonstrate the varieties of possible technique, practices, forms, and inspired expressions that do no harm. Not to contest, but to overcome the desire for contestation, not to dominate but to co-participate, not to shun, but to gather together in circles of peace for the well-being of each person. This book teaches an ethic of world and community cooperation and respect for differences that promotes reconciliation, forgiveness, and honorable behavior. Wisdom is a constant play of interactions that require the greatest discernment to find a response that best illumines the hidden potential of a given relationship. We may disagree, debate, or argue, but the passion that feeds our differences is one of reconciliation, partnership, and a need for greater maturity.

Holding to Wisdom means holding to inspiration in the heat of the struggle, to not despair but to repair, to not deny but to try another way, to find alternatives, new avenues of the possible, new horizons of the unseen. The praxis (practice) is in every moment, not bracketed to a special time or place; it is where you are, who you are with, in the present moment, now, because Wisdom is always active, always pressing us to acknowledge the possible reconciliation or recovery of meaning. Where is the place that Wisdom cannot enter? What are the circumstances where Wisdom is banished? Only where ignorance and torment dominate, only in the shadows where violence or aggression has become an addiction and lies a method of concealment is Wisdom unseen. Even so, Wisdom is there, hidden, triple veiled, gazing with sorrow-filled eyes at the self-betrayal of our human dignity.

Sometimes, in blind places, great courage is called for, an enactment or expression that holds the place of Wisdom as a sign of what cannot be violated or abandoned. Sometimes there is suffering and oppression, the twin brothers of dominance, and sometimes there is horror and predation. Sometimes there is illness and loss of ability, but these challenges do not erase Wisdom, they only offer an opportunity to stand firm in the face of social and personal illness as an example of dignity and grounded faith. A world in need of Wisdom reflects the very illness that must be healed and the brokenness that needs mending. Thus, no matter what the situation, we are challenged to find Wisdom and to apply it as best we can. Wisdom calls us now, today, to initiate a process of peaceful developmental change.

Wisdom requires education. We live in a complex world of multiple pathways, conflicting values, radically uneven wealth and poverty, illegal trafficking, abuse, addiction, excess and extremes of pleasure and want, need and desperation. Alienation, confusion, fear, and anxiety are common while patterns of dominance maintain their self-assigned, mostly male-created assertion of old values that do not recognize equality, partnership, or difference. To overcome the fractured nature of outmoded human relations, of imbalance between species and the natural world, requires deep commitment to education and the reformation of central values. Wisdom is found in the application of authentic education, in the assimilation of principles and values that shape mind, heart, and soul. The soul must learn, not simply exist, but develop and mature.

Education is a universal right, a primary expression of Wisdom, and all individuals should have the opportunity to learn to the highest degree their true capacities. But this means developing educational processes that are not coercive or corrupted by superficiality, shallow training, or dogmatic, ideological discrimination. It means developing a balanced, individualized, noncorporate process of education that serves to inspire and guide without imposition or autocracy. It means cultivating an education of mind and heart that is intimately related and inseparable from feelings, aesthetics, imagination, and creative approaches to learning. This book is also about education, laying out basic principles to guide a reformed and revitalized educational process. Education is a virtue if in the learning process we can distill the dross and impurities that attach to biased views and opinions. Sophia teaches discernment, clarity of thought, and self-analysis supported by intuitive insights, not just facts or data. Education requires spiritual commitment to continued, ongoing refinement.

Wisdom brings us full circle to face the challenge of our gender differences without regressing to an artificial and false idea of differences. Gender orientation is diverse and nuanced according to personal predisposition, the dialectic of male-female identity cannot be defined through the physical aspects of body but develops through alternative pathways to find a wide range of expressions and relations. What matters is not the orientation, but the values and care that is embodied in loving, nonmanipulative, respectful relations with others. Wisdom incorporates all orientations into the field of possible embodiments that do no harm, that seek expression through love and permissive relations between consenting adults. Wisdom is the guardian of all children and children are inviolable, sacred, and their sexuality must be guarded and protected against all predation and unhealthy attack. Wisdom teaches us to treat children with utmost respect, fostering in every way healthy, positive development and growth to full maturity.

The profound illness that results in child predation and abuse is one of the great illnesses of humanity; this illness must be healed universally for humanity to be able to reach its full potential. If we do not nurture every child, if we do not protect them from harm and injury in every way, then we are all stunted and impaired. Our children are a most precious gift, their happiness and health are an index of our maturity, their well-being a sign of our collective Wisdom. If we as a species wish to be whole and radiant, then children must be nurtured, educated, and protected; our task is to offer our children the utmost care and opportunity, worldwide, for health and maturity. Children need respect, love, and support without overburdening expectation, encouragement without denial, and hope that is not oppressed by bias or false truths.

And women must also be fully honored in every culture and given opportunity for full equality in all fields of human endeavor. This is not a matter of cultural differences, but of core values at the very heart of Wisdom. All women, regardless of cultural context or old values of abuse, marginalization, or repressive dominance, are the carriers of Wisdom and her children. The honoring of women is a mandate for world peace and cooperation because it is through women that we will establish a reformed and healthy world. Not women alone but in partnership with mature men who fully honor and recognize the differences and the values that women bring to our collective rebirth and integration. Only when we can create a world that fully honors the life-bearing, creative, inspirational, and loving heart of woman in creative relation with those she loves, her intimate friends and community, through her leadership, articulate analysis, and clarity of purpose will we begin to discover a more balanced world. This book is about Wisdom under the sign of the feminine because Sophia, as Wisdom, emerges from the recognition of the feminine heart as a loving, inclusive, healing presence. Through partnership, through balanced relationships, and male-female harmony, Wisdom grows, matures toward a full co-creative union. Wisdom is the third presence, dawning as the luminous aura of conjoined souls, sanctifying through grace and abundance, creative discovery and practical application.

This is a book about you and me. In your reading, you enter into a relationship with me as author, as a voice whose words seek to touch the place of Wisdom by giving Wisdom a place to emerge. And this emergence is between us, between writer and reader, in a context of sharing. Not always agreeing, but in a respectful way, considering, reflecting on possible truths wrapped in words, images, metaphors, and poetic expressions that seek to inspire. I cannot say that what I write is necessarily true for you the reader; but I can say that what I write is deeply true for me the writer. What I offer here is a distillation, an inscription written on the mirror of conscience, on the soft tissue of the heart and mind, in a partnership of the moment. Together we can take a journey toward Wisdom as she calls us, each in our own way, to be in relation through her as the third presence that offers insights through our creative relationship.

What I suggest to the reader is that what dawns through this work is not simply the sharing of ideas or thoughts, but the creation of a context for revelation. This revelation is not simply through the writer or the reader, but it is a dawning where sparks that fly from stone and striker ignite a fire, a warmth, a light given and sustained by inner Wisdom. Wisdom is the mother of revelation, the ecstatic bride, the sober wife, the strict parent, and the kind healer that gives us her presence in all our relations. She is present in this work because she is gracious and kind, able to give guidance and direction, because I fully honor her revelations. And that is what she asks of the reader, to honor the insights that come beyond the written words, the illuminations that spark your own creative growth, as self-surpassing discoveries leading to rebirth and reformulations. That transformation comes, as it must, through Wisdom and her gifts, beyond words, as instilled in the loving, receptive heart.

Finally, I am writing this work as a man and have a male perspective on the subject of wisdom based directly upon my experience of the Sophianic call. As "an apostle of wisdom" I find that the primal expression of that call is to protect and nurture life and, in particular, to recognize and support the creative union of feminine and masculine values and perspectives. Overall, my views on wisdom are based on a constant awareness of the value and worth of feminine perspectives as voicing primary values related to all areas of life and epitomized in intersubjective relations. There is a strong *eros* in my view of Feminine Wisdom, a sense of the presence of the body, of the sensual life, of the felt, lived, touched, and enacted vibrancy of a full celebration of our physical, emotional, and psychic beingness. The deep-down eros is found in soul that animates the body without creating any division or separation, that embraces the sensory, emotional, felt world, the passionately lived world, the visionary thought-world, in a soulful, unitary, centered way. Soulful eros is, for me, an expression of Spirit as an activating Wisdom, the deepest of all animate principles, an illuminating primal source forming a shared ground of feeling and participatory partnership. We cannot be whole without a full acknowledgment and realization of an integral harmony between masculine and feminine forms of wisdom.

Thus, my perspective in this work reflects many years of interactions with women and men, all as seekers of wisdom and all committed in various ways to the realization of latent potential. The curve or arc of wisdom gracefully expresses a nonlinear, adaptive response grounded in real circumstances, felt needs, and intuitions that manifest value affirmations in the support of life and the health of others. Such wisdom is embodied, not transcendental, deep-rooted in the earth in order to support a "tree of life" whose fruit will be sweet to the generations of the future. It is not based on a critique of any lack of wisdom, of insufficiency or malpractice that limits moral responsibilities. Rather, my goal is to offer inspirational reflections on a valued way of life whose activities support multiple paths of wisdom, diverse manifestations, even crazy wisdom that results in profound insights for the support and nurture of others.

There are many ways and modes of expression, many voices, poems, songs, dances, philosophies, or signs and symbols, all reflecting a glint of wisdom's light when seen with a clear eye. Thus, the wisdom I seek to express is shared, communal, co-gendered and finite, relative, and non-absolute. I seek openness not closure, dialogue not monologue, and community not isolation. The eros of this wisdom is meant to communicate inspiration and joy, a felt sense of presence, a comingling of essences for the purpose of creating life through partnership. Together we can discover wisdom and together we can refine it and make it a light for the guidance of others. Let us dance and sing together, to sit in prayer, and to embody in our way of life a Mystery whose contents continue to overflow even the worthiest vessel. May it be so!

PART ONE

The Lesser Mysteries

Praxis

Why do I call this section "The Lesser Mysteries"? I want to distinguish between what I consider immediate and accessible from what I experience as more difficult and demanding. That does not mean that Lesser Mysteries are easy! A spiritual path to be efficacious must challenge us to move beyond, on a regular basis, our current state of attainment. I see the spiritual path as a spiral, not a straight line, as an undulating and expanding circle of ups and downs that can lead, in a moment of inattention, to forgetfulness or distraction, to poor choices or habituated actions not supportive of our spiritual goals. As a spiral, the path leads to a return, to a series of recursive moments in which we visit yet again issues, concerns, or relationships already reflected and acted upon. Like a dream interpreted, then revisited and reinterpreted, like a new insight emerging out old ground, left fallow but still fertile, the spiritual path requires us to turn over the earth of our soulful life again and again, refreshing and reanimating our deeper capacities.

In the "lesser" sense, this refers to daily life, to spiritual praxis meant to enhance and deepen our work, our personal interactions, and the fulfillment of responsibilities in a responsible way. Nevertheless, these are still mysteries in the sense that they cannot be defined and strictly codified in language; they resist complete articulation and even in the most artistic and poetic forms of expression, they remain partially concealed. This is because Sophianic Wisdom is more inclusive than the limitations of language and resists contraction into the false concreteness that language always implies. To write about lesser or greater mysteries is a form of metaphor expressing a view that spiritual praxis is something more than what the words *lesser* or *greater* imply. Praxis in this sense is a process of discovery as well as patterns of actions and inner deliberations.

Specifically in part 1, I want to bring attention to body, mind, and soul—three unfathomable aspects of human experience, none of which can be fully described or defined through language. And yet, every person has some intuitions about the meaning of each, not based simply on reading or analysis, but based on lived experience whose modalities of expression and awareness are embodied, mental, emotional, and spiritual. What makes this section lesser is that it takes less discernment to recognize the importance of the spiritual aspects described; this does not imply that these aspects are any less significant than what I describe as greater mysteries. There is however an assumption in structuring the text this way as it implies a progression or series of steps that descend into the less tangible, less explicit, and more hidden aspects of Wisdom. What is greater is also lesser; that is, the greater is more encompassing and less directly observable, more complete but less recognizable in a common sense. The spiritual path, as I understand it, requires constant application of principles, a refinement of perceptions, a series of openings to the greater complexity of the transphysical domains expressed by human encounter and discovery.

Perhaps some readers will imagine, and a great deal of spirituality is imaginal, that Wisdom should be made plain and simple, immediately definite, explicit, and easily recognized judgments as to the quality and worth of one's practices. This desire for concreteness, for rule-bound explicit values and well-defined fixed principles issued in an authoritarian manner is not well suited to the direct experience of Sophianic Wisdom. The Lesser Mysteries are quite real, vividly actual, but not amenable to reduction through a defining logos; the map is not the territory, the territory is knowable only through living a creative life dedicated to finding those principles whose expressions are not simply fixed or formulaic. The power of the Word, the masculine desire for concise definition, must be subordinated to deeper impulses of Being that seek to express experiences that shape body, mind, and soul beyond the full reach of language. Like an arrow flying toward the target, the concern is to hit the mark, not to extol the virtues of the arrow. Like the arrows of Eros, when shot into the heart, they are meant to arouse the desire for love, passion, union, ecstasy, and transformation; it is not the words, but the target they aim at that matters. The Lesser Mysteries refer to immediate aspects that each hold their own kind of Wisdom and language that must point beyond itself to that content.

Even so, such description is an unveiling, a modest uncovering of inner depths whose reach extends into the unfathomable; this requires reverence and purity of mind, humility and caution. The question arises as to the appropriate state of receptivity for the reader. For the writer, the action of writing is a spiritual practice, and I hope that for the reader, reading is also a spiritual practice. In what sense then would reading be a spiritual practice? In part that depends on the stance of the author. My stance is not to persuade or convince the reader of the value of the work, I leave that assessment to the reader; my goal is to unveil, open a vista, share an intuition for the purpose of stimulating spiritual insights. What I write is true for me, an offering of reflections written in the quiet of my home, often in deep silence, and arising spontaneously through the practice of meditative reflection. My meditation practice is based on a lifetime of participation in inner reflections, stillness, one-pointed concentration, regular meditation, prayer, and the contemplation of perceptions arising from the depths of heart and mind through intentionally shaped desire. What is the core of that desire? The core is a search for gnosis or spiritual insight concerning the meaning, value, and purpose of human life and coexistence.

To read this work as a spiritual practice would mean to read with receptivity and genuine curiosity, to read without subjecting each line and phrase to judgment, to subdue critical attitudes and to take on an attitude of respect and appreciation. The reader may or may not agree or may find some agreement and sympathy and, in other parts, find less agreement; what matters is not agreement or disagreement, what matters is learning to listen and to read with respect. It seems so basic. If I were a real person in your presence, I would hope for a respectful, sensitive exchange, one that encouraged discovery and growth and avoided egoistic, conflictual affirmations or denials. When I read, I always read respectfully, even when I disagree with an authorial point of view, I still learn from and value our differences.

Reading in such a way is a Sophianic praxis, a wisdom practice meant to inspire learning and to correct educational values that place far too much emphasis on critical thinking and an aggressive attitude toward the text. Think of the text as a person because the text is an expression of personhood. Do you honor persons, even when they express views with which you disagree? The primary distinction is between the person and the idea or belief; I can honor the person even if I disagree with the idea or belief. Why? Because the Sophianic practice is to recognize the primacy of *personhood*, of embodied life, and the value that every person offers to the whole, consciously or not. To honor personhood when you read this text is to respect the effort and dedication shared as an expression of a sincere desire to communicate, even if you disagree with some ideas or beliefs. What matters is cultivating a practice that honors the other and your own worth as a responsive agent of Wisdom, as a seeker who understands the limits of words and individual ideas.

It is useful to consider four aspects of reading that apply to the study of heart-centered works offered as spiritual reflections. First to read with a *receptive attitude* that allows the reader to assimilate the description and analysis offered as an actual worldview held by another, as I describe in the previous paragraph. Second, it is necessary to read with *imagination and empathy* that allows the reader to enter into and participate to some degree with the author's thought-world regardless of the reader's own beliefs or values.

A third aspect of reading is to develop insight into the *foundational structures* that underlie the more descriptive account of the narrative. Whatever the actual states are that lead to a description of an encounter or interaction that is deeply affecting, the question, the inquiry, is to ask what psychic conditions support such an encounter or experience. This is not a matter of prejudging experience based on the reader's own values and views but seeking to better understand the written experience as given in a valid, meaningful worldview, however different or distant the author's view may be from the lived-world of the reader. The underlying structures or conditions that support a variety of participatory encounters cannot be reduced to beliefs or ideas; they reflect instead particular expressions of psychic sensitivity that may not be familiar to the reader.

A person who does not have a well-developed musical ability may not hear the musical structure, the key, the mode, the motifs that are evident in the experience of listening for a more musically aware individual. I am not speaking of quotidian experience but of refined sensibilities and a wide range of perceptions. The reader is under no compulsion to agree with the interpretation, or the consequences, drawn from the description, but a fair reading proceeds with the acknowledgment that the description, values, and beliefs arise from genuine perceptions and are not simply imagined or speculative.

The fourth aspect is to consider in what ways the *individual account* is relevant for others, to what degree it offers insights that apply more generally to those claiming to have similar or related experiences, including dream experiences.* I suggest this writing on Wisdom has significant correlation with others with a broad range of psychic and spiritual perceptions shared by those attuned to a diversity of spiritual experiences.

The Lesser Mysteries arise through perceptual encounter and participation in sensitive states of awareness that foster a more refined consciousness receptive to a wide range of phenomenal states often ignored or denied by less sensitive others. Some persons are simply born more sensitive; women in particular seem to have greater sensitivity in these areas than men, possibly due to cultural circumstances and the widespread denial by men of the value and worth of feminine sensitivities. And yet all human beings have these capacities, and we are in the process of a developmental shift toward increased psychospiritual awareness insofar as it is not repressed and denied by ideological attitudes closed to the value of such perception. These Mysteries can be described and written about, but no particular account can actually detail and fully express the entirety of the range of such sensibilities.

In part this is because such sensibility is changing, developing, expanding; simultaneously and ironically, such capacities have been more active in other cultures and historical periods where such sensitivity was highly valued, though inevitably embedded in a traditionalized patriarchal worldview. Part of the process of our mutual becoming is the liberation of psychic sensibility from dependence upon an authoritative framework that shapes such sensibilities into a more conservative and constricted belief system. I would not deny that such a shaping has its value or purpose, but I would challenge the belief that such sensibilities cannot evolve beyond a dependent collusion with traditional beliefs. Thus, Sophianic Wisdom,

*See Giovanni Stanghellini, "Clinical Phenomenology: A Method for Care?" for an interesting overview of co-participant reading and analysis.

as I understand its manifestations, is not reducible to any particular spiritual worldview, nor to any specific metatheory of mental development.

In many ways, there is no closure on Wisdom. Wisdom is not a content nor a system of beliefs; it is not reducible to an explicit set of maxims nor aligned with explicit states of mind. Wisdom is a free-flowing, spontaneous intuition that cuts through the morass of beliefs and mental fixations and gives birth to creative, generative patterns of meaning. Sometimes very specific and precise and at other times broad and inclusive. Wisdom is contextual and transcendent; it is fully present both within and beyond the rational boundary. Thus, a Wisdom text, in the most authentic sense, can have no closure and can never be complete or final. All such writings tend toward the aphoristic, the epitome, the brief summary that tags the burst of insight with a verbal marker but cannot exhaust its content in a thousand words of explanation. Such Wisdom is truly transverbal and its purpose is not to create a map but to open a page whose diagrams are saturated with visible ink holding a promise—a territory waiting exploration and discovery beyond drawings, words, and maps.

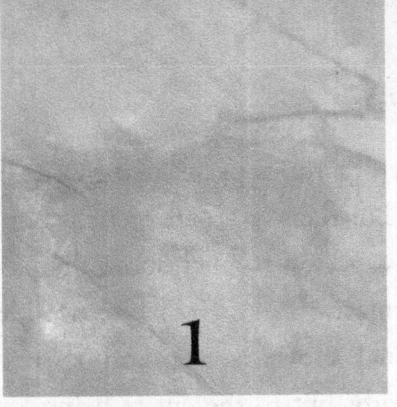

1

Praxis of Incarnation

BODY

The Sophiana approach to the first of the Lesser Mysteries is in and through the body, through incarnation. By *incarnation*, I mean the direct sensory experience of physical life, having and being a body. The complex relationship of body, soul, and mind is only partially unveiled by naming these three aspects. The most obvious and immediate aspect is our material, energetic, neural-chemical, animate, vital physicality, which is not reducible to an exclusively material form. We are not simply physical, and such a description misses the key point that our organic beingness is a complex of features, not a singular form and not simply material. As a complex of features, our incarnational, embodied qualities range from bone, muscle, and organs to nerves, chemistry, and electro-neural phenomena, which remarkably supports a field of feelings and consciousness whose identity is a subtle, immaterial feature of the embodied personhood. The mystery of the body is it complexity and its energetic, subtle nature; the organic is permeated by the energetic as well as by self-awareness, but the psycho-energetic is not well understood.*

In this sense, a person is much more than a body even though the body is a normative means by which we identify and locate a particular individual. However, the term *incarnation* does not simply refer to the body, but to the entire being and all of one's relations in a direct genetic, genomic sense as well as in a historically embodied social sense. We all have parents, ancestors, relatives, partners, relations, and intimate interactions with other similarly embodied beings. We are all part of a dynamic, energetic network of relations, embodied through family, friends, work, play, or by other circumstances in which we must constantly negotiate our identity as more-than-physical beings. Our embodiment is a shared social and cultural phenomena, however central or marginal an individual, we all participate in the social worlds of our heritage and existential circumstance.

Our physical, genetic heritage reflects a broad range of possible influences as seen in our appearance, bodily characteristics, ethnic inheritance, family resemblances, cultural location, and historical conditions. More profoundly, we are bodied by gender—male and female, though our sexual partnerships may be varied and diversely practiced. Gender is no small issue, and in terms of the Sophiana praxis, the feminine reflects a primordial, deep-rooted, core identity through the archetypal birth-mother paradigm of guardian, caretaker, teacher, and preserver of life. There is a primacy inherent in the female body that arises from the birthing ground and grows into a fertile garden of nurturing possibilities. This is the first of the Lesser Mysteries, the capacity to bear life, nurture another in

---

*On the energetic body, see Beverly Rubik, David Muehsam, Richard Hammerschlag, and Shamini Jain, "Biofield Science and Healing: History, Terminology, and Concepts."

the womb, and to give birth to a unique, sentient being. Because it is discernible and immediate, I call it "lesser" but in itself, it is profound, deep, miraculous, and the greatest blessing in the creative forthcoming of the cosmos. The origin of this capacity, its formative cause, reflects the Greater Mysteries, the very forthcoming of the universe, the cosmos itself as born out of a feminine nurturing process producing life, sentience, and new beings.

To use the term *incarnate* is to suggest a verb, not simply a noun, a spiritual *process* by which something comes into being, is born, grows to maturity, and attains a lifetime of experiential awareness.* As an incarnate being, I sense directly Sophianic qualities of my forthcoming, the inflow of Wisdom into my awareness as a maturing individual whose values reflect that Wisdom. We become what we contemplate; we are our thoughts and beliefs, if those thoughts and beliefs are fully embodied and valued as real, if they are enacted. To incarnate means to *embody and enact*, to commit to a set of values, goals, or ideals whose manifestations require a full dedication and a continual actualization, with inevitable self-correction, to better embody those ideals. Sophianic Wisdom is an enacted Wisdom, not an abstract idea or a mere belief or set of precepts, but an embodied attempt to fully live the values espoused. And this enactment requires a full recognition of the body as the means by which we actualize our inner beingness. Sophianic Wisdom is not world denying, not simply intellectual or overly rationalized, not detached or indifferent to suffering, not removed from the embodied world of others but deeply involved with all life, to preserve, enhance, foster, and animate fully interactive and cooperative relations between all sentient beings. The Wisdom of incarnation is not directed to some final end or world-transcending culmination, but to an ongoing, enduring,

---

*For more on incarnational spirituality, see David Spangler, *Introduction to Incarnational Spirituality*.

lasting world community of diverse beings whose values support life in a deeply multigenerational sense, as a long-term, enduring cycle of responsible relations.

By praxis of incarnation, I mean working with and through the body as a primary expression of Wisdom, not through body only, but also through the subtle relations of body-structured feelings, perceptions, sensitivities, and an interactive awareness of others fostered by a receptive heart and mind. The praxis of incarnation requires a commitment to self-development that encompasses the body as a primal ground for the cultivation of spiritual insight. The harmony of our many aspects requires a faithful appreciation of sensibilities; I see, feel, sense, engage, intuit, and react through body, through a felt sense of immediate perception and response. I trust this embodied response but know that I can improve, enhance, and extend my relations and like an athlete in training, I can develop an even more exquisite basis of perception by fully honoring and attending to, caring for, my embedded bodily processes. The body is a medium of spiritual development, not a mere physical organism.

But not body alone, as I am not only body; my mental and emotional life also require training and actualization, not simply as a given, but as a foreground for development. The full range of our self-capacities requires a mediated attention to all modes of perception and action, not simply thought or conception, but also doing and responding, feeling and sharing feelings. As a being-in-process, our cycles of development reflect a commitment to Wisdom, to become more aware, more spiritually educated, more responsible, and more refined in perception. Wisdom, as our metaphorical mentor, wants us to climb high enough on the hillside of embodiment to see a more expansive horizon than just the body alone. And there are mountains and valleys to explore and much greater vistas to know if we can train and prepare for the journey, find the inner discipline for scaling heights and descending into depths.

THE BODY AS TEMPLE

A good place to start our journey is to re-cognize, that is to rethink, the very nature of the body, its immediacy and natural-ness. The body is not a machine, that very masculine metaphor is completely inappropriate to describe what a body is. The heart is not a pump. We are nothing like machines nor is mind like some form of electronic, computational database. The body is a miracle and failing to realize this simple, obvious fact reveals the limitations of the material medical model. The body, as an expres-sion of nature—as an aesthetic form of organic life embedded in an ecological context—is a creation of great beauty and incred-ible complexity, supporting a wide array of perceptual capacities. The Sophianic view of the body is best expressed in the metaphor "body as temple" in which there is a sacred vitality, fully honored and revered, if very subtle, and best recognized through the felt life of the body itself. The mystery of the body is its sacredness, its ability to sustain awareness and feelings of connection through intimate intuitive perceptions. The beauty of the body, its primal eros, is not simply reducible to a sexual perspective, though sex-uality is certainly a core feature of our embodied existence. The eros of body is a set of aesthetic qualities that includes much more than the visible features of the physical body. The Sophianic eros manifests as inner vitality, a radiance whose aura and energies surround and penetrate the body to give it luster and a felt sense of life-presence. Without such presence, the body dies and while organically whole and complete, body's death is the very lack, the absence, of this vital presence.

This vital principle, taking many forms and diverse expressions, shaped by health, mood, attitudes, and a soulful embrace of embodied life, is a measure of our well-being. When this vitality shines forth, as luminous presence, then we can see how body is a medium for spiritual manifestations. Think of the body as held and animated by the subtle field of the soul, that is, body in the soul, not soul in the body. The animate field that holds the body is an index of the health and well-being of the physical media; if the soul is vital, alive, animate in a deeply lived sense, then the body also flourishes and is sustained in harmony and balance. By *soul* I mean the life principle, the animate (soulful) presence that acquires full conjunction and integration with the physical medium, through stages of maturation, from the molecular, pre-cellular level to the whole, integral organic structure of the person. The Sophianic view of body as temple means that every molecule of the temple is alive, therefore energetic, vital, all the way down into the vibrant submolecular base where cosmological principles form and unform continuously through arcane cycles of creation, destruction, and recreation. The identity of the being is not simply physical or psychic, but an integral field in which body-mind-spirit all play crucial formative roles.

We are complex beings, neither completely physical nor completely psychic or immaterial. Thus, my concept of soul is based on a theory of complexity; the soul is not one thing and the body another thing; I do not see the relationship as a form of dualism, nor even mediated dualism. The body is the ground that makes manifestations of soul possible; the soul is the ground that makes an animate body actual. The core reality is the body-mind-soul unity, as an intimately interpenetrated complex of features themselves inseparable from a cosmological truth: we are each a miracle, a cosmos in miniature, an image of the whole. This Hermetic, Sophianic teaching is fundamental; not that we are each all that is, but that we are each a particular manifestation of a vast potential made actual. As an image of the cosmos, we each reflect a larger cosmological process by which life comes into form, and further, by which life as conscious entity chooses development and a path expressive of our actual, even if latent, potential. From a process point of view, we are each an assembly of "actual occasions" of creative possibility through the layered conjunctions of large-scale cosmological interactions and small-scale individual choices.* Feminine Wisdom teaches us to honor and revere the body, all the way to its most invisible aspects.

This incarnational process is multigenerational, long-term, over eons of recursive embodiment. We have all lived through these cycles, forgotten our cyclical past, and become childlike in assuming a limited horizon of immediacy and physicality as a substitute for a more complex, ancestral, multi-life view. It is the cycles of nature that are our true measure and source, not simply human accomplishments or historical memories. There is a vaster process in which we all participate, the realization of what I term the evolving *World Soul*: a consciousness that incorporates every limited human awareness into the cosmological wholeness of conjoined actual occasions on a global scale. Our embodied life is an intimate part of that process as agents of instrumental transformation, inseparable from the life of every other being on the planet, visible or invisible.

The metaphor of body as temple finds its resonance with the creation of a sacred world, not one stripped, mined, desecrated, or plundered for human consumption, but a world in which the temple of the body is an image of the temple of the world. This revered, vast planetary home in which we dwell is also our body; if the world-body is not healthy, how can I as an embodied individual be

---

*For more on "actual occasions," see Alfred Whitehead, *Process and Reality*, 18; for an accessible overview, see Paul Stenner "A.N. Whitehead and Subjectivity."

healthy? Further, the reverence for body as a Wisdom teaching must include a deep reverence for the world-body, for terra firma, for all embodied creatures, each of which is a sacred participant in the creation and maintenance of an enduring World Soul. The continuity between the individual, the natural world, and the global community, with all its many diverse ecologies, reflects a context for shared spiritual enaction.

To leave a small footprint, to not mar or undermine the intrinsic beauty and wholeness of our planetary home is a Sophianic call, to be mature participants in the preservation and nurturance of all life, every ecology, and fully appreciative of the incredible miracle of a living world. To destroy the world is to destroy our own souls; to desecrate the body of the Earth is harmful to every living body. The body as temple includes in every way the temple of our planetary home; the very word *home* calls us to enactment—Healing Of My Environment—the necessary Sophianic action directed to preserve and not pervert the formation of a wholesome world. To honor our home is to honor the means by which we know the world, through embodied, embedded, extended, and enacted knowing; we are each a part, an image, of the whole and only by honoring the whole can we fully honor our embodied condition.*

The energetic radiance of the body, illumined by soulful response and disciplined living, expresses another intrinsic feature of relatedness, the qualitative expression of deep care and concern for the harmony of relations between all embodied species. It is not just a human world, but a world whose fullness and value lies in the multitude of species, types, kinds, of earth and sky and sea, all of whom contribute to the richness and value of our shared home. Every animal, every plant, every species contributes to the richness

---

*For more on embodied, embedded, and enacted cognition, see Albert Newen and Leon De Bruin, *The Oxford Handbook of 4E Cognitions*.

of the whole, regardless of its effect on human beings. Every species is a measure, every creature an example. Humans alone are not
the measure of what is worthy or valuable; we are only one species
among many. If we have the wisdom to recognize our place as co-
participants in a larger, more complex interactive and global field
of ongoing transformations, then we can take responsibility for
the preservation of species as an act of reverence for life. To live
in the world as a temple means to remove our shoes, to tread carefully, avoiding harm to others and cultivating Feminine Wisdom
practices that preserve life. This requires good health, good diet,
proper foods, not addicted to the death of creatures simply from
habitual taste or to satisfy a selfish appetite. The Wisdom of the
body requires a healthy self-conscious selection of proper food that
is not centered on the consumption of animal flesh. The Sophianic
teaching is that what you eat is what you become, what you consume
is transformed into your psycho-mental field, and the healthier the
food, the healthier the mind and heart of the consumer.

This is a matter of choice, of metabolism, genetics, bodily states
and conditions; each must choose according to needs, but those
needs should be assessed in terms of the impact of dietary choices.
By impact I mean the full range of what we support in terms of
what we eat; in eating we contribute to production, what we consume creates a market and that market dominates what it produces.
The quality of planetary life is directly impacted by the production
and marketing of food, clothing, of any animal product that requires
a life to make. Can we learn to live cooperatively, not through dominance but through reverence for life? A harmony of relations means
a select process of consumption, the lowest impact for the greatest
health. It means a dedicated practice that seeks to maximize health
and well-being, bodily grace and radiance, through select choices
that minimize harm. This is a matter of both moral conscience and

bodily temperament, of disciplined Sophianic selection and qualitative need, of overcoming learned habits and acquiring new attitudes. These are the principles of good diet, good health, and nonviolence for a vital, energetic body; it is the responsibility of the individual to make the appropriate choices. I have been a vegetarian for over forty years and my wife is a vegan.

The body ages, grows older, reaches maturity and passes into the later stages of life as a consequence of a certain way of living, thinking, and acting. Sophianic Wisdom teaches reverence for elders, an appreciation of the aged or infirm, of those less able to care for themselves. It is our responsibility to care for the elderly or infirm and to encourage a maturing population to seek a creative way of life that continues the process of maturation to the very doorway of death. There is no retirement from Wisdom, one only chooses to grow and to develop, or to decline as an expression of diminishing bodily functions. The body as temple certainly includes the body of the elderly, the body no longer fully vital as in youth and middle age, the body as a natural agent of change toward inevitable death. Death, however, is not the issue; the primary concern is to maintain a quality of life worthy of one's deepest potential, not through lonely self-indulgence but through a dedicated practice to persevere and to continue the art of inspired living. As elders, we should embrace the call to maturity. What kind of society can really develop if its elder members lack Wisdom, have no real insights, and remain self-centered and less adult as they age? The Sophianic call is for maturity in all stages of life, for responsible living as embodied beings, to work for the good of others, even in our oldest age.

If the body is a temple, then to what divinity might that temple be dedicated? I would suggest that it is like a temple dedicated to Hestia, the ancient Greek Goddess of health, home, and proper domestic relations. Associated with the temple at Delphi, with its oracular function, this Goddess represents a hearth-centered home whose central fire is a pure, bright flame of warmth, comfort, inspiration, and family gathering. There were also strong associations of honored Greek women (*Hestia poleos*) with Hestia who represented the highest ideals of successful domestic life.[1] When proper relations are established, when peace and respect prevail, and each person has a voice and contribution to make, then the Goddess of the hearth center is also present. The Sophianic principle is that the home is also a temple, a place of rest, renewal, creative work, feminine presence, and shared partnership in which each person has an opportunity to develop their unique gifts and abilities.

If these words connect, make an impression, contribute to the well-being of a reader, then Sophia is with us both, animating our relations, broadening the network of psychic connections, and opening the way for Wisdom. Of all sacred places, the home is one of the most intimate and personal, the private reservoir of dreaming, the oracular seat of inspiration, and the contemplative source of body's rest and recovery. The temple of the I Am is the temple of the home, shrouded in the Mystery of our collective aspirations and a collective desire for health and well-being. We each need our home, a place of retreat and renewal, and every path of Wisdom requires a temple where we can recover, rediscover, and regenerate the necessary vitality for the continuing renewal of our shared work. The body is where I dwell, my home is the place of body's rest, and the world is my arena of work, and when I look out beyond the horizon I see very clearly, a vast trans-solar and supracelestial domain, all part of nature in the most expansive sense. Health and well-being grow from the stability of home, the comfort of being in a place that is safe, creative, and alive.

PASSION AS SACRED EROS

Sexuality is a topic of central concern within the context of Sophianic Wisdom because it is the very basis through which life engenders more life. The body is a gendered media, purposefully formed to procreate, to give and receive seed and to womb a life into psychophysical being. The act of procreation is pleasurable, joyful, ecstatic because the creation of life is a spiritual activity. What is more sacred than the creation of life? This calling of soul into embodiment is a primordial, recurrent theme central to the reality of our living, planetary home. We live and have our being because we procreate; the Sophianic teaching is that sexuality is a sacred act, not only for the creation of life but for the communion of souls. Sexual relations as heart-centered praxis begin with reverence for body as temple, appreciation for the miracle and mystery of the body that moves through the rites of communion to reach the joys and pleasures that body can offer. But it is not only body, it is even more: hearts, minds, and souls that mingle in the fluids of passion for the purpose of union.

More than bodies intersecting, it is minds and hearts that meet and merge; sexual union as a meeting of equals, as a partnership, as a play of consciousness mediated through intense sensations meant to facilitate soulful awareness. And this awareness, this heightened state of soulful body-mind, propelled by sensations and deeper opening, leads to a threshold that maximizes soul-related states beyond the bodily condition. Sexual ecstasy is a deep mystery because it reveals the possibilities of union through pleasure and deep communion, it is Being-With in a profound sense when permeated with love and care for the other, when the third presence is active. Sexual union is a sacred opening, often masked by physical desires that never reach the true eros of soulful union.

The body is a medium of consciousness, this is fundamental; the core aspect of bodily life is its capacity to sustain awareness, conscience, a luminous sense of receptivity to multiple domains and states of perception. And reverent sexuality is a profound expressive activity that heightens and expands this awareness, leading in certain instances to true transpersonal perceptions and a unique transphysical condition open to a deep, interactive spiritual domain. The Sophianic teaching is that the body is an instrument of ecstasy, played by touch and caress, by warmth and care, to create a shared music of soul. This interactive play, intimate and arousing, is a stimulus in which eye and hand, lips and tongue, become the media for communicating love, connectivity; where a desire for shared experience is best realized through respect, sensitivity, and mutual interplay. Of all areas of human experience, this is certainly one in which the adage, "do no harm," is most appropriate.

Whatever the mutual play may be, the ethics of sexual love are based in the very inmost core of feminine values that propagate and protect life. Therefore, the spiritual practice of sexuality recognizes the primal sacred nature of our gendered differences and seeks to promote vitality and well-being in a context of pleasure. The ethic is clear: do not violate, force, harm, or in any way seek to dominate or to require the selfish satisfaction of only one partner. Sexuality is a mutual activity and only those relations that fully support the integrity, worth, and beauty of each partner, honoring the pleasures and fulfillment of both, reflect a Sophianic relation. Love is a form of partnership and sex without love cannot attain the fullness that love promotes.

The basis of sexual love is expressed in bodily passions. And passion is intrinsic to our human nature, an index of our ability to feel, sense, and resonate with others. Passion is a natural expression of vitality, life-force, animate interaction and relations that evoke emotional and felt conditions and moods reflecting our state of being in a moment-by-moment sense. When we direct those passions toward a creative, revelatory state, we open to a profound condition whose mystical depths are intimated in moments of soulful connection. There is a depth or fullness in sexuality that can lead to psychic transformation; sexual ecstasy can be transpersonal and transcendent in the more intimate moments of union. The fusion of soul with soul and heart with heart, body with body, and mind with mind, is a reality of deep sexual love; when this union is fully effected, it leads beyond body and into a vaster horizon of shared perceptions, a soulful opening to Being and Spirit.* For me the greatest blessing of sexuality is a celebration of partnership, co-union with one I love, a deep sharing; if on occasion this also leads to a more transpersonal horizon of awareness, I regard it as a blessing, a special gift that is not the goal, only an affirmation of a shared depth.

Bodily passions express various moods and attitudes, they reflect physical, emotional, and mental states and can arise unexpectedly when circumstances catalyze a response. Moods are conditional, not so much steady states as responsive reactions expressive of the deeper ocean of embodied being. A *mood* is not an expression of the full self, but a manifestation of an aspect or relative state that swells up in our struggles for coherence and meaningfulness. Our conditional being, our momentary status, is constantly mediated by mood, emotion, reaction, and states of mind that reflect our adaptation to the world in a present moment. I do not recommend living without passion or mood; the Sophianic teaching is to live passionately with concern and dedication to ideals that best promote harmony and

---

*Jenny Wade's *Transcendent Sex: When Lovemaking Opens the Veil* gives a good overview of the sacred nature of sexuality in the American context.

balance. Mood is not the core of beingness; however, it is a conditional body state that reflects our existential circumstance, a psychonoetic shaping of reaction and perception, not enduring but not inauthentic either.

Moods are relative to our deeper desires and needs, they disclose being, reveal the actualizations or frustrations of our intentions. Being aware of moods and what they reveal through bodily (as well as mental and emotional) states is a Sophianic praxis, our moods reveal in bodily conditions our state of relatedness to our lived-world.* Thus, cultivating moods that sustain, uphold, and creatively support primary values is a crucial spiritual practice and the accommodation of mood, as a revelatory, existential ground, requires us to shape intentions in response to moods, even when the mood is negative. Mood is primary, not secondary or merely psychic, an authentic source of response to lived conditions; moods manifest more primary responses, an immediacy that reveals our existential state. This changing conditionality, expressing our situated relations, informs our thoughts and self-awareness. Thus, working with mood creatively is a matter of attending to what arises even before thinking occurs.[2]

Sexuality has its moods, many diverse states and conditions that can impede or enhance sexual intimacy. Being "in the mood" is a statement of an existential condition, a willingness to engage or to wait, a sense of acclimation that requires sympathy in shared moods. Being in the mood for love and lovemaking is not always a spontaneous state but one that might require cultivation under circumstances that seek to enhance and attune moods to a more intimate interaction. This is not simply a matter of passion or feeling but more, in a feminine sense, an inner affirmation of receptivity to a penetrating

---

*See Matthew Ratcliffe, "Heidegger's Attunement and the Neuropsychology of Emotion," for a review of mood and its impact on the neurology of emotions.

intimacy whose effects can shake the soul and arouse deep feelings of connection. The violation of such intimacy through aggressive assault or overbearing domination is a mark of the contracted soul, one unwilling to acknowledge the negative impact of such assault. Male sexual predation is a form of deep social illness and mental disequilibrium, an aggressive impulse unmediated by patriarchal values that sees no wrong in such aggression. From the Sophianic perspective, the mood must be shared, equally respectful, and mediated by a feminine tempo congruent with shared desires.

Our passions are moderated by circumstances and should reflect our core values; we need to embody what we most value in terms of states and feelings. This requires a high degree of self-awareness, other-awareness, and world-awareness; all three are necessary for genuine balance. By self-awareness I mean a direct perception of my current state, my mood, in a moment-by-moment sense, not falling into unconscious reactions, blind mental habits, unconscious social behaviors, or emotional reactions predicated on former conditions. Being *present to yourself* means knowing your own strengths and weaknesses, your skills and lack thereof, your limits and your potential. No one is perfect, even spiritual teachers have their limitations and flaws.

I try to live as a seeker after Wisdom, and honoring her gifts, I receive guidance because I have learned how to listen, to receive, to hear the voices of others and find what I lack. Sophia does not teach perfection, but growth and development, relative maturity rather than ideal abstractions or ultimate ends. The conditional self reflects being-in-process, neither as a degraded ego nor as a perfect soul, but as a being *medias res*, in the midst of action, seeking greater development and mastery without seeking a false ideal or an absolute end. This requires humility and the recognition of limits; it means accepting the fact of *not knowing* even while seeking to know and feel more.* This means mediating personal needs and desires in relationship to the needs of others; it means moods are conditional, and self-knowledge can shape the quality and import of our moods.

The passion for self-knowledge is reflected through our knowledge of others; the belief that one can know self without also genuinely knowing others will result in a truncated view of what self is and can be. Self-knowledge proceeds through our relationships with others, through intimacy and sharing; only when we are confronted by our differences can we begin to see the limitations of a single point of view. Our passions are mediated collectively, not simply as felt responses to the world but as also shaped by the beliefs and attitudes of family, friends, relations, lovers, and those who might contest our values and feelings. The self-other relationship is a ground of primal education for the soul, the interactive field through which we discover our own worth or lack thereof. And this ground is often contested, an interactive field whose participants have many different points of views, and therefore, significantly, different passions or different investments of emotion in issues that might be quite unlike my own. Self-knowledge is linked to self-other relations in a very intimate way and the degree to which we allow others to enter into relation, our willingness to communicate, share, express empathy, even identify with the feelings and beliefs of others, is an index of Sophianic Wisdom.

Are we seeking a communal ground for belief, a community of like-minded others that requires a significant degree of passionate commitment, a shared eros that might override our own more intrinsic perspective? The mediation of our differences is a crucial aspect of our self-development and has an ethic of humility and relatedness that teaches respect, a willingness to listen, and to have

*For more on the conditional nature of self-awareness, see Lee Irwin, *The Labyrinths of Love: On Psyche, Soul, and Self.*

a realistic assessment of how these differences may impact others. In this sense, our passions and shared love should be mediated by the values we hold in terms of promoting or confronting the beliefs of others. There is a fundamental distinction between *integrity*, that is honorable commitment to a core set of values, and *respect* for the beliefs of others—both are important. Confrontation enters where harm or criticism of others is based on self-centered attitudes and moods that demonstrate commitment for only the preservation of a particular ideal, regardless of the beliefs of others or the harm such an ideal may cause. Sophianic love is flexible, receptive, and has integrity; it is based on a respectful caring for the well-being of others, not based on simple assent or desires, but on interactive dialogue, hearing the other, and listening with ears (and mind) open.

In turn, this leads to world awareness as it shapes our passions. There are numerous ideological platforms passionately and even violently promoted in the world—be they religious, scientific, political, sexual, or economic. The passionate avowal of any one of these ideologies, promoted by often dogmatic, male-centered, aggressive attitudes reflecting intolerance and self-aggrandizement, are not a basis of Wisdom. Sexual predation is not an acceptable form of behavior in the Sophianic context; what matters is a respectful honoring of the feminine above other desires that would seek to control the feminine. The development of world awareness is not a matter of conversion to a dominant ideology, but a realization of the creative ground by which diversity and differences can serve to create a more abundant, complex global field, a developing World Soul of diverse resources and capacities.

The process is not a dynamic of convergence to any particular (patriarchal) world order but much more a matter of differentiation, an emergence of complexity based on a shared ethics of respect and nondominance. This differentiation has an ethical base, one whose primary concern is the preservation of life and its flourishing in a world of peaceful, respectful coexistence—this will come, it is not an unrealizable ideal, but an emergent fact whose expressions can imbue our present choices. What must die is old-order thinking, passion invested in dominance, control, and rational objectivism. What must be born, and reborn, is the desire, the passion for a just, balanced, shared world of differences, plural views, and diverse concerns—dedicated to doing no harm through creative mediation. Sexuality becomes in this context a sign of maturity when there is no violence, no oppression, and no denying the value of intimacy as a means of deeper love and understanding.

Our passions can lead us toward balance and harmony, at the level of our personal and sexual relations, as well as our familial, communal, national, and global interactions. The guiding Sophianic ethic is based on the practice of care, concern, and genuine respect for others, at every level of coexistence—physical, sexual, emotional, mental, and spiritual—as well as fostering intimacy that supports a greater, more coherent field of creative relations. This ethic of respect and care is about nurturing development in both personal and communal actualizations without requiring conformity to any one ideological view. There is a difference between *guiding principles* and communal *ideology*; the first is about basic guidelines that require each individual to find the appropriate means for the application of those principles, including diverse interpretations of those same principles. Ideology refers to doctrines of universal application or systemic, putative descriptions meant to articulate an authoritative formation of social, religious, or political views usually requiring conformity on a collective scale.

Sophianic Wisdom, as I understand it, manifests through the articulation of guiding *principles* whose praxis and embodiment have many diverse applications. The goal is to provide a principled inquiry into the deeper mysteries of Wisdom without dogmatizing the application of those principles. The purpose and intention of correct principles is to provide a context for the development of Wisdom that is genuine, deep, and heartfelt. This Wisdom is passionate, erotic, and it comes forth through a desire for insight and community, not through conformity but through respect and a celebration of our shared diversities. What evolves through intimate sexual relations can grow into a deeper maturity that includes passion but also flourishes into a deeper understanding of the other, in respect and appreciation for all our moods and states. Sexuality is a metonym for human development, an intimate penetration of heart, mind, and womb, for the seeding of new understanding based on an ethos of shared respect, love, and collective care.

THOUGHT AS EMBODIED LOGOS

All our thinking is embodied thought, we think with and in relationship to our brain, our bodily emotions, our sensory perceptions, our passions and desires, and objectivity is a chimera of an elegantly displaced physicality. The claim that a masculine detachment from body and feeling is a superior basis for foundational thinking (rationalism) is not a viable theory for a fully embodied Sophianic existence. Embodied life is complex, layered, processual, developmental in bodily stages, and rational thought is only one index of our passionate commitments to certain beliefs and methodologies of inquiry. We are thinking beings, and we need to think clearly and meaningfully about the world, its operative processes and our relationship to those processes. However, there is a heart-centered way to engage in thinking that acknowledges our moods, feelings, and emotional states, our imaginings and envisioning of possibilities, as formative and foundational to our thinking processes.

There is no one methodology that best expresses the form that such thinking should take in understanding more thoroughly the intersubjective world in which we dwell and have our shared being. The Sophianic perspective honors intuitive insight as much as rational deliberations, poetic language as much as descriptive science, visionary art as much as technical blueprints. The approach to thinking as revelatory and ethically formative is not based in any one mode (or mood) of thought; thinking as mental activity is not fully separable from dreaming, inspired aspirations, or poetic exclamation. We become what we think and need to recognize the formative power of thought; we need to think creatively with variation in our methods and practices. Thought is multifocal, it has many centers and no one synthesis, it is a *process* and not a content; intuitive knowing is often spontaneous and syncretic, not simply rational.

A heart-centered process of thought is embodied and embedded; it requires a direct sense of the felt and lived-world, a sensory awareness of how circumstances, conditions, or influences can impact mental responses. As an embodied mind, embedded in a cultural context, as illustrated in the layered nature of our thinking organs, I do not have a single cognitive response to the world, but a many-layered structure of concomitant and linked, polycentric processes, all of which contribute to responsive mental activities. Whether it be hormones, bodily sensations, sensory stimulations, emotional reactions or moods, collective influences, social context, intuitive insights, or empathic feelings, cognitive activities are a synthesis whose processes are often subliminal, an undercurrent or assemblage of influences often noted only in a vague sense.

The conscious mind is not the index for assessing the full range of cognitive influences on mental processes. This is even more true of the heart-mind whose influence and impact on thinking has a very subtle and significant emotional impact on our entire bodily field and simultaneously on those with whom we interact.* These energetic aspects, whose subliminal influences can be directly observed through meditative training and a deep clarity of mind, genuinely impinge upon formative mental activities but in a subtle, less volitional sense. Our states and moods reflect our beingness, our purposeful conscious attitudes, our social context, and our subliminal, psychophysical condition. It is a complete artifice to imagine that consciousness, or being conscious, is all that matters and that rational thought is a superior function. The Sophianic perspective values all the layers, all the input, the subtle, the less conscious, the subconscious, the psychic, intuitive, the hyperconscious, and inspirational as all contributing to our shared knowing.

Thought, in the immediate conscious sense, is an outcome of an emphasis, a predisposition toward a particular form of praxis whose rational constructions are only one mode, a learned activity heavily imbedded in specific "language games" and methodologies. These games and methods reflect a historical, developmental process of maturation expressed through a specific kind of thinking and speaking (scientific, objective, aesthetic, literary, and so on) and they have appropriate applications and outcomes.[3] However, the practice of Sophianic Wisdom requires a different kind of thinking, a more heart-centered and body-based mediation whose contents are fully coherent and meaningful but whose method is more contemplative, intuitive, self-reflective, and empathic than a strictly rational, analytic, or science approach. Further, Sophianic

---

*For more on the heart-brain relationship, see McCraty Rollin, Mike Atkinson, Dana Tomasino, and Raymond Trevor Bradley, "The Coherent Heart, Heart–Brain Interactions, Psychophysiological Coherence, and the Emergence of System-Wide Order."

self-awareness takes an attitude toward process that includes the subliminal, dreaming, imagination, spontaneous imagery, and a holistic view of the embodied psyche. What matters is not only words or language, but also intuitions that strike the body-heart with a sense of connection and validation without offering a full disclosure of its possible rational or lingual constructions. And at times, this intuitive sense of rightness arises in a transrational mode whose expression may be more poetic and imagistic, more felt and energetically known, than as an explicit verbal idea or verbal thought.

Such intuitions may be processed and expressed in multiple ways, artistically, symbolically, or rationally and all of these modes have unique consequential outcomes. The voice of Wisdom can sing many songs, craft an artifact, or create a mathematical formula, and the source of this inspiration arises through complex knowing, a synthesis whose full integration is a bodily function that mind must learn to trust. The harmonization of body-mind-soul requires that body not be secondary to mind, that body have a central place in the processes of thought, that bodily response is trustworthy, valid, and naturally coherent based on tens of thousands of years of development, evolution, and ecological relatedness. The Sophianic phrase is "I think because I am embodied; body is my base, my teacher, my medium of knowing." This does not mean there is no Wisdom outside the body, there is, vastly so, but as incarnate beings we know this Wisdom through body, through memory, and through an imaginal sense of place and time.

I know myself through my embeddedness in a way of life, extended through all my relations, my home and family, through friends and colleagues, through a dedication to enacted and extended study, research, and constant engagement with the hearts and minds of others. I am a being in relation to others, not simply a reflection of collective beliefs or patterns, but a unique individual among other equally differentiated individuals in search of our common ground, our shared potential to create a world worthy of inheritance. The articulation and enactment of this shared desire for coherence requires many voices, many modes, many diverse forms of knowing whose harmony is not submerged into subconscious reactions or dogmatic authority. Language plays a secondary role in this Wisdom process, a means but not a source or end.

The Sophianic search is for an *embodied logos*—that is, for verbal expressions that will communicate a sense of embodied Wisdom open to the future, a receptive in-gathering of insights whose seeds may serve to germinate growth and development in others. Thought in this sense is a heart-centered activity whose process is one of slow growth mixed with spontaneous insight, of steady application through reflections and dialogue amplified by dreams, imaginings, and transrational intuitions. There is a discipline in this form of activity; one must enter the heart-center as a temple, a mystery, a place of revelation whose flame is responsive to a purity of intent. My intent is to receive, discover, to be an acolyte of Wisdom's grace, to be capable of a generative articulation or enactment that resists the tendency to merely speculate.

What Wisdom communicates is an existential call, an authentic expression of being through lived words, born out of my masculine embodiment, that results in a clarity that does not overreach or exclaim universals but meaningfully opens a way forward. An inspired, embodied logos, partnered with embodied eros, does not seek closure in one time or place, but greater openness to possibilities informed by the cares and concerns of others. What matters is sincerity and genuine concern, the intention to receive and create for a common good, a clear intelligence that encourages the development of every person's gifts and abilities.

The Sophianic *eros-logos*, in all its many forms, as poetry, prose, artistic symbolism or philosophic expression, is recognizable by its primary heart-centeredness, by a felt sense of deep concern arising from an inner, adaptive response to our many-layeredness. It embodies language as accessible, not overly abstract, and has a Wisdom concern to communicate the role of values in the formation of any enterprise or goal. Such speech is instructive, offers guidance without demanding conformity, and reveals a larger territory whose topography can only be known by direct exploration and engaged living. Such an eros-logos points beyond the words to the post-rational sources of Wisdom that are radiant in the heart and unitary to the larger cosmos. In a post-rational context, the value of reason and language is seconded to a more interior affirmation of depths of meaning that arise out of a direct relationship to the subtle, spiritual, and soulful.

Always these primary intuitions bring us back to the very ground of our beingness, saturated with deeply felt eros, in order to encourage engagement, passion, a celestial marriage whose beauty and symbolism is an alchemical sign of a deeper, more fundamental unity, beyond what words can convey. The poetry of such communication arises through its transparency for presence, words that sing us into a state of receptivity for insight. However small the spark, what matters is the light it confirms, the vibrant touch of Wisdom's gift, the grace that words cannot explain. Thought as inspired logos is an oracular medium; it suggests, provokes, challenges, and inspires reflection, meditation, and a deeper sensitivity for the subjects of its discourse. It does not so much explain as propose, offer a direction, and provide a sketch that only the reader or listener can bring to life by assimilating what is useful to find the color and texture through their own personal commitments, to fully realize and reshape a possibility.

Eros-logos also encourages us to cultivate *kallos*, "beauty" derived through cultivated virtues of soul, such that thinking is informed by those qualities of soul we value as most expressive of our utmost being. This kind of beauty informs the body not based on artificial standards or cultural norms but through luminous qualities that give meaning and worthiness to our words. By *beauty* I do not refer to "ideal" forms or thinking, not at all. Existential beauty derives from a heart-centered depth that informs thought as inspired words, sacred words seeking to express deeper Being. These virtues of soul, as based in Feminine Wisdom, require effort, self-discipline, and yet, an openness to spontaneity that expresses creative insight. Beauty of soul encourages spontaneity in speech, not reasoned argument, though that too is a possible expression, but more commonly a living sense of presence that informs thought as guided by inner intuitions because soul is aligned with the deepest sources of that intuition.

Clarity of mind, lucid thinking, soulful sensitivity, and mental focus all contribute to kallos—a certain beauty of thought and insight. This reflects soul grounded in Being-With and not simply in self; a soulful approach is one that is receptive to subtle influences derived from the integrity and wholeness of shared cosmic life. The soul becomes a means through which the inherent unity of Being-With can flow forth into minds and hearts open to the incredible beauty that informs the creative process. This inherent beauty is embodied, not simply in physical form, but also it shines forth, an aura of sanctity, a halo of light that enshrines thought with its own unique, luminous qualities. And this light is differentiated by the soulfulness of each individual such that its refracted rays can illumine a vast spectrum of possible expressions and forms. The eyes reflect this intelligible light, the kallos of soul, an immanence radiant within the heart-mind distilled by soul development into a purity of gaze whose nature is oracular and poetic. In Feminine Wisdom, Sophia embodies this beauty of thought and soul, as her luminous gaze, love filled, encourages us to

continue to develop our soulful life that we may merge and individuate our own version of her gaze, her love, her sacred well-being. Such
is the challenge of embodied eros-logos.

INCARNATE KNOWING AS STORY

We all have a story, the story of our life, our loves, successes and
failures, accomplishments and disappointments; and every story is
unique. The metaphor of a "life story," of memories and memoirs,
points toward an embodied Wisdom text whose telling requires
reflection and self-awareness. I call it a metaphor because every
life story is selective, punctuated by explicit moments, encounters, interpretations, select events, influences from dreams, visions,
imaginings, and our many distinct relationships with others. The
telling is an art form, more than gossip and rote repetitions; it is, or
can be, a creative narrative of life incidents, a form of sharing that
amplifies a perspective. And no story is complete, the only complete version is the actual life that is lived, moment by moment.

The Sophianic approach to the life story is one meant to illustrate a pathway, an interwoven series of perspectives whose complex
narrative and intersubjective relationships reveal bodily encounter,
injury, illness, success, accomplishments and failures, inner transformation, awakenings, aspirations, and discoveries in the process
of daily living. How we creatively face all the challenges of self-
awareness in the context of social, communal, familial life is the context for the story. And every story has a family, a childhood, social
locations, and historical embeddedness whose collective impact is
often crucial for an understanding of the story. Each of these aspects
are part of the story, the story is never simply about the individual,
but also about the collective period of that life, the historical context that matters in the processes of individuation, the struggles and

accommodations that shape a life and result in a visible outcome, worthy of memory and study.*

What then is the Sophianic praxis of narrating even an instant from one's life, or more fully sharing a select review? The praxis begins with self-awareness of purpose, an attitude toward the value of embodied experience shared in a context of trust, with an intention to create resonance, to illustrate a response to life situations, to communicate values and aspirations. The embodied sharing of stories is a vital element of how we negotiate our lives in relationship with others; our degree of empathy, detachment, engagement, calm, or excitement are all part of how we illustrate a stance, our attitudes toward others, our desires for soulful communion, and our most deeply held values. The primary narrative is the deep Sophianic story, the telling of a soulful journey in search of meaning and fulfillment, not simply talk or day-to-day interactions, gossip, or reactionary criticism or approvals. The spiritual inquiry is "What is your soul story?" and "What are the most deeply held values that give your story a soulful, lived meaning?" And perhaps even more crucial, "What are the stories that illustrate the key values of your life, including frustrations, failures, and unrealized goals?" The Sophianic story is not an idealization, not the story of ideal dreams or hopes, but lived-world, embodied experience as a vivid, existential account of growth and development with all the slippage we normally encounter in a spiritual journey or quest. And of course, highlighted by the many experiences that confirm, validate, and support that valued way of life.†

---

*An excellent example would be Carl G. Jung's *Memories, Dreams, Reflections*. My own story is found in *Anatolia: A Spiritual Memoir*, unpublished.

†For a brief account of the story of Sophia, see Lee Irwin, "The Divine Sophia, Isis, Achamoth and Ialdabaoth," and "Appendix: The Divine Sophia," in *Awakening to Spirit*, 355–58.

The Sophianic story is the embodied story, not the story of mind alone or desire only, but the actual lived, felt experiences that are formative in the realization of core values. A life-story incident is like a painting, not in the realistic, digital image sense, but more like a dream image, a bit surreal insofar as the narrative reaches beyond the everyday world of quotidian experience and offers something more, a glimpse of soul-life, of deeper encounters, of a door opening into other domains and revealing a synchronic illustration of Wisdom manifesting. The painting is highly symbolic even if it has a literal sense; there are metaphors hidden in the commonplace and analogies concealed in explicit imagery. The artist, that is the narrator, must be selective, giving the right color, shading, emphasis, and structure to bring out the inner domain of the experience or vision or value concern. At the same time, the Sophianic narrator must avoid excessive elaboration, falsification for entertainment, and a tendency to tell what is expected. Genuine narratives have a quality of *meta-realism*, offering both real-world experience and also deeper, less apparent implications less accessible to external observation. The deep inner life can never be fully illustrated but is only offered in tales of encounter and exploratory manifestations not fabricated for entertainment but to reflect actual experiences that shape and craft personhood. Always, there is an intangible depth, an inner privacy whose existential contents can never be fully stated or shared.

The dynamics of the lived-world are constantly forming and unforming as we choose or respond to circumstances and our choices reverberate within the multilayered psyche, constructed through our habitual tendencies. To narrate, we must select from embodied memory the virtual illustrations that best epitomize the values we wish to communicate. The role of consciousness is to assemble through memory a narrative of the ways in which body absorbs and integrates experience in the direct felt or lived sense. Body holds memory, body is basic to our narratives of spiritual development, body is the ground of our incarnate awareness and thus, body is the media that holds the memory of our story. Disembodied stories, that is stories that do not connect with body, with direct incarnational experience, may illustrate transphysical capacities, and yet, often those stories strongly reflect bodily image, sensory perceptions, and other bodily aspects—like a flying dream or out-of-body experience in which the nature of the experience seems to be through an image identical to the physical body, thus an embodied image. In Sophianic perceptions there are very profound transphysical aspects that are an intimate expression of our deep soul capacities, and yet, we start and end with body, we come back to body, we return to the embodied state, changed, but still a unified psychophysical entity.

The story of these encounters and transformations turns the normally physical body into a more Proteus-like being, capable of changes of a very dramatic kind; the Sophianic view is that the body is a metamorphic entity, an embodied story must accommodate its transformative capacities. We are body, we are much more than body; we are mind, we are much more than mind; we are spirit, and we are much more than spirit. We do not know our self-capacities in the fullest sense, we know only a very limited bodily sense; we are also capable of healing others through touch; we can induce remarkable physical changes; we have miraculous capacities and radical soul qualities still latent and awaiting a visionary call to actualization. Embodied knowing must not be a captive of any cultural narrative or material ideology that would deny or suppress embodied capacities of the more paranormal types or dismiss our capabilities for supraconscious states that are fully bodied and more. Our soulful being encompasses our bodily nature, the body is contained in the field of the soul and as such this encompassing field can shape and reshape the body. But this requires skillful living, self-discipline, and a soulful way of life that does not put body first to satisfy appetites or tendencies, which accelerates aging and decline.

Our bodies do age, but the soul ages also, and in maturity psychic discipline can support bodily health and well-being by drawing upon deeper psychic resources of a soulful type while also maintaining healthy bodily practices. What is the story of aging in a spiritual sense? How can a person age with grace guided by Sophianic Wisdom? These are key questions for aging. The story we tell ourself about our state or stage is crucial. What are the core values of aging? Beyond good health and positive loving relationships, those values include continual education, discovery, and the cultivation of a deep inner calm, a stability of personhood open to possibility and embodying a soulful luster whose effects are tranquil, uplifting, and luminous with insight. The story of a life is not concluded until death, and even then there is more to the story; the Sophianic emphasis is on living fully into death, in continual growth in which death is a learning stage.

Death is not a fearful marker but a threshold to even greater development; but this requires training and the cultivation of practices that support dying as a spiritual act. Death is natural, an intimate partner in the actualizations of soulful living. We die as we live, with grace and wisdom, or not, depending on soul's condition and attitudes. Our story must include the narrative of dying, and of return, for having lived once, we can live again, in our narrative and through the gift of metempsychosis. Death and rebirth, this is the true Sophianic cycle. The Wisdom praxis of the body includes recognizing and developing all the latent tendencies of embodied knowing and acting, body as temple, body as source of Wisdom, and body as the healthy support of mind. The body is central to Wisdom, not peripheral. But body is mortal, death inevitable, and this is good and natural. Death is part of our story, a closing chapter.

The Wisdom of dying is based in overcoming fear and uncertainty in the face of radical change. Dying, like living, is an art, a creative process of letting go in order to move forward to new awareness and insight. The Sophianic view is one of an expansive horizon in which death is a boundary we must all cross that requires letting go of the body. The body is mortal and fallible, a vitality that can lose its tenacity to live, give up its grasp, and allow the natural processes of destabilization to manifest a transition. Soul and mind can continue, with great clarity and the aid of other entities; it can enter a post-death state and pursue new goals and states.* Death is release and a turn toward greater possible becoming, not a loss or end, but a stage of transformation guided by the intent and attitudes of the postmortem individual. And even then, there is a "body" as a soul-minded awareness in subtle form, free from the tether of organic being but not lacking in embodied attitudes or perception based on organic sensation. There is a mystery there, how dying is not entirely a loss of body because perceptions carry sensory habits and embodied memories. The body may be released but its constitutional factors travel with us, into spirit and then back again.

Our story can include narratives of past lives, a sense of having lived before in a different body, a different gender, a different ethnicity, and in different social-historical contexts. In this sense, death is a repeating theme, a cycle in which multiple

---

*Research in Near Death (NDE) has assembled significant data of the after-death state; see Bruce Greyson, "Implications of Near-Death Experiences for a Post-Materialist Psychology," and Janice M. Holden, Bruce Greyson, and Debbie James, *The Handbook of Near-Death Experiences*.

deaths contribute to our current life story. Here we must reach into soul memory as a resource for understanding life beyond the body, even if the cycle is one of constant incarnations. Not many people remember past lives, and often false memories can create inflated versions of those lives. But psychotherapeutic techniques have revealed the most common memories of past lives are those that are often the most traumatic, a possible reason why people do not wish to remember those lives.* Childhood memories of past lives have also been thoroughly studied and it is notable that those studies reveal that children at adolescence tend to forget and even deny such memories recorded earlier by researchers.[4] The issue is one of denial and cultural values that either reject the idea based on Christian theologies or materialist theory, which also believes in only "one life, one death." And yet many people have life stories that include past-life memories, scenes, and persons once known, or visits to places that seem vividly familiar. Dreams are a primary basis for past-life memories because dreaming taps soul knowledge through altered states that access our past experiences.

The Sophianic perspective is to simply open a horizon on the possibility of such memories, because if we have lived before, then surely there is much to be learned from those memories. Our life stories, plural, are intrinsic to the self-narrative that seeks to truly understand soul as a repository of lessons and encounters that have shaped beliefs and attitudes in our present life. The undercurrent, the subconscious influence is there, working below the threshold of everyday awareness that would deny or dismiss such dreams and memories. Short-sighted pragmatism is impatient with the imaginal, with possible influence of such past contents. The Sophianic praxis is to imagine the possibility of multiple lives, then to have

---

*Morris Netherton's *Past Lives Therapy* gives impressive accounts of such memories; see also Helen Wambach, *Reliving Past Lives*.

the honesty to evaluate introspectively the value and worth of such "memories." The life story, its scope, does not simply end at death but merges into a vaster reality where becoming is an ongoing process of development and self-reflection in cooperation with others. Death as transition is a chapter rather than an end, a concluding moment in a long series of experiences with many other such moments.

Another aspect of story is the disjunction between actual events and how we reconstruct them through narrative, this includes the problem of false memories and fabrication. Do we actually remember what happened? Or do we construct a version of what happened that accords with our own self-understanding? We can fabricate memory through the process of tacit association and the syncretic nature of multimodal knowing. Unlike an electronic recording, the impact of experience does not leave a verbatim record, instead, personalized effects remain inseparable from mental and emotional attitudes and personality dispositions. This is why the comparison with artificial intelligence through supercomputing with human mentality is a false analogy; we do not record facts or data, we remember experience as seen from a personal point of view, both as factual but also subjective and immediately interpreted. These interpretations are not true or false, they are value-laden assessments concurrent with emotional reactions, variable moods, and cherished beliefs. Because mind is multilayered, the impact of experience is filtered through awareness that is already shaped by previous experiences. There is no mental *tabula rasa* ("blank slate") on which lived experience is inscribed in perfect fidelity. Instead of this abstract philosophical notion, our minds are carrying impressions that are not only personal but also collective, through a long series of transformations, that leave soul knowledge briming with possible insights and ideas, even at the moment of birth.

Our stories are always selective, not simply by conscious choice, but also strongly influenced by organic, neurological, emotional, and hormonic influences. The many-layered brain, like the many-layered mind, reflects subtle influences that may not all be conscious. Thus what we claim to remember may be a neuropsychic response, a conditional assembly of aspects influenced by tacit associations operative below the liminal threshold. Desire can shape memory, aspiration can shape memory, fear and loathing, anger and hatred can shape memory—there is no pure objectivity in memory. Everything is circumstantial and relative to our own existential stance and beliefs. The Sophianic praxis is to acknowledge the relative nature of memory in the shaping of our story and then to practice self-honesty to a high degree, aware of the tendencies to shape the story in terms of what motives the narrative. This means accepting fallibility, the capacity for misunderstanding, and an ability to reshape the past through new insights, as a means of self-surpassing.

Our story is not fixed, but like life itself, the story evolves, including the development of past understanding and old narratives. The real story is ongoing, it does not necessarily move to some preordained conclusion nor does its origin remain unchanged. The entire human story may shift and radically change in ways unforeseen by current beliefs and attitudes. Through the metaphysics of discovery, we may uncover new and radical aspects of embodied awareness that will change the entire narrative of human history and global culture. Such a change is demonstrated in the impact of scientific theories of evolution in contrast to religious theologies. The same is true for the personal story as well, Feminine Wisdom comprehends this transparency of boundaries, how we can "see through" the limitations of our current narratives for more dynamic perceptions that can shift our understanding to whole new patterns of social and cosmic life. Future narratives will be diverse but they will share an important feature in dissembling the past and offering new insights into the relevance of past creative events. For example, the death of the father god and the rebirth of the feminine spirit as foundational and primary, not secondary, but as a revelation based in a co-gendered matrix, giving life and intelligence to all species and worlds. The true story is far more profound than the old male narratives, because giving birth means bringing forth life in all its possibilities and creative nuances.

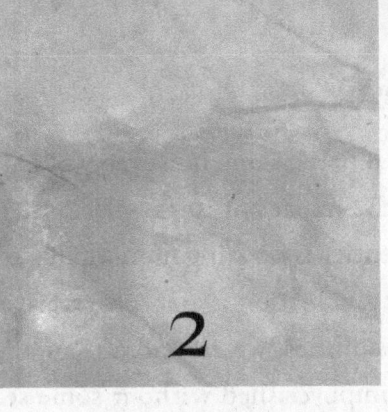

2

Praxis of Relatedness

SOUL

The lived-world is a shared world, and our sharing extends across a spectrum from intimate beloved to unknown strangers, from family to community to many diverse others. This fact of relatedness and sharing is not limited to known living individuals but extends, through text and media, to a multitude of others—authors, writers, actors, creators, artists, many long deceased. It includes all our animal relations, our interactions with other living creatures, and reaches into the subliminal domains of dreaming with its own populations and archetypal entities. But even more subtle, our relatedness collapses the artifice of the supposed subject-object separation and participates in an interactive, co-creative, shared sentience all the way down to the subtlest creative occasion and all the way up to the macrocosmic All. We are all related; we are all relatives within a living universe of others whose similarities are in many profound ways more similar than our obvious and often conflictual differences.

The Sophianic praxis of relatedness is grounded in a fundamental premise: we all participate in relatedness, and we are deeply influenced by all our relations however we may choose to modify or radically alter the impact of those relations. This does not mean that individual identity is nothing more than a consequence of these relations; as our individuation is a deeply creative realization of multigenerational possibilities, we are more than all our relations. And yet, we would be impoverished without some select influence from others, however much we may resist the beliefs or attitudes of those more intimately part of our life journey. We are all related, and we can choose which of those relationships best correlate and support the realizations of deeper potential and this choice is an ongoing process of selectivity from birth to death. This relatedness also includes animals and a sense of responsibility for their well-being.

Further, we influence others in all our relations; we are each a living example of what a human being can become; even in the most trying circumstances, we exemplify a possible mode of embodiment. This process of interaction and relatedness begins in infancy, through childhood and adolescence, into young adulthood, to the prime of life, and into advanced maturity and elderhood. And every stage has its unique characteristics and possibilities of relatedness; we can learn and grow in maturity with others, or we can become fixated at a plateau of development or regress in times of crisis or during loss of incentive. Greater population means greater impact of mass events; we are not isolated from the struggles and sufferings of others; the more massive the event, the greater the felt impact by all. In a world interconnected through complex technologies of communication and media, the collapse of distance has a direct psychic impact; we are surrounded by world events, inundated by information from and about others, deluged with visual, aural, and literate textuality that threatens to overwhelm the sensitive participant. And this communicative interface fosters new forms of intimacy, discovery, encounter, and face-to-face, eye-to-eye, ear-to-ear meetings.

There are few local communities that exist apart from this media of interaction and few individuals who will not or cannot participate. Increasingly, the norm is greater interactions, more frequent communication, an enhanced field of possible connections. It has its dangers, abuses, alienating aspects; it can degrade as well as enhance; but the Sophianic significance is found in the noosphere of increasing complexity and information density.* We all participate in a shared matrix of interactions, subconsciously and consciously, through which subtle psychic influences flow continuously. Wisdom is not simple, it is complex, deep, and inseparable from the inter-related, interactive processes of nature, culture, and human development in all areas of life. A person may nevertheless cultivate simplicity of life and modest virtues, a sincere reduction of waste and accumulation; this would be a manifestation of Wisdom, in the applied, practical, lived sense. As beings in relation to the Whole, such a reduction is not a limitation on the contents and depths of complexity that actually sustain and animate the Whole.

Knowledge of shared processes, of creative occasions, means there is a deep sense of the actuality of how those processes work, correlate, and interact in order to sustain life and awareness. Such knowledge reaches far beyond current paradigms of relatedness; our participation in and through the intersubjective field, as inseparable from nature, requires Wisdom in a higher degree. Complexity is a mystery, a stochastic probability whose processes and outcomes cannot be fully predicted. Wisdom is not simply an assembly of moral or spiritual prescriptions; it requires an understanding of the very processes in which we all participate. This means the integration of nature and culture, rural and urban, simple and complex, sensory and trans-sensory, normal and paranormal; it includes tracking the

---

*By *noosphere*, I refer to the concept articulated by P. Teilhard de Chardin in *The Phenomenon of Man*, that he defines as "the thinking envelope of the biosphere."

processes far beyond the immediacy of felt participation, all the way down to the most animate vibrant string and all the way out into the vast multidimensional macrocosm.

However, relatedness begins at home, in the heart, in the immediacy of our actual relationships and in the struggle for mutual understanding and acceptance. If relatedness is a basic existential condition, one that is a necessary aspect of our success as an enduring species, then an index or measure of our Wisdom is the success through which we manifest and maintain a wide array of positive relationships. I do not simply mean relationships that reflect similarity of views and beliefs, but successful relationships that embody significant, often challenging differences. The index of our mutual development is surely measured by our capacity for more than tolerance; our creative interaction, the authenticity of our engagement, the integrity of negotiating diverse worlds and values all reflect our Sophianic commitments.

The concept of salvation through gnosis is not simply a mystical tenet, it is also a call for more authentic relatedness and understanding of all our relations. The Sophianic gnosis is relational and interactive; it is "this world" knowledge and includes all areas of investigation in a deep ethos of nonviolence and respect, not as simply bracketed perceptions or a particular ideological construction. A fully participant knowing through living relations requires skill, maturity, and a flexible appreciation of our unique differences. What we have to resist is the authority of imposition and a didactic insistence on a single practice or closed value system. Flexibility in our relations expresses a soul quality, a genuine appreciation of differences. If we are all related then we must do the work of reconciling our difference in order to bring about a new integration and wholeness, this is both a local and a global challenge.

LOVE AS LIVING KINDNESS

Love begins in the family and if it does not begin there, family relatedness can cause great suffering and lifelong struggles to adapt and overcome neglect, abuse, or repression as well as overindulgence and unmediated gratifications. It is our childhood context that strongly shapes our capacities for giving and receiving love; an unloving family or one whose concept of love is hierarchic and dogmatic, is not a context for the acquisition of Wisdom. Indulging children with no discipline or supporting self-centeredness can also create incapacities in love. The deep soul-core of love is empathy for, and interest in, the well-being of others without sacrificing one's own well-being. The key Sophiana soul principle is "to love and to be loved" through interactive, mature relationships that enhance both the lover and the beloved. The model for this love is the primal relationship between mother and child, a healthy, respectful relation that honors the integrity, abilities, and unique qualities of each person. Such a Sophianic relationship is not based on a hierarchy of worth, that a parent is always right or that a parental view is the only valid view; in a Sophiana relation, each person has the right to be themself, even if immature and undeveloped.

Love is the great teacher, not discipline or punishment; deeply held respect for every being, openness to and responsibility for assessment and reevaluation of one's own views and wants sustains the creative aspect of the process. Such development requires guidance and boundaries that will help the child recognize the limits of their own desires. The praxis of Sophianic love requires us to model the very discipline that we believe is necessary for the health and well-being of our children. Such praxis is not based on what we say, but on what we do, who we really are, such that "actions speak louder than words." Maturation is shaped by values and attitudes communicated to the child, values often embedded in prejudice, discrimination, and bias regarding the values or worth of others. Unless we can assess our own limits, be open to the challenge of differences, and constantly work to refine and improve our own value orientation, we foster a limited bias and offer only a constrained, contracted, and conditional love.

Such conformity is not love, it is obedience, a slavish imitation of mind and heart that overrides the felt sense of empathy that is naturally present in an open, healthy mind when relating to strange and different others. The principle of love as kindness, as a Sophianic virtue, requires an open mind and heart, a clear sense of soulfulness fostered through positive relations, one not conditioned to reject or discriminate against others based on family bias, collective social reactions, and inherited preconceptions. Social attitudes toward women by men are a common example, racial prejudice is another unexamined bias. There are discriminatory attitudes sustained in broad cultural patterns that arise as reactionary responses to those who think, act, or value differently; this discrimination often acts to conceal self-righteous belief in one's own superiority. And such discrimination also conceals a fear of the other as a threat that might challenge or unravel such attitudes and thereby throw into question an entire worldview of beliefs.

The conservative mind, the dogmatic affirmation incapable of negotiation, dialogue, and change, is the birthing ground of unexamined prejudice for untold generations of children. "Do not think, reflect, or debate—only conform, obey, and repeat the patterns—or you will not be loved." But this is not love, it is not kindness; it is a form of emotional manipulation and an attempt to control thought and belief. It is an aggressive desire to dominate, to re-create, to shape another into an image of the contracted self, regardless of what that other self may desire, believe, or feel. And the pattern is multigenerational, ingrained through conditional ignorance, and transmitted with self-righteous certitude in its correctness. This unconscious, blind expectation is a true mark of ignorance, a complete lack of self-assessment based on inherited, constricted attitudes that only serve to reinforce a rigid posture closed to negotiation. This close-mindedness is a generational problem, an entrapment whose justification relies on the "way of the fathers"—an ancestral bias that supports a narrow, oppressive hierarchy of values.

The Sophianic path is far more challenging. It does not begin, proceed, or end with authority or traditional, dogmatic values over the worth and importance of our individual differences. It seeks to promote love and kindness without imposing in-group structure on who is, or is not, deserving of such love. All creatures deserve love, without demand and expectations of conformity to a closed set of unjust values. Love proceeds, in the deep, soulful sense, through a constantly negotiated relationship between the lover and the beloved; every moment is a potential moment of change, discovery, and new insight or realization that may enhance the relationship. This does not mean there is no contestation, no conflict or disagreement; the struggle for self-realization requires that we confront our own limitations, our prejudices, our undeveloped thinking or false beliefs, in order to become a more open and loving being. The Sophianic praxis is to be as loving as possible with all others without sacrificing integrity and core values. This is the concept of *responsible love*, that is, a love that can stand with integrity in the center of one's being and still be open to and empathic with the views and values of others.

The Sophianic path as I understand it embraces a primary commitment to nonviolence, peaceful negotiations, restorative justice, cooperation, and resolution of conflict through mediated adaptations. And it also requires that we recognize the maturity, insights, and Wisdom of others who might guide, assist, and help us to clarify and develop our values and qualities of love. I do not mean to suggest that all relationships are equal in terms of maturity, education, training, or spiritual development; they are not, and love in this context is differentiated according to one's development. Therefore, responsible love is developmental and requires continual work and refinement to fully actualize the deepest spiritual potentials of that love. The core of responsibility is hearing the other and acting in accord with values that seek mediation and just, cooperative relations.

In a profound sense, the Sophiana of love is a divine gift, an inherent soul capacity for the manifestation of Being, as a transformative presence in a consciously loving person whose effects have an immediate, spontaneous impact on those receptive to such love. Receptivity in such a case is a matter of attaining the necessary degree of sensitivity to feel and participate in such love as a *sacred relationship*. Being open to and in negotiation with the values and beliefs of others is not a matter of accepting all manner of cultural bias or ingrained patterns of mistreatment, violence, or prejudice. It is instead a capacity to treat others with love while also holding the Sophianic values that genuinely express purpose and positive being in the world. All values are not equally valid, many values reflect a less mature, more defensive or aggressive mentality whose capacities for love are conditional, reductive, and often rigidly hierarchical. Value assessment is intrinsic to love as more than feeling. Love is a stance toward right-mindedness, just relations, and a willingness to be guided by a Feminine Wisdom that honors our difference while calling us to embody the highest standards of spiritual integrity.

The practice of loving kindness arises from feelings of interest, empathy, and concern for those in need of responsible, meaningful relationships. This includes all our relationships with children, humans, animals, plant life, and the many diverse ecologies of the Earth. The metaphor I use for this relationship is "heart-centered love" where the organ of perception is the felt reality of care and concern for others within the deep body center, not in mind or abstract thought. Mind and thought have their place and must enter into the search for viable alternatives, strategies, and creative solutions to problems. However, heart-centered love is a gift of empathic knowing, a felt soulful sense of relatedness, invoking the "third presence" by which Sophia makes herself known. This goes beyond values, while including those values, and enters into the metaphysics and mystery of our capacity to love and to be loved. This love is not simply an emotional or feeling-based, bodily response; it is that and more. It is an opening to an active spiritual presence or Being-With whose origins are transrational, mystical, and a fundamental source of life. We do not create love, we transmit love; we become vessels through which a greater and more profound love can flow unimpeded into the world for the good of the lover, the beloved, and the witness presence of that loving relationship.

Such a soulful love is kind. This means that the Sophiana praxis starts in conscious right-minded love, in acts of kindness to others, and then grows into something more, a sharing, a co-participation in an ontological process by which the world is made and unmade.* If love is developmental, if it requires ever-greater alignment between heart, mind, soul, and well-being, then by stages we advance to a more open horizon through which Being and Spirit dawn as inspirations for the formation of a more loving world. We are the agents of change and transformation, we are the makers of our worlds, and we are the means by which those worlds become known. We must learn to discard the less sufficient and to amplify the hidden fullness

---

*For more on "making and unmaking," see Lee Irwin, *Visionary Worlds*.

that is even now seeking new manifestation. Love must be embodied, enacted, and encouraged.

The medium for this change is kindness, altruism, generous feminine-masculine efforts of aid and support for others, a willingness to become transparent and a genuine source of love without discrimination. It is not through individual willing but through loving relations, partnership, and committed actions in a shared process of becoming that shapes intention and will toward goals that require many diverse agents of change. We are not alone, we are working together with agency that is both visible and invisible, both many and one, seeking creative expression for the benefit of all those whose love can support a peaceful, harmonious world of differences. And Spirit is working with us, through us, to instrumentalize a more loving world.

This does not mean we must join various groups or form alliances with organizations dedicated to principled action—we can join, we can form and organize—but the real task is to be a loving person and, in that love, to be linked with all other loving beings who share similar goals. This is part of the *metaphysic of love*, that our loving kindness places us into immediate partnership with other agents of change and transformation, wherever we are and whatever our circumstances. As I write this, I feel loving regard rising in the hearts of some readers as a spontaneous manifestation of connection and a sharing of vision. Such perception is not bound by time or locale, it is part of a much vaster spectrum of consciousness and co-participation; as such, those perceptions extend into the past and into the future, on occasion with great vividness. Love and compassion are transphysical; they extend beyond the present and create a context for connection across the vast spectrum of all conscious beings.

This sharing of perspectives, this merging of mind and heart, is an expression of soulful love no longer bound by temporal condition but embodied through an alert psychic perception of a shared matrix of values. Love is not simply an emotion of the body, it is also a quality of consciousness and Being, an awareness whose subtle influences extend far beyond the bound conditions of a single bodily life. The conjunctive nature of such love is a prime dynamic for creative transformation; it is not bound by physical limitations but overflows into shared networks of other loving beings all of whom help to amplify, without effort, the cumulative, global effects of such loving kindness.

The Sophiana of love, that is the Wisdom Love that can guide and inform the heart and mind, is a shared reality of soul, not simply a personal experience. My love is made stronger by the love I receive and my capacity to give or share love is a living, deep well whose soulful depths are infinite, not individual. The depth of the well is measured by my capacity to open and receive, not just to give or make sacrifice, but to be a vessel through which love flows into the world without effort or precondition. This requires the discipline of *transparency*. There is no ownership in Sophianic love, only the free exchange of care, concern, and kindness directed toward the growth, maturity, and health of self and others. Love is a dynamic field, one that is co-created and can fill a home, a workspace, a public arena with inspirational quality and depths of support that foster an even stronger field. This is what I mean by loving kindness—it is a dynamic of love that is fully alive, consciously present, right-minded, and transparently communicated as life-vitality, as soulfulness, through an energizing, nurturing presence. This field is co-created by loving individuals, persons and animals, whose presence and warmth creates a feeling of openness and a welcoming sense of support. It is the quality of our love, its depth and fullness, that is the means for the creation of a loving world; through such soulful love, the world is transformed.

THE EARTH AND HER CHILDREN

Many Indigenous peoples hold the view that "all my relatives" refers to not only humans but also to animals, plants, and other aspects of nature: the rivers, the seas, the clouds, the mountains, the rocks, gems, and elements of earth, water, air, fire, and spirit. And these aspects of nature are often considered to be ensouled, that is as having qualities of being that are unique and psychically related to human beings through dreams, visions, and ceremonies. The significance of this belief is that the human-other relationship is a soulful relation, one in which the creatures and beings of nature can and do communicate and form relations with receptive humans. This is the world as animate and sentient, fully alive, where no agent, no being or entity, lacks sentience, where each and every creature, element, and aspect reflects sentience. I believe in pan-sentience as a pervasive manifestation of Being and Spirit that infuses and animates each distinct entity with just those qualities of sentience that are necessary for its individual existence. This means that all the way down to the vibrant strings that form various elementary particles and all the way up to macroforms like galaxies and galactic clusters, to the universe as a whole, there is sentience relative to the form and quality of the specific entity.

Sentience is thus inherent in and inseparable from energy, matter, and light; sentience is a characteristic of the "initial conditions" for cosmic becoming or, as an alternate premise, sentience is inseparable from our "existential conditions" if we view cosmology from the perspective of the current observable universe. In a pan-sentient view, all elemental matter, however rarified, as plasma, gas, liquid, or solid, or as discreet atomic structures, is imbued with sentience. This does not mean they have a particular form of consciousness, but rather that every entity sustains a vitality whose qualities can cohere to form unique expressive and responsive relations for that particular entity. Thus, sentience is qualitative, unique, adaptive, responsive, and suited to the actual form and creative occasion that represents a particular entity.

Humans have human sentience and tigers have tiger sentience and stones have stone sentience and lithium has lithium sentience—and they are by no means the same or similar. However, insofar as entities interact and can form relationships and connections, the qualities of sentience can change, mutate, and form new complexes of sentient interaction. In the simplest terms, sentience is a capacity for relationship through positive, neutral, or negative responses; attraction, repulsion, and neutrality are fundamental reactions, even at the particle level. This interactive capacity is the very basis of the arising of all forms of sentience; this is not an expression of consciousness but a more simple, direct sense of primal response. While sentience is primary, consciousness is a later derivative of that basic sentient capacity.

If we think of *soul* as an entity that is a subtle form of self-aware sentience, and in some way separable from a specific material form, then our vision of the cosmos must also include genuine psychic dimensionality. Traditionally speaking, such dimensionality is considered far greater and vaster than the physical matter-energy universe. To quote Sri Yogananda, the distinction is "like a material basket held up by the much more expansive balloon of the immaterial universe."[1] My own view is that in a sentient universe the ultradimensional aspects of the cosmos are an intrinsic feature of "all our relations" and are in no way separate nor distinct from what we call the material world. To put it a bit differently, the world is saturated with sentience "all the way down" and as such, forms a unitary field or matrix of ever-increasing degrees of subtlety, complexity, and awareness in which all dualities are simply a medium for creative, dynamic interaction.

The world changes constantly; everything interacts, merging, separating, combining, and disintegrating without loss of wholeness in the process, including the transformable qualities of pan-sentience that infuses each and every being. Soul in this context is an ultradimensional aspect of the lived field of embodied conscious awareness. As a self-reflective center its very existence and operations, even if not visible, are quite receptive to and interactive with other soulful beings. In this context, the term *psyche* refers to the embodied soul, intimately unified with body and separable only by death. There are subtle domains of interaction between sentient beings, embodied and disembodied, including sentient beings who are not human, yet sentient. This is because we inhabit a truly sentient universe. From a feminine perspective, we can call it "living nature" as a pervasive, universal aspect of the pan-sentient Whole.

The most obvious co-relationship is with animals. Animals as members of distinct species have unique qualities of sentience that are by no means identical but nevertheless share "family resemblances" that make them obvious members of a particular group. As I regard all sentience as specific to and formed by individual creatures, each creature has unique and distinctive qualities of sentience that create an identity within the context of shared species traits. The human-animal relationship expresses a third field that reflects the nature and quality of interaction between species— such that animal companions are co-participants in forming that shared field. Individual attitudes toward animals of every type, both attractive and repulsive, create a psychic context for interaction. Fear of spiders or snakes creates a field when encountering those creatures and love of cats or dogs likewise creates interactive potential. The Sophianic, Feminine Wisdom view of animals is to see them as partners in shared species relationships in which each species offers unique perspectives on the nature of sentience and through interactions, creates a complex field of shared sentient relations.

If we live with responsible love then our relationship with all animal species should be one of loving concern, conscientious caretaking, and a deep respect for the worth and value of every species. Managing our animal-human relationships can be a form of incarnational spirituality; the Sophianic principle of "love all beings" does not exclude any species if all species represent the creative potential of intrinsic sentience. What is possible becomes visible in what is actual. The snake, the spider, the biting insect, the shark, or rat are all sentient beings whose very existence is a testimony to the possibilities of sentience. Not from only a human point of view but also from a more process view of creation dynamics overall, animals of land, sea, and sky are a precious expression of life abundant. We all are diminished by the loss of a single species, the richer our environment, the more complex the possibilities of manifest sentience. Love and partnership, or caretaking and loving kindness, is the medium for the fruition of sentience; our animal-human relations epitomize our ability to think, act, and show concern for nonhuman beings whose value is no less than our own. Humans are also animals, and in the best sense intelligible and loving; thus, our animal nature is a natural soulful aspect of our co-relations with all other animals. The Sophianic perspective, as Feminine Wisdom, seeks to provide care and well-being for all species.

There is also an imaginal aspect to soul relations between humans and animals, a psychic relation whose creative consequences help to guide human beings to a more conscious state of being. Many cultures have valued animal guides, animals as teachers, as spirit beings capable of enhancing human abilities through partnership. Like the Comanche woman healer Sanapia, whose healing power was amplified by her psychic connection with "eagle spirit" that would manifest to her as a spirit eagle who wrapped its wings around her to empower a successful healing. This visionary connection was manifested in her trembling, sweating, rapid heartbeat, and the disappearance of her surroundings; then the power would fill her body and transmit through her arms into the feathers she used for healing and then out into the ill person.[2]

There is a distinct relationship between healer and spirit helper, one is not assimilated into the other, but each remains linked through specific states of consciousness that were, in Sanapia's case, "kindled" after four intensive years of training, by a four-day final fast and a successful vision that transferred her mother's healing power to her through the eagle imagery. The animal power remained consistent between mother and daughter, the imagery was shared and transferred and, in a world of empowering animal relations, was fully believed to originate with the eagle species, one of whose members initiated the original contact. The transpersonal capacity to heal was thus a "gift of power" linked to specific practices and a reverent attitude toward animal beings believed capable of transhuman abilities.

Animal powers are not reducible to human projection. There is something mysterious here that is captured in the image of the gift of power inaccessible without the necessary human-animal connection. In turn, this introduces the theme of transpersonal agency whose manifestations are frequently linked to nonhuman sources. It is generally true that in many cultures closely connected to and dependent upon animal relationships, select animals are seen as having greater than human capacities, which can be transmitted to human agents, often through dreams and visions. The opening sphere of transpersonal agency, through visionary and imaginative encounter, reflects a Sophianic soul principle—the Mother of Animals—as an empowering agency that can take many different forms, as in goddess images, but is by no means always human and may in fact frequently take animal forms as well. I am reminded of the multi-armed Goddess Durga, riding a Tiger in order to subdue all powers that seduce and mislead a seeker from the spiritual path. The animal companion (Tiger) assists and adds its strength and capacities to those of a divinized human woman as a sacred conjunction of human-animal partnership. Animal powers, broadly assessed, reflect the natural ecology of the community and represent abilities unique to a particular species even though different dreamers of the same animal species may have very different enhanced abilities.[3]

These transhuman partnerships can also be made with plants, trees, herbs, and living nature in many diverse forms; for human seekers after wisdom, sources of inspiration and guidance are not limited to only other humans. The metaphor here is the capacity of natural forms to hold sentience as viable manifestations of latent potential discovered through an intimacy of shared connection, a psychically charged, animate sense of vital insight and knowledge. This connection with living nature is not simply one of empowering humans, but also of sharing knowledge or qualities of sentience; the mint plant, the honeybee, the lotus flower, all offer sentient qualities that can complement, enhance, and even purify human awareness. The inverse of this relationship is to offer care and consideration for the preservation of diverse plant life, to value with Sophianic feminine respect the worth of every living thing. And it implies something more than agriculture for mass consumption and the artifice of claiming corporate ownership of reproductive means, in seeds and other genetic aspects of plant life. A responsible love develops through reverence and respect, not ownership and control, and its fruition is through a generous gifting of discovery for the well-being of others, including respect for the very earth that so abundantly offers us sustenance. The gifts should be shared and not owned for economic benefit.

The Earth itself may be regarded as sentient, a Gaian soul field whose latent capacities manifest in and through all actual species. As a holistic field of related beings, held by all Earth inhabitants, our shared species life is precious beyond counting and an immeasurable gift in the face of a vaster cosmos where such a living, sentient world is rare and valuable. What we may term *animate nature* is really a limited concept of *actual nature* in all its rich, complex, and interactive relations in which humanity now plays a dominant and, at times, destructive role. The greatest problem is overpopulation, the unchecked proliferation of one species overburdening the resources and natural relations that have for so long sustained and nurtured life in a planetary sense. To acquire balance we must limit our reproduction to harmonize with resources necessary for the whole of the planet, all species, not just the human.

Eventually this overpopulation will pass, so I believe, but not soon and not without tremendous impact on our planetary wholeness. The Gaia principle, as a Sophianic concept, expresses the belief that life on this world forms an integral whole that requires a balanced relationship between what we use and what we contribute. By contribution I mean for the good and worth of every ecological niche and zone, what we do to sustain, protect, and nurture health and sustainability. The Sophia of good ecology, as a feminine principle, is based on contributions to and respect for all life; the very sentience of the whole is inseparable from our actions, choices, and the possible good we can create to preserve and protect our natural heritages.

The "earth and all her children" are not centered on the human species, the field is much larger, all-encompassing, all-inclusive. However, human dominance can create massive imbalance, illness, and exhaustion among all species. If we overpopulate, poison the oceans, strip the land, cut down the tropical forests, and cater to the appetites and indulgences of profit-driven economies, then we can expect to suffer. Unless we can teach present and future generations to limit our needs, to preserve, respect, and love the world for all its rich diversities and uniquely evolved local ecologies, then the "terror of history" will certainly show how our collective immaturity destroyed a world through selfishness, neglect, and indifference.

The Sophia of planetary concern is manifest in a Feminine Wisdom that seeks to preserve, nurture, and protect the tremendous gifts we have inherited from Gaia, from the life-world of all living beings, and from each and every species. Our human-animal-plant-ecology relations are not simply there to serve our selfish interests; what is required in Wisdom is to move beyond self-centeredness and to seek a partnership of shared integrity with each and every living creature and environment. This is more than stewardship—it is a Wisdom born of mutuality, not a hierarchy of relations, in which we dominate or decide—and it requires transparency and the sublimation of self to a larger more complex process of becoming. A soulful Wisdom seeks respectful partnership that honors the value and worth of every creature and ecology. My hope is that we will find the Wisdom necessary to preserve the richness and to reduce our demands and needs to a more balanced and respectful way of life.

HIDDEN SPIRITS, SACRED WORLDS

If sentience is a property of every entity and even the base elements hold sentience from the simplest to the most complex, then each expresses unique features of sentient possibility. A diamond or ruby may hold certain qualities of sentience, very refined and pure, as might various kinds of stones, crystals, of other very simple, basic materials. The old Hermetic tradition often engaged in correspondent ritual activity by gathering together various objects—flowers, herbs, materials, precious stones, crystals, and so on—each assembly representing a particular set of qualities (occult virtues) that together amplified the overall subtle effects when performing various rites. Further, the timing of rites with these objects was connected to planetary movements, times of day or night, lunar cycles, and other astral alignments to create the exact circumstances to heighten the effects of the correspondences. The underlying theory of conjunctive ritual using very select natural objects, often accompanied by music or singing, was all part of creating a sacred sentient field whose subtle energies could have a direct impact on the human participants.* These kinds of conjunctive rituals are common in many spiritual traditions, particularly those related to an embodied, earth-based spirituality, and often related to healing and transformative rites to rebalance and realign participants with the local cosmos.

Alchemy as the art of spiritual transformation is another example that engages with many types of elemental matter in the practice of often rigorous, reiterative stages of refinement meant to produce an elixir or inner essence of the conjoint materials.† The alchemical motto, *Solve et Coagula* ("dissolve and coagulate"), reflects the necessary cycles of refinement, the dynamics of disassemble and reassemble, required for the gradual creation of an ever-more subtle elemental synthesis. We dissolve old beliefs, old ideas and practices, then form a new integration, a more refined thinking, better practices. A similar motif, "to separate and to conjoin," reflects the necessity of construction and deconstruction, as both creation and destruction are necessary aspects of the overall creative process of discovery.

---

*See Marsilio Ficino, *Book of Life*, 85–183, for an excellent example of magical correspondence.

†For more on alchemy as related to personal development, see Irwin, *The Alchemy of Soul*.

It is not simply a matter of building or constructing an elemental synthesis, but of creating and then *uncreating* when one sees the limitations of a given construction that has not yet fully expressed the deeper, purest qualities of sentience.* The art of transformation is not based on a final outcome or teleological given, but on the exploration and discovery of how elemental matter can be used, adapted, shaped, and reshaped for a wide range of soulful outcomes. The theory of the philosophers stone, which takes so many diverse forms, is a Grail-like symbol expressing the process of purification through psychospiritual cycles linked to nature and elemental matter—like carbon compressed to an allotrope diamond. Human development is not separate from nature but deeply entwined and intrinsically part of the natural world, which is the medium of our spiritual realizations.

The Sophiana of embodied existence can be imaged as a pilgrimage, a search for a mysterious Grail that symbolizes our most profound soulful potential. In this sense, nature, by which I mean the natural environment of woods, trees, plants, fields, streams, rivers, mountains, and ocean beaches, all free from the clutter of human habitation, is the healing ground of our alchemical development. The Sophianic Wisdom is nature based, world immersed, and finds inspiration in the natural beauty, power, and essential vitality of primordial ecologies, in flora and fauna, unshaped by human control or dominance. The pilgrim on this journey, the seeker after Wisdom, must ask the appropriate question: not "What is the Grail?" Ask rather, "Who am I and how may I serve in the manifestation of the Grail?" The Grail is not one thing; it is not a cup or a spear or a stone, it is more like a transformed world vibrant with healthy embodied beings positively related and mutually supported.

---

*For more on creation and recreation, see Lee Irwin, *Visionary Worlds*.

The Grail emerges through a process of discovery, as a manifestation of Higher Wisdom, and it has no one form; its forms are as diverse as the beings who embody the actual living Wisdom that the Grail represents.[4] And the context of this discovery and its embodiment is the natural world, our home, terra firma, our balanced planetary communities living in respectful harmony and celebrating our diversity.

If elemental matter is uniquely sentient and if sentient beings can develop greater awareness and sensitivity to this implicit sentience, then the alchemical integration, as a creative process, will be unique for each person. My relationship to others, to the natural world, to expanded sense perception and subtle world awareness, cannot be imitated or reproduced. We do not, on our pilgrimage, seek to reduplicate but to share and to discover possible, multiple insights arising from our diverse journeys. We must each undertake the appropriate alchemical work, undergo the fires of transformation for refinement, to continue the Great Work in contributing to the well-being of the whole.[5] And elemental matter, in its most minute integer, also contributes to the whole by adding the qualitative synthesis of its own being to that whole. Working with elemental matter might be an actual path, the chemistry of focused research on the very nature of matter as a spiritual journey, not simply as a detached observer but as a participant consciousness whose mental states reflect insight into the actual processes of chemical interaction. The same might be said for physics and astronomy, as well as other life sciences, as researched by seekers on a path of Wisdom based in a respectful and sensitive approach to understanding the sacred nature of matter, energy, and consciousness.

Traditional religions hold a variety of views on the sentience of nature, though many demote nature to a lower stratum in transcendent models that overvalue the etheric, spiritual, and nonmaterial subtle worlds. Sophianic Wisdom is embodied, a this-world orientation, not excluding transcendent aspects but valuing embodiment as a central focus for the work of becoming. Religious views are not paramount, they simply represent alternative traditions embedded in a particular type of spirituality; each offers a path, and each can be differentiated according to its goals. As Sophianic Wisdom is inclusive and incorporative, any spiritual path may serve to promote Sophianic development if that path corresponds to an embodied and transformative, ethical perspective that fully honors the world and all its creatures.

Most contemporary spiritual traditions do contain some expression of emergent Feminine Wisdom, not always as central but at least visible in a variety of symbols, images, concepts, and practices. However, what is now emerging is a forthcoming of Sophia in her own right, as a path that is distinct and recognizable however incorporative in its scope. The sacred world of Sophia is the natural world, the body is the natural temple, and the heart is the organ of central perception, linked to mind and soul in service of meaningful relationship with others. And the emphasis falls on personal development and shared transformations, not through doctrine, but through the alchemy of continual refinement and the cultivation of interconnected perceptions and insights. It is not a one-way path, but a multipath pilgrimage whose travelers intersect with and learn from the paths and insights of others.

The "hidden spirits" of the natural world are those subtle influences that act upon us, and through us, to facilitate alchemical interconnection and relatedness to the web of life. Every spiritual tradition notes the impact and effects of nonvisible, soulful influences that originate in a spiritually defined cosmos of entities with no discernible physical form. Earth-based spirituality, as noted above, links these influences with actual animals, plants, minerals, stones, and elements of earth, water, air, and fire, as seen in many alchemical schools. The Sophianic perspective is, as I see it, a confirmation of subtle alchemical influences that impact and motivate our actions but whose origins are not reducible to the individual psyche. The "web of life" metaphor, the shared matrix, suggests a transpersonal interconnectedness of participants through a variety of media including dreams, intuitions, mental or emotional impressions, paranormal perceptions, and explicitly shared images or thoughts. A thought-world is a subtle world, a school of thought sustained through the mental-emotive awareness of its members. There are spiritual connections in the sense that similarity in thought or belief forms an open matrix of psychic impressions whose contents surpass any one individual synthesis.

A Sophianic view is one that is invisibly shared among many hearts and minds, a sharing that creates a context for the transmission of insight across the field and between members. The Wisdom-field is a *spiritual matrix*, a field constructed by conscious meanings and values, subject to revision and reformation, and open to other larger, more complex thought-belief worlds. Sophianic thought-worlds are not all the same, there are many differences in signs and images and ideas, but at the heart of the differences is a similarity of respect, love, and cooperation. In turn, a Sophianic thought-world, like all thought-worlds, attracts (and repels) various other psychic influences that are extrasensory sources of empowerment. For example, specific beliefs resonant within explicit collective attitudes create a subconscious flow between the individual and certain psychic configurations within the collective.

A materialist attitude creates sympathy within the collective for materialism and its adherents concur on a subconscious plane of subtle interactions, the same for all schools of thought. Various thought-worlds are formed as a subnet of shared ideas and resources that act to stimulate thought and actions. A spiritual belief system is a resonance sustained by collective mentality and a shared context for insights based on the nature, symbolism, and practices of that tradition. The Sophianic perspective is emergent and formative, creating a variety of new contexts for relatedness and opening unique wisdom fields of subtle influence within the collective to support each perspective. The Sophianic perspective is emergent but also ancient because it valorizes certain spiritual teachings long known to humanity in diverse cultures.

However, subtle influences cannot be simply reduced to the "collective" if that implies a strictly human mentality, excluding all other forms of psychic influence. Few people have genuine creative insight into the actual nature and contents of the psychic world and the construct of the *Mundus Imaginalis* (Imaginal World) remains an open horizon for further explorations.* Agency within that open domain may, as noted, include the sentient influences of all living creatures—such that animal minds may well interact with and influence, invisibly, human behavior and thought. The sentience of any entity is a possible source of subtle influence; a particular plant, like white sage, may have nonvisible influences that support, for example, calm, clarity, and inner purification. If we give up our chauvinism and self-centered anthropomorphic attitudes, we can discover a much larger world of psychic influences that incorporates many forms of sentience and does not make human consciousness the center of the universe. In this open horizon of shared sentience, the nature of human development may well depend upon our ability to overcome the bias that would deny shared sentient influences of nonhuman beings, or the influence of other-than-human beings.

---

*Henri Corbin's concept of the Mundus Imaginalis is discussed in Tom Cheetham's *Imaginal Love.*

In this development, dreams are the mediating context for discovery and influence in the Mundus Imaginalis. What we dream, in terms of our relatedness to other species, beings, entities, spirits, or angelic manifestations, is a sign of the possible seeking confirmation and expression. I do not literalize my dreams in an explicit concrete sense, but I do not deny the transpersonal contents that specific figures in my dreams represent. In the visionary world, beings do appear, manifest independence, and offer guidance and direction, sometimes quite oblique, that contributes to self-conscious development or reveals a fracture or conflict in need of healing. The vast array of spirit beings found in all religious traditions suggests the pervasiveness of transpersonal agency as enacted through vivid, direct personal dream and waking encounter. My own visions and dreams challenge me to acknowledge these agents as something other than subjective mental creations and to recognize the validity of sentience in subtle forms and beings distinct from my own mentality.* In a spiritual cosmos, agency and impact are linked to our mental processes and perceptions and they extend beyond the sphere of the material or the personal subjective psyche.

The larger cosmos, as mesocosm or macrocosm, manifests subtle agency of a highly complex nature, fluid, adaptive, and sentient beyond mere projection or speculation. The actuality of that agency is directly experienced and known by a very large population of dreamers, visionaries, psychics, and sensitives whose experience is indicative of a greater and more complex multidimensionality. The Sophiana of this complex is a feature of unfolding, an opening up to or a reclaiming of innate psychic capacities that are absolutely necessary for full human development. And these latent psychic abilities are an essential feature of our relatedness to a more complex, subtle, invisible world (or worlds) of

*For more on dreams and spirit encounters, see Lee Irwin, *Dreams Beyond Time*, 191–201.

agents, also sentient and independent but linked to our evolving, collective planetary life. The Wisdom approach is to take a soulful view, to open heart and mind to the invisible, subtle, and transpersonal as an intrinsic feature of our natural beingness. Sophianic Wisdom is intuitive and subtle, not a hard rationalism, but a soft imaginative receptivity to the possible as well as a gentle acknowledgment of the actual and immediate being. Both matter—the soulful perception of the subtle world and a pragmatic commitment to solving real-world problems—and both are needed for real solutions.

Spiritual beings represent their own wisdom and understanding, not based on forms of absolute knowledge but rather reflecting their own learning experiences. The question of subjectivity raises the issue of autonomy as both an expression of inner self-awareness and shared mentality with others, this includes all spirit beings. They are no more autonomous in thinking and understanding than we are as individual embodied human beings; they too participate in the shared matrix of thought-worlds that shape emergent wisdom. Nor do they seem distinct from the personalities and thought-worlds of the mediators who receive instructions from them; there is a matrix of interests and intentions that shape how those relationships evolve and form. And they go through stages, just as in any developmental process, thereby suggesting that development is indeed a norm for even the most refined spiritual entities. These stages reflect a process ontology, how evolution is a universal aspect of sentient relations, how things and beings evolve through interactions leading to new understanding. Sophianic knowledge is transitive, not final or fixed.

THE WEB OF LIVING LIGHTS

When I look up into the heavens, see the span of stars that represent our galactic home, see the punctuated vastness lit by distant starlight, and observe the brilliant fullness of our own star, I am stunned by the beauty and the Infinitude. We are not alone; the cosmos is filled with life, not just energy and matter, but with consciousness and intelligence as well. As long as we search only the visible spectrum we will find little evidence of the actual living cosmos; only when we open our perceptions to the full spectrum of sentience, to all other living minds, will we begin to find direct evidence of the many worlds that coexist with us. The Sophianic perspective is that we inhabit and coexist within a continuum of shared consciousness whose nature and scope far exceed human mentality. By *continuum* I mean a range of psychonoetic perceptions, a soul-knowing of the heart-mind that spans a field far greater than physical perceptions and connects to other forms of consciousness beyond the material realm.

My intuition is that we are inseparably part of this continuum, and our soulful relations reflect the degree of our preparedness to actually open to and receive from that vastly shared consciousness. Not all worlds succeed in attaining the necessary degree of openness and receptivity that allows for profound global transformations; some worlds may never acquire the appropriate mentality nor the necessary cooperative, harmonic global resonance that signals true world awakening. Some worlds seem darker, more closed, constricted by mentalities that choose control, dominance, obscurity over clarity, and deny all alternative worlds in order to promote narrow, rigid structures of consciousness suited only to a one-world theory. There is a range of worlds from the most contracted to the most open, and we stand in the middle, not yet mature but moving toward a possible fully conscious awareness beyond this one world.

The living universe is so much broader, vaster, multilayered, and filled with precious life and awareness on a scale far beyond any local cosmology. Nevertheless, this world, our world, is the place where embodied life holds the promise of possible fluorescence into a truly intelligible world of self-awakened beings. And the Sophia of this awakening is expressed through a feminine metaphor, a flowering, an opening to beauty, reverence, and appreciation for all sentient life, through the development of our own beauty and well-being. We cannot behold the beauty unless we become beautiful within our own life, within our own well-tended world; to see beauty (kallos) is to be beauty. This beauty is a *soulful beauty*, an openness to the larger cosmos through soulful, deeply felt, fully enacted participation in the creation of a better, more beautiful world. This is our challenge, not to destroy, deface, and abuse, but to honor, create, and revere life and all life-forms for the good of the whole. The Wisdom approach is not so difficult, it simply begins by honoring the worth of others, preserving relations, and genuinely expressing reverence for the very fact of life, your own and all others.

By *soul* I mean the sentient field that surrounds and penetrates the body, an identity formation that is capable of surviving death and has a capacity for rebirth. The soul, as noted in NDE research, retains cognitive ability and may have enhanced cognitive capacities once liberated from the body.[6] It is soul that is the basis of intelligence as carried in memory, sensate impressions, and *samskaras* (habit energies) that form the personality core of each individual. I believe soul is an evolute, that is, an entity that came into being over time through evolutionary processes until it reached a capacity to retain individual identity after death. In the larger cosmological sense, soul precedes mind, insofar as soul is a ground-of-being identity developed through intimate partnership with body evolution. Body-soul evolves from the most basic conditions while mind reflects a later self-reflective stage. For me, this is Sophianic because it prioritizes incarnational development with body-soul as the root cause of our shared self-aware mentality.

In keeping with a Sophianic view, I believe soul development is a *collective* phenomena—meaning, soul is a subtle field of shared awareness that links us with other beings (not just human) to form a matrix of relationship that can then sustain (or harm) future soul development. Cultural values reflect soul development; what a culture values, promotes, enforces, or represses rises from the inner domain of internalized values passed through generational (collective) learning and bias. In this context soul is not a pure entity created by a divine being, but a process identity evolved through multiple shared incarnations and cultural immersions in a variety of social contexts and diverse gender orientations.

The medium of soul expression and enhanced soul awareness is linked to dreams, such that soul knowledge comes vividly from dreams that are less conditioned by the social ego. Soul wisdom is a consequential accumulation of insights gained through lived experience, education, training, cultural immersion, and multiple incarnations. As we grow into the dawning of a renewed Feminine Wisdom we can draw upon the deep roots of soul to inform and shape our shared current understanding. Soul knowledge is developmental; through thought, feelings, perceptions, and experience, soul can become more aware and more fully able to access the deeper intuitive knowing that soul holds through its many incarnations.

Is this inner Wisdom the same as intelligence? I do not believe that the Sophianic Wisdom is simply an expression of intelligence, though intelligence can bring luster to that Wisdom. The Wisdom I refer to is the wisdom of the soulful heart—the capacity to sense, feel, know, and respond to the life and value of others, the world, the cosmos, without aggrandizing one's own worth or value. And we should not minimize self-worth either; it is a matter of balance, of standing with integrity and dignity in the face of the Infinite, so much greater than any individual, and seeing within that Infinite something more profound than our own image. The male idea of man made in the image of God is only one image among many other images that do not glorify human maleness nor require anything remotely humanlike in appearance. And the sacred source of that image is not female either; the divine nature is a very profound Mystery, and no image (of any gender) can represent the fullness from which all life comes, all species, all worlds, through all time. One image of Infinitude is nothing more than an affirmation of a particular creative occasion, one to be valued and revered, but only one among so many more.

This wisdom of the soulful heart does not lack intelligence, if we assume that all sentient beings reflect some degree of intelligence in their very nature as distinct entities. Sentience as a property of nature is a pervasive quality of soul whose actualization requires, in a distinct species, evidently millions of years to actually reach a significant degree of self-reflective intelligibility. I would argue, somewhat metaphorically, that the wisdom of the heart is old, a primordial soul wisdom that sustains the grounding relatedness to the world and to others that then, through sharing, fosters intelligibility of mind. First, I imagine we cohabit and coexist and create rudimentary forms of community and interdependence, which then leads to an increased degree of leisure and surplus that allows for the cultivation of more reflective, aesthetic, and symbolic expression. Our relationship to life-forms, animals, plants, and other creatures, including the spirit world, is thus more primal and more ingrained in a deep relational, soulful sense than our capacity for abstraction, logic, and later forms of mental development. However, this does not imply that Wisdom is regressive because the principle of Sophia as "living wisdom" is adaptive to and fully correspondent with contemporary, current mentality. As intelligibility evolves so too does Wisdom adapt; the integration of heart, soul, and mind is dynamically correspondent with our relatedness to others and the world at large and reflects the varying stages of our collective maturation.

The very nature of intelligence is by no means fully understood. If Wisdom is a deep participant aspect of Being and Spirit, and I believe it is, then its manifestation in the form of intelligibility is not restricted to simply mental activity. There are perhaps many kinds of intelligence and while some forms may be more developed in one person as compared to another, they may be equally intelligent and yet have very different skills and abilities.* Excellence in some skills, unique abilities of mind, psychic sensitivities, body-centered perceptions, relational intuitions, may all be expressions of intelligence and reflect a larger spectrum of consciousness that is irreducible to simple, discreet mental acts. A logical intelligence is simply a type, not the epitome of what constitutes intelligence more fully or completely. Abstract thinking is a specific activity that may be highly developed but very limited and narrow in scope. And certain types of intelligence may reflect, as in some forms of autism or savant capacity, remarkable and even astonishing ability isolated from normative patterns of social interaction.

The wisdom of the soulful heart may also have multiple expressions, but its grounding metaphor requires "a felt sense of the other" as an embodied, consciously aware being. The overdeveloped mind tends to dominate perceptions through excessive mentalizations. The heart, as a living organ of life-giving vitality, as a neural complex sharing cellular continuity with the brain and other organs, is more fundamentally body-centered and holistic. Because heart-centered perceptions are body felt, emotionally sensitive, and generative of a larger field of energetic influences, both receptive to and

---

*For more on various types of intelligence, see Howard Gardner's *Five Minds for the Future*; he has many other published works on this topic as well.

influential on others, it has a generative capacity far greater than the brain or any other organ.* Thus heart-centered awareness, expressive of our deepest and most enduring sense of connectivity with others, the world, and even the cosmos at large, is a primordial knowing-through-relatedness, a soulful knowing based on shared perceptions (not always in agreement!).

The radiant field, the electromagnetic heart pulse and rhythm, impacts those around us and we are also impacted by the heart-states of those with whom we interact. This is why a "loving heart" is one that calms, soothes, and brings a feeling of acceptance and support when one enters the field of a truly loving person. The generative power of the heart, expressive of reverence, compassion, loving kindness, or thankfulness, creates a powerful field that can immediately impact and influence others. This is a matter of something more than intelligence, it is a state-specific condition linked to the heart as a rhythmic center of well-being broadcast into the world to the benefit of others. The soulful heart when healthy and calm is integral to this sense of well-being, it creates a shared field of soul-presence because the roots of soul reach into the depths of true Being and Mystery. The soulful heart solicits third presence.

Heart-centered Wisdom is a light unto the world; it is a luminous source for world transformation in a very subtle, psycho-energetic sense. The heart-soul field expressing Wisdom is an intelligible field of a certain type. It is the *intelligence of relatedness*, both morally developed and psychically imbued with qualities of shared consciousness. Those qualities are unique to each individual but, in a shared sense, they reflect a genuineness of concern for the well-being of others and a dedicated co-participation in an interactive process that is supportive and loving. The qualities of consciousness are not

---

*The website of the HeartMath Institute contains much research on the nature and field of the heart.

simply mental but existential, that is, based on lived values embodied through actual *soul praxis* in support of creating a more loving
world. The grounded praxis is simply to be loving and compassionate, to express care and concern that is heart-centered, in the most
direct and genuine sense. It is found in the practice of responsible
love and in a creative willingness to be thankful for the opportunities to be loving and supportive. One of the healthiest states is
the state of soulful *gratitude*, and to live without gratitude, without
thankfulness or the recognition of our need for others and the ways
in which others act to support and foster our growth is to live in
contraction, with a closed, contracted heart.*

The "web of living lights" refers to the interconnected fields
that link loving individuals in the shared matrix of soulful, heart-
centered world transformation. That web is not restricted to simply the obvious material world, but extends into the subtle worlds
of psychic perception, and includes agents of a more transpersonal
nature also contributing to our collective well-being. Even further,
that web can link to other worlds where diverse beings also support the developmental process of creating a balanced planet of
embodied, cooperative species. We do not yet comprehend the
actual scope of world awakening and world transformation; we see
myopically only our own problems, conflicts, and unresolved tensions, aggressions, and competing theories of world creation. What
we do not see is the larger scale of the transformation in a cosmogenesis whose paradigms are by no means unique to our processes,
but which contribute to a far greater scale of change and development. Cosmogenesis refers to world transformation in a "many
worlds" context such that our human evolution is not singular or
unique but an index of a vaster evolutionary becoming on a cosmic

---

*For more on the crucial importance of gratitude and its relation to the heart, see
Robert Emmons and Michael McCullough, *The Psychology of Gratitude*.

scale that requires whole worlds to evolve beyond their local and self-absorbed concerns.

In the larger sense, the Sophianic Wisdom comes back to the embodied practices of the loving heart, to the soulful center of the transformation, however obtuse the theory of cosmological development may appear. What matters is not the overall cosmic context as much as the immediate, effective application of Sophianic praxis in and through our relationships. The web of lights in the human-animal-world scale is great enough; our connectivity through the soulful heart is a source of light that brings spontaneous illumination as hearts touch and souls commune. Love of others, love of animals, love of nature, love of the world, love of the unseen powers of spiritual life, all contribute to the soulful awakening of the Heart's Wisdom. Sophiana sings in our blood when the heart circulates loving, soul-centered concern for more than our self; we can infuse the very energy of our life field with psychic qualities that directly impact the states of others. The qualities we cultivate and embody, those virtues that best represent our loving concerns, are animate within and through the field of the heart and that field extends to the hearts of others. And when we touch, heart to heart, there is light . . . subtle, soft, infusive, and world transforming.

3

Praxis of Awareness

MIND

Mind is not less important than the heart but it is perhaps somewhat less primordial in our developmental evolution. I would suggest that "mind linked to brain" is only a partial description of mind and that mind, in the full sense, is more thoroughly body based than simply described in terms of discreet activities of one organ, the brain. The entirety of the neural system, the complete energetic field of embodied mentality, is centered in the brain but not reducible to brain-only activity. I believe that the heart center, as an organ of relatedness, has its own intelligence; and perhaps, as many Indigenous peoples teach, other bodily organs also embody qualities of intelligence. Perhaps we can intuit that intelligence is not strictly a mental property as much as it is a quality of Being whose sentient adaptation to a particular complex function results in a qualitative awareness unique to that function. Thus, the liver may have unique qualities of sentience that actually contribute to the overall sentience of the entire being and so on for every organ. Perhaps this functional adaptation of sentience goes all the way down to the cells, the neural networks, and the energetic transmissions of consciousness throughout the entirety of the living being, extending into a transphysical field that reflects consciousness as an auric or energetic soul-field phenomenon.

In this complex of meshed sentience, in the qualitative sense of shared awareness, specific "mental" functions may be appropriately described as reflexive and analytic abilities arising from the constitution of the whole person, as a conjoined synthesis or alchemy of all participant organic structures. Could one think without a heart? Does the liver contribute to qualities of consciousness? Does my sexuality influence my mentality? Does the very quality of my blood constitute particular attributes of mind, or at least affect heart-mind in some subtle ways? Does what I eat or drink result in mental consequences? If the mind is body based, then mental activities we denoted as "head-centered" or "brain based" may be only a theoretical portion of a much more comprehensive totality. Mind in the larger sense can also be related to soul, in which case, mind is not in fact utterly dependent upon brain or body, opening the door to a vaster process of mentality than even body can support.*

As a "relative non-dualist" I do not emphasize the difference as much as the similarity and fit between body, mind, and the soulful heart in forming human identity in the immediate existential sense. My concern is to articulate the Sophianic principles of heart-mind as intrinsic to embodied life in the world, not as a transphysical entity, even though I do believe that death is a transition, not an end. Feminine Wisdom is here and now in the immediate bodily sense, and what matters in terms of mentality is the cultivation of mind in harmony with body as temple. The three most fundamental aspects of mind are thought, memory, and imagination; each is

*See Lee Irwin, *The Labyrinths of Love*, for more on this topic.

influenced by emotion and mood. For me, these properties of mind are body based, not brain based, even if the brain is the obvious site for specific mental activities. Having an organic center for mental activities does not mean that those activities are restricted to and only created by that organ.

The brain as I see it is more a mediating and transmitting organ, one that coordinates and processes sensation, perceptions, and discreet mental activities. As an organizing center, it is surely the hub or nexus through which mental activities occur as webbed into larger neural networks. But the reach of intelligence as intrinsic to the development of sentience in specific form and function suggests that as an organizing center, the brain is receiving information and "intelligence" from multiple sources intrinsic to the body in all its organic complexity even down to the cellular and pre-cellular, possibly molecular and submolecular levels. In a subtle sense, the brain also receives information extrinsically from the nonphysical world, through psychic sensitivity that is more than brain based.[1] The brain, as I see it, mediates and coordinates, transmits and receives, reacts and responds, but is not the source of intelligence.

Awareness, in the broad sense, is the combined synthesis of all perceptive organs and activities intrinsic to my bodily life. If I cut my finger, I feel it, know it, experience the impact, and assimilate information that modifies my behavior. My entire body is involved, my stomach reacts, my heart speeds up, certain emotions are triggered, energy flows, shock is felt, and mind may be blank, overwhelmed by other sensations and inflow. If I imagine vividly, I feel it in a direct bodily sense; if I remember an incident in the past, I feel it and it may even have location in specific muscles or bodily locations. If I think clearly and inspirationally, the effect is an energetic uplift of body-mind-heart integration, insight may dawn and transform my mental horizon in ways that impact my entire being, mood, sense of self, and result in mental reorganization of habits and attitudes.

I see thought as manifest through the qualitative context of bodily life, such that my thinking is a dynamic part of my felt world and inseparable from my sense of well-being and meaningful interactions with others. We do not think in a vacuum, we are always in relationship, even if only to the thoughts and ideas of others. Our entire mental life pilgrimage is a search for mental stability, creative freedom, and self-discovery linked to our ability to articulate and communicate what we discover. In this process, Wisdom can infuse and guide our mental activity and in so doing, open the doors of perceptions to new vistas of thought and inspiring visionary horizons of what is and what may become.

HEALING OLD WOUNDS

Mental life is not separable from emotional life; mind and heart, in a metaphorical sense as well as in an actual existential sense, work in harmony with the whole body to support genuine Wisdom. If the body is hurt, that hurt can harm heart and mind; if the body is nurtured and disciplined, mind and heart are nurtured and disciplined. Mental development is a body-based process and a healthy mind requires a healthy body, such is the Wisdom path. The Sophianic approach to mind is to truly respect and honor mental life and development but to do so by bringing body and mind into harmony with the heart and with all our relations. Purely mental development is a chimera of mind cut off from bodily life; mental development in the holistic, Sophianic, feminine sense requires training and education that is integral to the whole person, not just to the development of mental skills and technical languages. Such a holistic approach requires a full integration of emotional life in support of meaningful intelligence, an intelligence that is unique for each individual and is as diverse as the interests of each person.

There really is no standard measure for education or for mental training in a fixed systemic sense. A soulful education is one that honors and recognizes the capacities of each individual in a context of development through partnership that fosters interest and motivates exploration. Educational training requires flexibility and adaptation to meet the needs of different individuals in order to discover the unique gifts, capacities, and a possible skill set that best promotes individual intelligence and insight. Can we educate the whole person? Can intelligence be cultivated that is unique and expressive of individual skills and abilities? How do we train people in difficult, demanding disciplines and also honor those skills as indicating success without overdramatizing or excessively overvaluing such accomplishments?

My response to all these questions is that what matters is the whole person, not simply an intelligible skill nor a particular expertise. What truly matters is the entire person, the quality of all their relations, and the goodness that is evident in how they live and act, in the goals they seek. To educate the whole person means that no area of life is exempt from development and that special skills are only a narrow expression of a much larger spectrum of intelligibility. Education in the most complete sense is about drawing out potential in all areas of human life and teaching the appropriate values and behaviors that best solicit a creative world of loving relations and genuine heart-centered partnerships. The whole person is an image of the cosmos in a specific sense, an integration of unique potentials as embodied by cultural and historic location, and yet, reaches beyond that locality into the very foundations of intelligence and awareness.

However, many people have been deformed and repressed, mass educated and conventionally taught to act according to prejudicial values or narrow spectrums of intelligibility that do not foster cooperation or mutual discovery. Education is not about teaching competition or encouraging success only among those who demonstrate special abilities. Education in the full sense is about more than learning particular skills or disciplinary expertise; it is more about the value and worth of every aspect of our human situation: body, diet, health habits, emotional well-being, friendship, skill in dialogue, quality interactions with others, mutual respect, moral values, a fertile imagination, cultivating creativity and curiosity, overcoming bias, and gaining comparative perspectives without overvaluing one's own accomplishments or insights. Sophianic Wisdom requires soulful education, education of the body and heart, not just the mind; it is more than learning to reason and judge because judgment requires maturity in life experience in all areas of human endeavor, not just in the application of abstract ideas within a particular thought-world. Such education is not about specialized vocabulary and the techgnosis of disciplinary specialization; deep education requires the full participation of all our abilities, of body, mind, soul, and spirit.

The deformation of soul, the psychic impact of narrowly routinized education, in terms of family values, attitudes toward others, emotional abuse, or verbal aggression, all contribute to a diminishment of soul. A soulful individual seeks to discover within themself a deeply felt relationship to the value and worth of others, who may embody very different values and attitudes. A soulful life is heart-centered, an awareness that senses and interacts with the heart-centered concerns of others distinct from one's self; a soulful life implies an ability to love in a nondiscriminatory way beyond the confines of one's home or community. But such love is rare and often only learned much later in life because of the deformation and lack of emphasis on love and compassion in conventional education and learning. We learn to compete, to excel, to *conquer* fears, and to *repress* unwanted feelings that interfere with "success" in the external, outward sense. We cultivate mind but not empathy, analysis but not synthesis, deconstruction but not creativity. Even with specific successes the inner life is often very immature, diminished, under-developed, or submerged in conventional beliefs that dislocate soul from the center and substitute a narrow intellectual expertise based on unexamined attitudes as sufficient for worldly success.

In a less soul-centered life, social recognition often becomes a substitute for a more personal sense of connection to diverse others whose skills may be quite different and not pragmatic or external. A kind person, a gentle or deeply feeling person, or a creative and eccentric person may have intelligible qualities far more important than expert knowledge or technical skills. That is not to say that expertise and technical skills are not important or necessary but rather that Wisdom is not simply a matter of such expertise. Pragmatic abilities should be recognized and valued but not set forth as a substitute for a more soulful life; one can be technically developed, expert in explicit areas, and still be soulful, creative, and caring. What matters is the quality of life and the depth of perception, not simply learned skills or admirable abilities. So often, the inner life is buried beneath the demands for conformity, expertise, worldly success, or even more aggressive, critical attitudes eulogizing a specific worldview as superior to most other perspectives. In a shared world of multiple and diverse views, education of soul requires flexibility, openness, and maturity in negotiating our relations within that diversity.*

Unfortunately, many people are wounded by their family, community, personal relations, or education in the external, competitive

---

*For more on education and the soul, see John Miller, *Education and the Soul*.

sense. We do not teach spiritual values or heart-centered development in a broad cultural sense; we tend to teach pragmatic skills and to value competitive success without reference to "private" or "personal" life as though personhood was based on adaptation and conformity to existing social norms. But personhood, in the Sophianic sense, is about finding and developing personal integrity, inner qualities of soulful being, and genuine skills in relating to others, however different their thinking or beliefs. The wounded soul, that is the deformed psyche, can and does react, often with disturbing violence, as a consequence of loss of soul, loss of personhood, repressed by social values that fail to recognize and foster what is truly valuable and worthy in each person. Violence is an illness of soul, a state of being that falsely believes that aggression, lies, deception, and even mass destruction can bring about some ill-formed good whose manifestation would serve only a very limited and repressive minority. In this context, the victim is also the perpetuator; the cycle of violence is an inherited set of stunted values whose enactment serves only narrow, self-centered goals accomplished through the repression of often innocent others.

The greater good, the good that serves the intelligible uplift of humanity through right-minded, heart-centered education, is the good that recognizes the value of the individual in the context of shared responsibilities based on an embodied praxis of social harmony. But social harmony requires healthy minds; social integration must support the healthy development of personhood, of individual worth, and the recognition of innate abilities, not determined by functional values. Such education requires mental-emotive training and self-discovery, the worth of dream knowledge and the imagination, the value of creative expression and skill in variable modes of communication and self-reflection. The praxis of social harmony is born and cultivated by education of soul that acknowledges the necessity of both individual development and social well-being.

The Sophianic path requires self-knowledge as part of our education and mindful awareness that is fully engaged in exploring and developing qualities of consciousness discernible through inner attention. Wisdom develops through a stage-by-stage realization of the interplay between inner life and outer expectations and between psychic sensitivity and committed social action. Such Wisdom is not simply "inner," but it does recognize the value and worth of direct personal insight based on feelings, intuitions, and imaginal mental activity that can then be aligned with more pragmatic concerns and responsibilities. Education should teach transformation and adaptation, not simply the unreflective assimilation of information or depersonalized training in expert skills.[2]

Wisdom requires *mental clarity* as a fundamental quality of mind applied to what arises within the field of consciousness, not as socially constructed, but as personally perceived. I do not believe, nor experience, the world as didactically formative in the shaping of my mental-emotive life. What I experience is a living, interactive relationship between my soulful personhood and my lived-world. That lived-world, as expressed here, is complex, cosmological, and not reducible to any particular social or cultural model even though it is influenced by and consistent with my cultural and historical location. But the context for me is global, not local, and transhistorical, not simply a lineal account of my current embodied life. By *transhistorical* I mean that my personhood is not reducible to my immediate embodied experience but extends beyond my present incarnational life and accesses information that reveals a more distant past and a more extensive future than my immediate lived-world. And I see this greater past and future clearly, in a state of calm, as extending beyond the horizon of my current physical embodiment and yet acting to inform my personhood through insights that I would call psychic and Sophianic. The interplay between personhood and social expectation, between being a self-aware individual and a socially responsible participant in communal life, is a partnership that requires a significant degree of both education and enhanced self-awareness.

The value of *clarity* in mental life should not be underestimated because often what arises in a subtle sense, as informative and guiding insight, appears spontaneously when mind is able to sustain a clear and open state. As a lifelong practitioner of meditation, for over fifty years, my praxis is to cultivate meditative stillness of mind, a calming of mental activity, and the cultivation of quiet concentration without object, sound, or thought. In this lifelong practice, I discovered early that mental well-being and balance was impossible without an accompanying effort to distill, refine, examine, and rebalance my psychic life. The complementary practice to meditation is self-analysis directed toward greater maturity. What is necessary is to engage in an ongoing and thorough examination of self, an unpacking of attitudes, beliefs, values, mental habits, and acquired learning in order to reach a more integrated, inwardly consistent, and balanced mind.

The attainment of mental clarity requires lifelong praxis in the synthesis of feeling, thought, imagination, and value orientation in a dynamic context of mature development, which includes training the mind in stillness. It is quite possible in this process to reach a stable condition, one that is fully functional and self-aware and then to imagine that such a state is the goal of mental life. That is not my view. My view as a follower of Sophia is that mental, emotive, heart-centered life is an unending process of discovery and continuing transformation. Thus, a stable condition is always subject to challenge and greater awareness; mastery is gaining the necessary expertise to revise, reformulate, and shift the gestalt, a flexibility that fosters new insights leading to a more mature Wisdom.

The healing of old wounds requires mental transformation and rebirth in the direct psychonoetic sense. The goal is to liberate the "old self" from narrow thinking, outer authority, and a lack of inner sensitivity for an ongoing process of discovery and the development of intuitive insights beyond a current state of relative stability. It is a spiral path, one that can recycle and recover former states, beliefs, and mental-emotive conditions and nuance what is coming-to-be with greater depth and fullness. And it is a path of discovery for what is emerging, not yet manifest, but seeking embodiment through personhood that is able to sustain those insights and offer them for reflection and consideration to others. Healing is primarily a matter of bringing greater consciousness to the subliminal, to the not-yet-recognized influences that bear on particular states, moods, and reactions of a personal kind and that are irreducible to one's explicit beliefs or ordinary attitudes.

The "unexplored country" is where the healing is needed because the conscious mind is only the surface of our complex personhood and we require deeper self-awareness than simple conformity to the unexamined life. The challenge is to take up the task and to maintain an ever-deepening self-awareness that is both socially valuable and personally fulfilling. This requires intelligence, training, and self-discipline as they contribute to our pilgrimage to a more complete realization of Wisdom. The feminine aspect of this process is based on supportive love, a nurturing that is not overdemanding nor overly critical. This is a process of patient uncovering, of necessary asides and occasional detours, a cycle not an inflexible straight line. Developing self-awareness in the feminine context requires substantial relations with others, and a deep sense of one's own relativity; we work together toward the realization of individual goals. The path is one of creative discovery, it has playfulness, good humor, and lightheartedness as well; it is not simply sobriety without a smile. A good laugh is a sign of deepening wisdom!

TAKING FULL RESPONSIBILITY

The person most responsible for your personal development and integration is you, not a teacher or friend or master. And every person is a teacher and not all masters are helpful. The theme of mastery often obscures the process of self-development. The traditional view of the "master" is one who knows and has attained the highest states on a given path, a person imbued with gnosis, and a living example of spiritual personhood, a "realized being" representing an ideal. And this is good and valuable and such a person can be a trustworthy teacher, guide, and friend. But on the Sophianic path, each person seeks to walk their own walk and the challenge is to find an intelligible way of life that best supports the unique path you choose. We can all learn from masters, teachers, and guides but this does not mean that a seeker's will should be surrendered to another, nor does it require conformity to ideas or values that might conflict with an intrinsic sense of one's own self-worth or positive beliefs.

A person may freely choose to accept the guidance and spiritual direction of another because that respected other offers soulful guidance felt to enhance awareness and insight. But the deeper challenge is to take full and complete responsibility for one's own spiritual life, to honor all the teachings that inspire and give direction, and then to assimilate those teachings and to amplify, develop, and creatively apply them in a unique synthesis of soul-making.*

---

*On "soul-making," see James Hillman's *Re-Visioning Psychology*.

And this process is one that requires mental clarity, applied intelligence, and continuing self-examination. What the teacher offers is an alternative for self-knowledge, instructions for a way of life that may be better and more integral than the current life. However, the more feminine approach places emphasis on multiple relations, seeing the teacher in every person, and not necessarily submitting to the authority of another.

In this process of taking responsibility, mind plays a critical and central role. It is fundamental that we must think about our life, values, responsibilities, and core beliefs. The assumption of beliefs is not simply a matter of a transmitted teaching or a value set learned from family, community, or personal study. The Sophianic praxis is to think carefully and critically about one's lived-world, in all its various aspects and dimensions. There is a creative tension often found between values that one holds to be necessary as they inform and give direction for a spiritual path and, alternatively, received ideas or beliefs that are celebrated as expressions of wisdom and insight within a particular tradition or social context. A thoughtful approach requires an engagement with traditions and belief systems whose importance cannot be simply determined by collective assent or epitomized by celebrated, distinguished teachers and guides.

A person might consciously choose to follow a tradition, to assimilate the teachings of a tradition as a member of a distinct community; however, even that decision requires some degree of personal adaptation to what is received and then personalized. I believe that every person can contribute to the embodiment of tradition in a historical process of self-discovery that requires the synthesis of multiple fields of intelligible research and discovery. We can no longer define *post-religious* spirituality in terms of any one tradition but face the challenge of multiple traditions, multiple fields of discourse

on topics critical of tradition, and a host of discoveries not assimilated or addressed by those traditions. From a post-traditional perspective, there are many teachers and guides but no exclusive loyalty
is required to legitimize a spiritual view.[3] Why? Because feminine
spirituality is not a matter of sanctions by external authority; instead
it rises through the integrity and soulfulness of its lived expression
and dedicated embodiment.

Wisdom, as a realization of deeper truth and fulfillment, is
not reducible to any one, or any combination of, traditions. The
very concept of a traditional thinker or of a person whose thoughts
are directed and informed by an explicit historically grounded religious (or secular) philosophy or thought-world, however sophisti-
cated, reflects the past, not the future. I do not mean to suggest
that such a thinker cannot contribute significantly to the present
or to the future, nor am I challenging the value attributed to a
tradition. But a traditional orientation is based on a mentality of
multiple generations of thinkers immersed in a long sequence of
thoughts and values often limited by inherited prejudice, dogmatism, cultural particularity, and male-centered thinking.

In a deep Sophianic sense, present and future thinking challenges attitudes or faith claims that are restricted to or dedicated to
doctrines whose intelligibility is more a matter of inherited thinking
and belief, and less a matter of actual direct perception and creative
self-realization. The Sophianic path requires utmost authenticity in
the present, not encumbered by the past, but informed by the past in
ways that offer insight and guidance consistent with a larger scale of
values whose full range encompasses human knowledge and discovery in all areas of life. We can draw upon a wide array of resources
for investigation and actualization of a Wisdom path and this array
includes all fields of knowledge. Select areas of knowledge may be
reconciled with more traditional thinking or those areas may offer

utmost challenge to traditional beliefs and values. In post-traditional spirituality, what matters most is direct personal insights and how those insights contribute to a better, more mature world.

The issue as I see it is not the past value of tradition, certainly not as a template for future becoming, but the credible thought, reflections, and spiritual realizations that traditions offer as informing the processes of human development, regardless of the future. There are transpersonal aspects inherent in all spiritual traditions and those aspects offer profound insight into our human capacities and latent potential. The value of traditional teachings is found, as I see it, not in the constructs of doctrine and required beliefs, but in the living realizations of spiritual embodiment that demonstrate our inseparable relatedness to a profound ontological depth. Our full human beingness is realized through intelligible access to and encounter with Being and Spirit as embodied in various states and stages of shared illumination. Yet, these illuminations do not conform to a singular pattern, nor is their manifestation limited to a strictly traditional practice or path. A thoughtful approach to deep potential can value tradition as a resource and manifestation of spiritual capacity and yet also see those same capacities realized through practices and insights not defined by any particular tradition or religious value system. The intelligible future reveals a panoramic view of human capacity, unfolding and developing along multiple lines of exploration by no means confined to past traditions or conventional belief systems, including the limited beliefs found within the material or more traditional sciences.

Taking responsibility for spiritual life, as authentic existence, requires a genuine commitment to actual values, beliefs, and attitudes of mind as illustrated in embodied practices. But this commitment also requires serious thought and reflection; the Sophianic path is not a path of simple beliefs or conformity to fixed ideas and values. It is a path of *discovery*, a pilgrim's journey reverently undertaken as a life work, not through an inflexible belief system, but through an ongoing search for insight and understanding that informs and guides an exemplary way of life. The luminous example is seen in the quality of life, the depth of insight, the creative expression, and a skillful and compassionate ability to work with and genuinely love, and to be loved by, others. The thoughtful Wisdom of such a path is through creative expression and depth of insight arising from a disciplined mind, loving heart, and an honorable, enacted human sensitivity for the value and worth of others. It is a path both self-reflective and socially conscious, intelligible through thoughtful mental application and enriched through emotional depths and creative adaptation. It is not an exclusive path of conformity to a particular doctrine nor subject to communal or traditional consensus—creative discovery and bold insight need an open context for expression.

But what does it mean to be responsible? And how does such responsibility relate to clarity of mind and thought? There is an old logion, or saying, that I would phrase as "consistent in thought, word, and deed" as a fundamental basis for the development of responsible relations and positive self-expression. The term *consistent* implies several important attributes: that we do what we say we will do, in a timely and dependable way; that what we say or think is not contradicted by our actions or behaviors; and that there is a capacity to assess the continuity between thought, word, and deed. In short, that we do more than we promise and do so in a positive and patient frame of mind. Conversely, consistent does not mean lacking change or creative transformation. As we proceed on the path, our views, values, and attitudes may shift or change, and it is exactly this feature of transformation that requires clarity and self-analysis.

There is a significant difference between moods and impulses and clear insights and the re-evaluation of key values. Being responsible means acknowledging limitations, lack of clarity, befuddlement, and confusion, all normative on any spiritual path. One gains consistency through practice, and in sliding back or wandering off the path, by taking cognizance of loss of center and finding a way back. We are far from perfect beings; everyone makes mistakes, occasional poor judgments, and at times self-absorbed decisions insensitive to the needs or hopes of others. Being responsible means recognizing these slips, failures, and missteps in order to rectify and redress an attitude or act in ways that will lead to better judgment in the future. It means having a capacity to apologize and to change behavior in ways that support growth and positive insights. It means being reliable, even if fallible, and still dedicated to improvement and co-development.

Honesty in this context is crucial and heart-centered thinking requires a keen awareness of our personal limitations that may cause discontent, anger, or pain in others. The praxis is grounded in self-knowledge on the one hand and in the ability to hear and to listen with an open mind, the response, criticism, or reactions of others impacted by our behavior. And there is a distinction here between the impact of a behavior and the qualitative intent that motivated that behavior. Insofar as reactions are shaped by moods and impulses that arise and express subconscious or less-conscious attitudes, the context of blame or pain may reflect a lack of clarity between action and intention. Our intent may not be clear or even conscious and subconscious impulses may result in less-than-optimal behavior; the goal is to gain greater awareness of what motivates our behavior and how we might solicit a luminous third presence.

Intentions are shaped in highly diverse ways, not simply by conscious thought, which more often than not manifests as an after-effect seeking to "explain" actions or intentions. We act or react, respond or express intent often without forethought or reflection, calling upon mind as a means to legitimate or justify what has already been enacted. But a clear, calm mind can mediate reaction and impulse, can overcome transitory mood, and can shape intentions in a conscious, value-centered way that reflects maturity and does not lack spontaneity. I note that people often tend to believe, falsely as I see it, that clarity of mind and intent inhibits spontaneity, but a beautiful, utterly spontaneous work of art is often a creation of a very disciplined and well-practiced artist. The art of self-knowledge and clear intent can foster spontaneity and creative expression because mind becomes a disciplined medium of clarity that promotes intuition and fluid response free of repression, inhibition, false attitudes, and limited self-concepts.

The Sophianic work is a work of liberation from constraints that might impair creativity or repress development that is unique and additive to human maturity. The mental aspect in this process is less informed by abstract ideas, though at time such ideas can be very inspirational, and more informed by the cultivation of spiritual intelligence.[4] I believe that intelligence is not a fixed quantity and can be developed much more fully. The core of education is to develop intelligence that can be applied to human circumstances that genuinely matter and in so doing, leads to even greater insight and intelligibility. We inherit a rich ancestral past of thinking and creating, soulful in many cases and conformist in many others, that suggests a multitude of unanswered questions in the past that those embodied in the present have an opportunity to explore and investigate. We each can add to this intelligible past through our own thinking and embodied actions. Taking responsibility is not simply a task based on personal development but also encompasses the collective inheritance and unexamined possibilities of what has yet to be understood in that inheritance.

I feel a responsibility to address the issue of Wisdom not in a historical or traditional sense, but as a practice and orientation in the living present. There is a collective aspect to Wisdom, a history and representation as symbolized in the very term *Sophia*, a feminized emphasis. But for me, that history is secondary to a current, living presence of Wisdom as embodied in and through an intelligible recasting of our inheritance as adapted to shared, emergent discovery that can transform human understanding. Each person can add to or challenge the content of this writing but the real issue is how your own Wisdom is embodied and visible to others as an intelligible and accessible knowing. We can share perspectives, but we cannot live another's life, so each intelligible expression adds to the qualitative contents of Wisdom and none of those expressions are final or complete.

DREAMS AND INSPIRATIONS

For over fifty years I have kept a dream journal, recording dreams in detail, often with commentary, in electronic format for easy access and analysis. Dreams express variable modes of intelligibility, often synthetic with emotional states and amplified by, at times, powerful, affective dramatizations. And dreams are not all of one type but have many variants and reflect a wide range of psychic capacities often unrealized by the ordinary waking mind. This disjunction between the waking mind and the dreaming mind indexes our capacity to assimilate varying states of awareness that range beyond the boundaries of a strictly functional consciousness. The Sophianic approach to dreams is to treat them as viable expressions of meaningful psychic content, messages that need interpretation but whose origins are ontological and not just subconscious.[5]

For those who do not remember dreams or do not consider them relevant for self-development, the index is one of closure and denial of possibility. For those who make the effort to assimilate dreaming contexts into their waking awareness, the index is one of positive continuity between variable states. And for those who accept dreaming as an expressive manifestation of creative, guiding intelligence, the index is one of cyclical variability in a continuity of mind that seeks to sustain dreaming contents in the waking state and remain open to alternative states beyond dreaming. The Sophianic approach emphasizes the import of the *content* in dreams, which lead to insights about our individual, collective, global situation, but also on the *states* of dreaming that lead to transpersonal encounter. Such insight requires constant work with dreams and a living sense of continuity with ongoing dreaming cycles in relation to waking experiences, shaping and guiding our spiritual intentions.

Dreams are not easy to understand because they reflect trans-egoic processes of mind and feeling whose expressions dramatize inner struggles, aspirations, frustrations, hopes, daily impressions, and longing of soul often not recognized or fully acknowledged by the conscious self. Dreams are often inflated and overly dramatized as a means of directing conscious attention to latent issues of concern unrecognized, or in need of attention, in the life of the dreamer. Often dreams are simply a release for inner tensions and emotionally charged reactions or responses to daily life; other dreams are cyclical in expressing long-term issues or themes unresolved by the dreamer, put away but by no means inactive. Other dreams are reflections of collective impact, from family, community, culture, or contexts relevant to the life of the dreamer. No particular type of dream is a "wisdom dream" as the Sophianic aspect, for me, is a sense of presence and insight that may appear even in the most mundane dream. However, certain dreams epitomize this sense of presence by highlighting the dream as sacred encounter in which the dreamer feels and embodies the direct, often subtle, transformative impact of the dream.

Some dreams, a small percentage, are experienced as spiritual enactments of latent potential that unites both the dreamer and the living cosmos in a harmony of encounter often stunning and profound in impacts and implied significance. And some dreams are pronouncedly mystical and charged with reverence and even awe in the face of genuinely transcendent encounters beyond the normative frame of everyday thinking.[6] Alternatively, spiritual themes and images can appear in any dream type, representing presence even in small ways notable by a felt sense of importance even if not fully comprehended. The range of dreaming types is vast and individualized, but the Sophianic aspect is a pervasive feature of the more expansive, "sacred" encounter dreams, which are at times quite subtle and yet infused with revelatory insights.

In terms of the individual basis of dreaming, a large majority of dreams express the immediate circumstances of daily life, both in conscious and subconscious attitudes, as a consequence of actions taken, thoughts reflected, interpersonal relations, and the stimulus of imagined possibility. Dreams in this sense are psychic impressions or "imprints" whose emotional and intellective contents are animated with variable themes reflecting both lived experience and underlying psychic attitudes or dispositions. While these dreams may seem ordinary as a creative replay of daily occurrence, they often reveal something fundamental about human nature. The ever-active mind or psyche is constantly processing lived-world experience, at the same time that outer events impinge, inner responses also correlate to shape our moment-by-moment condition.[7] And this process of adaptive response continues while we sleep and when we dream.

However, in sleep the mediating "reality" of the moment is no longer dominated by a conscious mentality and instead, subliminal influences shape emergent dream scenarios into something not quite normal. These subliminal influences can present the self in an alternate context and open the possibility of new perspectives on how we think, respond, interact, or express possible asocial or eccentric elements of identity. Dreams express the *atypical self* as well as the daily self, and this atypical self is an entry point for Wisdom. When psychic impressions are shaped into a non-ordinary stance, into a surreal or altered reaction or response, then what is revealed is an implicit capacity for change and adaptation. The atypical self is a surreal aspect of identity representing not just the shadow side (unintegrated elements) but also potential spiritual aspects awaiting further development.

Dreams are not simply random expressions of psychophysical processes, they are in a more complete sense, a product of psychic interactions between body-brain, self-other awareness, and soul identity—between domains of experience in which the whole person as an embodied soul is made aware of subtle, interactive potential. A Sophianic, heart-centered approach to dreams requires a willingness to hold the dream, its contents, emotions, symbols, and ideas as intrinsically meaningful; dreams are not a result of random mental processing, but an expression of internal mental-emotive response and the arbitrariness of the dream reflects arbitrary attitudes of the waking mind. We are constantly processing experience, waking or sleeping, seeking to integrate or assimilate events and interactions in ways that inform our ongoing sense of identity and purpose.

Incoherent, contradictory values, feelings, or thoughts will produce the same in dreaming; I often note how those who deny the value of dreams live a surface life strongly identified with values that highlight the rational conventions of the everyday mind. This clinging to immediacy, to conventional thinking, to the obvious present, marginalizes subliminal processes that constitute a far greater influence on human life than any form of rational thought. Dreaming is fundamentally transrational; dreams are meaningful and yet irreducible to obvious, immediate corollaries. This is why dreams are filled with symbolic nuance, surreal images, implicit intuitions whose contents reflect awareness and relatedness "beyond the brain"—beyond the obvious and immediately objective.

The Sophianic Wisdom of dream praxis recognizes their oracular nature, the prophetic elements, the paranormal aspects and the heart-centered transformative experiences of lived-world impact. Dreams can tap into deep human potentials, which is why they can be sources of inspiration and revelation—crossing the boundaries of everyday rationality into the complex textures of multilevel perception. Dreams can open the path of Wisdom to the cosmological and metaphysical, to our own deeper capacities of perceptions and intuition, to reveal new modes of being consistent with soul-life, with the deeper stratum of our ontological inheritance, our collective being, and our as yet unrealized mystical capacities.

Wisdom in this sense is not simply pragmatic or functional but, encompassing these qualities, wisdom extends into a vaster complexity of Being and Spirit in which the full scale of human ability can manifest through the medium of higher dreaming types. These higher dreaming types remain marginal to the everyday life of dreaming; most dreaming is quotidian, normal, rational in reflecting everyday life—and Wisdom can be gleaned from such dreams. However, some dreams are more profound, mythic, archetypal, transpersonal, and revelatory.[8] These higher types are the very sources of Wisdom, they spring full grown from the forehead of the dreamer, they leap out in mythical, psychic, and mystical forms and seize the ordinary personality with a fearsome awe—a gripping encounter with an unknown sacred depth. These dreams require study, reflection, analysis, and appreciation for their implicit values and significance. But they resist strictly rational interpretation because of their transrational nature; the implications point toward Sophianic Mystery, toward the unrealized potential of higher being.[9]

However, such dreaming is not strictly personal. Wisdom dreaming inevitably reflects communal, collective, and global issues, tension, struggles, and the search for integration and harmonization between dreamers. The Wisdom praxis is to record, study, and reflect upon the dream content and upon the dream experience as distinctive aspects of self-development. There are three elements of dream praxis that are basic to Wisdom reflection: the recorded *dream* (a written record); the recorded *experience* (feelings, emotions, associations, and qualities accompanying the contents); and the *interpretation* in terms of personal, communal, and collective aspects. The distinction between the communal and the collective is based on local family and community in contrast to more global cultural aspects. Dreams are not merely subjective, but reflect shared concerns, group issues, family patterns, local context, and on a larger scale, global tensions, struggles, and interactions endemic to our interactive global cultures. The dream is inseparable from the lived-world and social-cultural context of the dreamer; it is a dynamic enactment in virtual form, an imaginative dramatization of possible outcomes or often recurrent themes that reflect developmental possibilities. Some themes may challenge an existing worldview or dramatize unresolved conflict or negative relations or self-attitudes in need of change.

Higher dreaming types often reflect lifelong patterns, a developmental arc that can be positive or regressive depending upon personal circumstances and cultural location in impactful social events. The Sophianic approach is to look at every remembered dream as having some value and worth, however mundane, that ties to larger themes and developmental patterns indexed by any specific dream.

By indexed, I mean the dream reflects states and conditions that are participant in larger identity patterns—how does this dream reflect my current state in relationship to ongoing developmental themes? Such indexing implies that the dreamer knows their themes, can see some relationship between a current dream and lived-world values and patterns. Further, how does the dream reflect communal and collective issues? What is the outcome that the dream points toward, not only personally, but also communally? Dreams can unite personal, communal, collective, and global themes into a single dramatic representation.

Another important aspect of dreaming is the way in which dreams offer various forms of virtual enactment. The capacity of mind to exercise abilities of a psychic nature are frequently expressed in the dreaming context, though easily ignored or missed by the dreamer's preoccupation with other contents. In my own life, dreaming has been a major activity for the exercise of psychic abilities, which have then manifested in waking life; abilities such as telepathy, precognition, clairvoyance, or distance viewing, as well as psychokinesis and psychometry, out-of-body flights, communication with the dead, and so on, have all occurred repeatedly, and in a developmental fashion, in my dreaming. There is nothing unusual about this, many people record paranormal activity in dreaming.[10] Thus dreaming is a developmental condition for the exercise of latent psychic capacities whose actualization can lead to waking manifestations of those very same abilities as exercised in the dream context. What is required is a willingness to attend to, record, reflect upon, and value such dreams as a means to strengthen the development process.

Ignoring them, dismissing them, and denying them inevitably leads to repression and only low-level functionality in regard to symbolic and psychic potential. This does not mean dreamers must embrace some form of programmatic belief; it only requires an openness to the phenomena and a willingness to attend to its manifestations and to encourage through affirmation the possible expression of such ability in the waking life of the dreamer. Wisdom teaches us to recognize the paranormal as operative and valid forms of human perception and dreams are the media through which such perceptions can be enhanced and developed. Attending to dreams, remembering, and reflecting includes the assimilation of paranormal aspects as expressing latent capacities within the dreamer (not just in others).

One-quarter of the world is dreaming right now; some large segment of the human population is always sleeping where day for us is night for them. This constant large percentage of active dreamers reflects a human condition that underlies the waking state. Mental activity in the human condition is subtly subject to dream integration, replay, assimilation, and subliminal influence through dreaming states that cycle through the rounds of sleep on a daily basis. Dreaming is not occasional but a *thematic constant*, a normative process by which experience is internalized and social and psychic events are in variable ways processed by mind and heart. Sophianic Wisdom recognizes the pervasiveness and legitimacy of dreaming as a rich, complex human activity whose roots draw not only on the collective but also on the sacred sources of human development.

Where the collective meets the sacred is in and through dreaming, where the paranormal content connects us with other dreamers in a vast field of dream sharing whose interplay and intimations bring us into subtle contact with the psychic worlds of others. Dreaming is not an isolated act but a co-participation in a continuum of dreaming activity in a global context. We have little recognition of the dreaming matrix as a shared psychonoetic condition, of how subtle dreaming influences cross the boundaries of dreaming in and with others. This undercurrent of psychic influences is also active in waking states but even more so in dreaming. Awareness, lucidity, subtle perception expresses our capacity for interactive dreaming where even in an unconscious condition, dreamers touch, interact, and influence events and persons based on a shared psychic continuity (and contestation). Wisdom seeks to comprehend this matrix of shared dreaming as a resource for shared human development.

This is part of the Sophianic Mystery, that the ground of All Being is active within and through our psychic life, both waking and sleeping. Feminine Wisdom recognizes the import of dreaming, and its shared and communal aspects, dream groups, dream sharing, and dream recording are all part of such a wisdom. Women have long attended to dreaming as a meaningful activity in a direct personal sense, open to dream guidance and inspiration. Dreams can be teachers, not just expressions of subliminal impressions, but a wholistic assimilation that reveals a larger, more complex world of associations. Tacit knowledge is a part of dreaming and discovering the latent associations requires the development of skillful interpretation and a better understanding of personal symbolism. Such an understanding is not only personal but also communal and resonates with the dreams of others; together we can better understand the value of dreaming as a shared matrix of vibrant connection and co-learning.

VISIONARY KNOWLEDGE

If some dreams are revelatory and a source of insight, the waking dream or vision is a primary context for acquiring a direct, participatory knowledge of deeper Being. This refers to lived experience, an awakening to our capacity for spiritual perceptions founded on the radiance and fullness of a direct encounter with the Sophianic

Mystery. The transrational nature of this encounter makes it difficult to describe and the variable nature of the encounter precludes any fixed array of traits or contents. The epistemic basis of such knowledge is as rich, complex, and diverse as the heart and mind of each individual; it has no closure in any form of typological morphology. Its manifestations take on the contours of the individual, perhaps at a soul level, and therefore express unique characteristics and forms. There is a creative tension between the knower, knowing, and not knowing.

In some spiritual traditions the goal, such as *nirvana* (or enlightenment) or *moksha* (or liberation), predicates certain realizations or insights that express a successful realization of the goal. And yet, in an individual sense there can be and often is, variability and diversity in experience. Further, the praxis of this knowing is highly variable; there is no one way to assure a successful realization. In a less traditional context, mystical experience has an open horizon where the possible disclosure of Being, in a deep encounter, can and does take a multitude of forms and expressions. Thus, visionary knowledge is not a content or a particular set of insights as much as an exploration of possible ways of knowing, an epistemic exploration, a series of encounters leading to a more comprehensive understanding. And some visionary aspects remain unknown, not understood or comprehended, such is the Mystery of Being.

In my own life, I have had numerous sacred encounters of a mystical kind, and as an independent thinker and not as a member of any religious tradition, these experiences mark a trajectory toward an ever-deepening appreciation of the Sophianic Mystery. By this I mean that the experiences have not resulted in a specific "traditional" or theological set of realizations; instead, I have acquired a direct appreciation of the phenomenology of mystical encounter without the burden of theological or philosophical conformity.

This does not mean to imply that I escape the limitation of context and educational training; far from it, my interpretation of experience conforms to beliefs and values that are conjointly formed by my social context, education, innate ability, and multiple encounters. The outcome remains open, the interpretative horizon is by no means reducible to unchanging ideas or beliefs. The more I experience, the more open the horizon becomes as each immersive encounter adds nuance, complexity, and diversity to the overall phenomenal context.

The qualitative aspects of these encounters range from shock, awe, and amazement to wonder, reverence, and humility in the face of an Infinite that I do not comprehend but that I recognize as the source of many religious and spiritual teachings. The primary foundational aspect of these encounters is a direct awareness of a unitary ground of Being whose creative capacities overflow that unity into an immeasurable complexity of diverse beings, worlds, and planes all capable of sustaining life in forms suitable to their existential circumstance. And these diverse beings have their own capacities for knowledge of that unitary ground, without need to mimic the traditional forms of any given human tradition. And yet, traditional forms can be a means to a visionary knowledge of that same unitary ground, infinite in capacity and yet specific in actualization. What I experience does not contradict traditional teachings but is by no means confined to those teachings; there is so much more to learn and experience, particularly in the higher mystical types.

From a Sophianic perspective, visionary knowledge is a unique kind of knowing (gnosis) in three different ways: first as subjective experience; second as a reflection of shared or similar experience with other accomplished experients; and third, as an expression of Being and Spirit in the context of a particular social context, place, period of time, cultural location, or historical moment. The

Sophianic perspective as I see it, places emphasis on the individual, the social context, and the shared experience of others, illustrating the ways in which our own encounters coordinate or synchronize with the experiences of others to create an exchange of insights whose co-creative integration helps to build a sense of community.

The Sophianic community is not based in doctrine or dogma, but in the affirmation of similar experiences, as for example in dreaming, that reveal significant themes, goals, or ideals and values central to the praxis of Wisdom. Such Wisdom is fluid, adaptive, nonaggressive, and not invested in the need for conformity to rigidly determined doctrines. What matters is the shared experience that confirms the complexity, diversity, and yet complementary nature of Wisdom as applied to maintaining a better, more mature, and harmonious world. The flexibility is not arbitrary or merely subjective but is grounded in real visionary knowledge, in direct encounter with Being and Spirit leading to more complex but diverse views on how Wisdom applies to a given situation.

In terms of themes within visionary knowledge, beyond the unity theme noted above, another obvious corollary is that of *interpretive flexibility* grounded in direct experiential knowing. Wisdom as praxis, not simply as theory, places emphasis on the immediacy of experience in relationship to the application and outcome of that experience. Wisdom in this sense is not built by experiential encounters alone, but by the application of those encounters to issues of human development and social integration. However diverse or complex the experiences, the goal is not the accrual of mystical moments but a more pragmatic application of Wisdom insights to real-world problems.* The demonstration of Wisdom is through creative activities, compassion toward others, actions and

---

*Jorge Ferrer, *Revisioning Transpersonal Theory*, 125, discusses the problem of narcissism when placing too much emphasis on spiritual experience.

teachings that lead to a better appreciation of individual and collective well-being.

An individual can demonstrate great Wisdom without claiming any exceptional experiences, a Wisdom one grows into over a lifetime of dedication to values and principles reflecting Wisdom ideals. Visionary knowledge in this sense is a special category of Wisdom, a reference to the reality of direct perception and immersion in Being and Spirit as source and ground of ontological claims about the nature of self-becoming. My experience leads me to believe that this ground is universal but not reducible to any particular system of metaphysical claims. Every system reflects that ground, so the question is on what basis is the system constructed, what is the hermeneutical perspective for any kind of systemic construction of Wisdom? How applicable is that Wisdom? Wisdom is a construct of perception and the integration of experience into meaningful patterns of insight; there are many nuances to Wisdom and a variety of gestalt patterns that reflect specific forms of such insight.

My own view on this question is pragmatic, and the question can be reframed as, "How does my experience contribute to insights and actions that lead to positive, creative, *shared* outcomes?" The emphasis falls on the application of visionary knowledge to human (and species-wide) problems in trying to create a more healthy, well-balanced, harmonious world. And this action is not isolated to the individual but applies to others in the creation of community and task-oriented work in which others fully participate and contribute their Wisdom as well. Wisdom is not reducible to a single experience or insight but grows and develops through testing multiple insights in real-world situations and relations to others whose own views matter and may challenge the very nature of those insights. This book is my contribution to the importance of shared Feminine Wisdom as a necessary revolution leading to new, more mature understanding.

Thus no one experience, nor one type of experience, can be sufficient for the development of mature Wisdom; rather what is required is an ongoing process of integration and application of experience to developmental challenges that do not have any immediate or easy solution. How do we overcome prejudice? What is the role of gender in spiritual development? Can we create a nonviolent solution to injustice? How can equality be made a right of every human being? What is our responsibility in relationship to animals? How will we treat the Earth and its resources to provide for the happiness of future generation? These are spiritual problems, not simply social concerns, and they require genuine, mature Wisdom for their solutions, a shared Wisdom whose participants can each bring the uniqueness of their lived experiences to the problem.

The praxis of visionary knowledge is to seek, through a variety of spiritual disciplines, greater knowledge of the unitary ground, through direct encounter and genuine transpersonal participation in the Mystery of that ground. The reason I call it Mystery is because it cannot be easily fathomed in its fullness and in the extent of its influence, nor can it be known in a complete sense, no matter how profound the experiential encounter. There may indeed be enlightened beings, mystical personalities, saintly figures with extraordinary knowledge and ability, but that does not mean that the Mystery is fully known or comprehended. There are ways to know that Mystery that are valid forms of mystical, visionary knowledge but such knowledge is always adapted to the context and lived-world of the experient. Therefore such knowledge is relative to the knowledge of others, even if the basis of that knowledge is self-similar and unitary.

The praxis is to find the way forward to the depths, to immersive encounter, to the transformation of self in a sea of Being, to a true awakening to higher knowing and perception. And then, to bring back into the embodied human context the teaching, practice, and application of that knowing as adapted to circumstances where that knowing is valued and appreciated. Perhaps there are silent sages, unspeaking examples of mystical realizations whose teaching is manifest through their presence, somewhat like Mata Amritanandamayi (Amma), the hugging woman saint of India, whose inborn nature "flows with love" toward all others.[11] Even these silent ones offer the gift of presence without speech or actions other than the very Being they manifest, such is the Mystery, where presence surpasses words or any systemic form of teaching.

The depth and complexity of visionary knowledge also refers to the mental predisposition of the experient; my own tendency is toward theory and reflection in the context of teaching and research. But there are many other ways including social activism, therapeutic healing, medicine, science, and every discipline and perspective that contributes to a better and more harmonious world. The relative nature of experience is complemented by dispositional characteristics inseparable from embodied life (though at a soul level, such dispositions may be far more relative in relation to the soul's multiple cycles of embodiment). The application of Wisdom resulting from experience is amplified by education, gender, family and social context, moral concerns, and cultural relations formative for the individual.

These extrinsic influences do not determine but may well influence the visionary encounter, the interpretation, and the application. There is perhaps a probability factor involved in how, where, and why such outcomes manifest in specific forms and with certain others. Sophianic Wisdom embraces *relativity* as a necessary aspect of individuation; we each play our part in the greater efforts to cocreate a just, harmonious, mature world. What matters is not the experience but cycles of application that lead to maturity in practices shared with others. Visionary knowledge has innumerable applications, but those applications often require practice, repeated efforts, and cycles of renewal that bring new insights to bear on complex problems. The Wisdom path is never finished, always in process.

Visionary knowledge has a creative role, similar to the prophetic ability to foresee possible outcomes and results of current actions. This "seeing into" is a probability, not a necessity or unquestionable truth, but a stochastic glance, an intuitive psychic image of a possible outcome. In forming a pathway, visionary knowledge is a marker of possible directions and consequences, but not necessarily actual, more as potential. The relative nature of this knowing is its "fit" with actual historical and developmental processes, how the actual is shaped into reality through the cautionary predictions of probable outcomes. The imaginal aspect of such knowing is a creative feature of what might be or might become, a warning or a promise, a dramatic sign of danger or success. The certainty comes with the actualization, through choice or at least responsible reaction, that results in collapse of the possible into the real and actual. The creative aspect is seen in the probable nature of the vision, its predictive value, and its capacity for synthesis, drawing together aspects of knowledge and awareness into a unique gestalt, as a prophetic possibility. Wisdom requires this ability, a forecasting that can see both the probable and the improbable, and then make appropriate choices.

PART TWO

The Greater Mysteries
Sophiana

To speak of the Greater Mysteries is to remove a veil, to uncover a hidden domain of experience whose contents and forms are less substantial in terms of everyday meaning but more powerful in terms of application and embodiment. While such Mysteries can be codified, therefore limiting the scope of their meaning and possibilities, in this work I refer to them in principle, not by definition or doctrine but through the prism of actual experience and practice. I say prism because the light refracted through the crystal of embodied life takes on unique characteristics and refractions based on the quality of the crystal and its specific properties. The soul is a prism, an energetic form whose qualities and attributes reflect multiple incarnations and a psychonoetic history of emergence and transformation ever modulating and attuning the refraction pattern of the now moment. The purity of the crystal results in a greater clarity of light and subtle gradations of light wave differences, as imaged in what the alchemists called the Peacocks Tail. The fan of colors reflecting qualities of body, soul, mind, and spirit—murky or clear, distinct or blurred, based on the life choices and actions of the individual. Sophianic Wisdom is the source and implicit capacity of that Light, shaded by human actions, choices, and beliefs. The crystal of the soul is formed under the pressure and impact of the embodied context: how we live, what we choose, our thoughts, words, and deeds. And the goal is to reflect that light in its purest and most complete form, however relative to the light of others.

This Wisdom Light is refracted through the attitudes, beliefs, and actions of our embodied life and its gradations reflect the personal qualities of our understanding. It is not a given content nor even a specific state, but an amalgamation of intuitions unified by the coherence of our internal well-being. This amalgamation combines knowledge, faith, and experience into a horizon of perceptions related to our actual embodied social and personal interactions. Unlike the metaphor of light and its refraction, the actual gradations of insight are adaptive and relative to our lived experience, our receptivity to infused knowing, and our ability to respond creatively to what arises through spiritual encounter. I will discuss such knowing in the next chapter, but it is important to clarify that faith is fundamental to Sophianic knowledge. In the Sophiana sense, *faith* is a disposition to hold open a horizon of possible knowing as yet unseen but forthcoming. By faith I do not mean a content, not a belief system, nor a set of specific truths that remain unproven.

A process understanding of *Pistis Sophia* ("Faithful Wisdom," also known as the Virgin Light) is based in a revelatory condition open to creative discovery and emergent insights built on previous experience and discovery.* It manifests as a form of *hieros logos* or sacred teaching whose depths cannot be reached by faith alone but require faith as an ongoing stability in the process of creative encounter and assimilation. When a teacher offers instruction, they do not start with the most challenging aspects of the teaching but with simple truths and encourage the student to accept those truths as a basis for later discovery that may well surpass and transform those simple truths. The student must believe in the value of the teaching even when they do not comprehend the goals toward which the teaching points. This requires faith in the teacher and in the teachings, faith guided by self-motivated thought, not dependence.

---

*For more on the Pistis Sophia as manifest in the women disciples of Jesus, see George R. S. Mead, *Pistis Sophia: The Gnostic Tradition of Mary Magdalene, Jesus, and His Disciples*; see also excerpts 23–27 in the *Stobaei Hermetica* on Kore Kosmou ("Maid of Heaven") as found in Walter Scott, *Hermetica* 1:457–531.

Pistis Sophia is an esoteric path of faith whose center or heart is a deep commitment to the femininized sacred perspective, an embodied, emotionally attuned development leading to an expansive knowing applicable to worldly life and struggles. The nature of this faith is a willingness to trust feminine nurturance through the cultivation of an inner, intuitive awareness, a womb-based conception whose birth is a Mystery unveiled through the contractions of dedicated, consistent efforts and strengthened through sacred praxis. Trust is at the heart of this process. In attuning to a sacred feminine presence, the seeker becomes pregnant through the touch of Spirit, through the initiatic grace of Sophiana, through the inspiring Light of that presence. Faith is more of an attitude, a receptivity and openness to presence, an understanding that emergent Wisdom must grow in and through the soul's life and become gradually embodied in action, speech, and thought.

My meditative name for Sophiana is Holy Mother Spirit, as source of life, being, and becoming, that Light that illumines the heart-mind and instills Wisdom based on the capacities and receptivity of the seeker. And yet, that Light is more than feminine, more than the named vessel, more than any one form—it is a Light that is multiform, multidimensional, and vast in capacity beyond conception or image. The Mystery is the capacity of that Light to adapt in form and function, to reveal and to conceal, to manifest a form and to exceedingly surpass that form. She is all form and no form; implicit and explicit; hidden and manifest; individual and collective; worldly and transworldly.[1] All becoming is through her deep and sacred Presence and Being; and the term *her* cannot contain that Mystery. Nevertheless, in a direct persona sense, I know her as Holy Mother Spirit, divine source and Guiding Light.

Faith leading to experience means that this faith is not abstract or intellectual but embodied through direct insights into the very nature of our shared becoming. There is no wisdom without insight and this "seeing into" must take the form of an illumination of heart, soul, and mind through direct intuitive knowing. The preparation for this knowing is a receptive heart, mind, and soul open to the Mystery, like the parable of the ten virgins at the wedding, all of whom carried lamps to light the way for the groom. But they waited long into evening, and some even fell asleep and the oil in their lamps burned low. Then the groom came, smiling, and five of the virgins in their wisdom had extra oil (and five did not); those five with oil retrimmed their lamps and lit the way for the groom while the other five missed the groom while seeking to replace their oil (Matt. 25:1–13).

The oil is a sufficient faith, even in the darkness and deep of night, sufficient to light a path leading to the sacred wedding, the reserve that serves those who are well prepared even in the long wait for revelation. Wisdom is not attained simply through learning and study, it requires something deeper and subtler, an immersion and initiation, a baptism in Spirit that demonstrates the reality of the Sophianic Mystery, not the idea, but the lived actuality. This initiation is not gained in a ritual act, nor through a code or symbolic gesture. Such a baptism requires a clear conscience, no guilt or doubt, a committed attitude of dedicated devotion to a realization that is beyond words and not reducible to the approval or actions of others, nor to a narrow prescription of outcomes or results. This initiation cannot be demanded or solicited by will but requires deep patience and an enduring stability and a loving heart, coming unexpectedly like a sudden soft breeze in spring, full of life and vitality.

Faith itself is a Mystery because we do not fully know how that in which we believe will emerge or manifest. But as the above parable illustrates, we can apply intelligence to faith in order to better prepare ourselves for whatever may become. A surplus of faith does not mean ungrounded belief but instead a pragmatic acceptance of our own limitations. This grounded faith is directed by a need to be prepared for the unexpected, to realize that the path is not predictable, and to be adaptive to circumstances that might change how that faith evolves. Unlike masculine ideas of faith as inflexible adherence to doctrine, feminine gnosis seeks direct realization of inner potential with an understanding that the emergence of such potential is individualized, adaptive, and often unique. Faith must be flexible but hold to core values, open but not easily distracted, not rigid in expectation of what may or may not manifest. Such faith is creative, not didactic.

The beauty of Sophiana is the fluid depths and energetic expanse of what is possible in the context of loving care and concern for others, all others, not a select group, not a community or collective, but all beings, all living creatures. The correct Sophianic attitude includes all, without constriction or limitations of kind, species, or type, because the very source of life is the supreme gift of that Light and Wisdom. And if all matter contains the seeds of sentience, even to the most minute subparticle, then the very earth, the soil, mountains, trees, plants, and animals, the stars, suns, moons, and multiplanetary worlds reflect that most precious gift—life and awareness, shared sentience, inseparably One. This gift of life is the supreme Mystery, the most valued attribute through which arises a multitude of beings, all expressions of what life might be, embodied and made actual through the ongoing continuity of that gift.

Therefore, *thankfulness* is at the heart of this faith, a deep gratitude that life is your gift, your responsibility, and your challenge— to make the gift into an exemplary expression of what is possible, specifically to become an embodied manifestation of that Light and Wisdom. It takes a lifetime to fully realize the possible ramifications of exemplary being, regardless of experience or mystical immersions, however early in the life path. It is not the experiences that matter, but the outcome as manifest in a life well lived in service to the well-being of others, to creative discovery, and to the development of a loving heart and disciplined mind, a soul rich with insight and faithful to its Source.

What follows is an exploration of what I am calling the Greater Mysteries, specific aspects of the spiritual path illumined by a Sophianic process of discovery, articulation, and relative insight. There is nothing final here, only an opening into the Mystery, which must by its very nature surpass what is written here by a great measure. In reflecting on these greater aspects, I have selected four aspects to explore out of a myriad of possible others. First, I will explore the Mystery of salvation, the necessary direction of the soul's transformation in awaking to the call of the Divine Feminine. This is salvation gained through sacred teachings (hieros logos) and the baptisms of initiation.

Second, I will reflect on the alchemical marriage as a symbol and sign of maturation including issues of gender, sexual identity, inner integration, and the dissolution of the masculine-feminine paradox. This union passes through sacred marriage (hieros gamos) as a blessing of children and family, to death and renewal. Third, I will give an overview of the relationship of the individual and community to the World Soul and how that greater identity involves a superconscious aspect of awareness inseparable from the Sophiana gift of life. This Mystery will take us into multilevel reality (hieros psychia) and hyperdimensional perceptions, normal, paranormal, and transpersonal. Finally, I will discuss the importance of reincarnation and rebirth (metempsychosis) both within the cycle of one life and in the larger cycle of multiple lives, in shared soul relations, and in the relationship between worlds and domains of this life, afterlife, and future becoming. I will then close this work with some reflections of the reborn masculine, and the responsibilities of a fully integral Sophiana approach to embodied community.

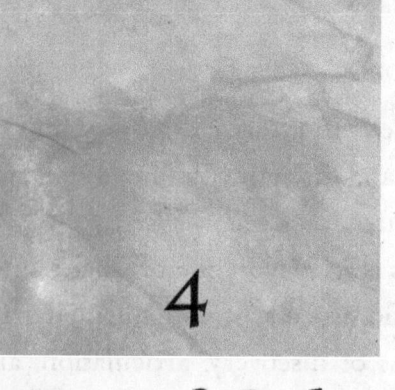

4

Mystery of Salvation

HIEROS LOGOS

If Wisdom is not a specific content, then it requires something more than study and education in the history of the soul's life. However, study and education are intrinsic to the path. Too often I hear seekers wanting only simple truths and easy access to the goals of the path. There is a naive notion that true Wisdom is simple and uncomplicated, and there is a truth in such an assumption. Wisdom can be reduced to simple axioms as guides to live by, as signposts on a pathway whose goals lie hidden in the mist and clouds. Love and be loved. Act with compassion and concern for the well-being of others. Learn to listen more and to speak less. Be willing to make a sacrifice for a greater good. Love your neighbor and the stranger as family. Love nature. Act with humility. Have pure motives. The list goes on. These sayings are simply ethical guidelines for worthy behavior and not the means by which one attains true Sophianic insight.

The cosmos we inhabit is not simple and it is not reducible to simple ideas without tremendous loss of insight into the actual workings of a complex multilevel, multidimensional reality whose core is not reducible to one-dimensional theories of unity and one-ness. The actual reality is so much more than what we comprehend and so much more complex than the reductive truths we claim to live by. A wisdom seeker must stand in awe of the greatness of Infinity and know, deep down, the insufficiency of personal understanding. No description can assimilate the fullness and no written account can contain the depths and nuances that make up the ever-active currents of souls becoming. We grow into wisdom slowly by degrees, depending upon how well we comprehend the complexity that surrounds and penetrates our shared awarenesses. Wisdom requires effort and self-discipline, not just the accumula-tion of sayings and ideas.*

Therefore, we must start with humility in the face of the Infinite. How difficult it is for embodied beings to comprehend the scope of the Infinite! The word *infinite* points to the limitless, unbound, utterly surpassable reality of all-becoming, to the cre-ative capacity for deeper awareness and understanding. However we codify or symbolize or contract our descriptions and theories, the infinite remains uncontainable and irreducible to not only a given system of thought or belief, but irreducible to all thought and all belief, specifically or universally. The very meaning of Infinite Being is a paradox in words, an arrow flying toward the sun whose slender mass and structure will vanish in a brief burst of light leaving no ashes, no trace. It is so much more than the thought we direct toward its actual content—the Infinite has no containment.

Wisdom expresses the Infinite in its scope and applications. We may personalize and codify, we may taste the essence of its

---

*The theory of wisdom and humility has a long history and is found in Plato where Socrates asks why the Delphic Oracle claimed he was the wisest of men (*Apology* 22e–23c).

presence, but we cannot contain it through words, or thoughts, or deeds. And yet, we can manifest Wisdom through the clarity of our perceptions and the quality of our beliefs and how they inform our actions and relationships with others. And education is important, a sense of the past, the history of ideas, the complexity of multidisciplinary theories, all reflect the ongoing challenges of developing wisdom not simply in behavior and social interaction, but in the sciences, arts, in social and political applications and in the formation of governments, institutions, and religious and spiritual communities. In all areas of life, Wisdom can be brought to illumine problems and to find solutions that endure if we have the courage to authentically ground that Wisdom in its Infinite source, with humility and awareness of our own limitations.

Aristotle, in his *Nicomachean Ethics* (4.1141b), claimed there were two kinds of wisdom, practical and theoretical, where practical wisdom requires actions leading to well-being or happiness (*eudaimonia*) and theoretical wisdom requires "scientific knowledge combined with intuitive reason." While extensive theoretical knowledge or expertise is certainly an important aspect of wisdom in a general sense, such knowledge is usually limited by area expertise that does not map easily to other areas of expertise—mathematical knowledge is not particularly applicable to expertise in cooking or gardening! And the application of expert knowledge to actual practical needs and outcomes is often lacking, for example, the need for a philosopher to fix a broken window. Hire someone with practical window skills! But the solution is usually not that I should apply my learning to the problem—because that learning has little or no application to the problem. Knowledge of the theoretical type is limited by its lack of applicability to many other areas of life.

General wisdom, of a practical sort, is also limited by the scope of one's lived experience and areas of work or action even if one is happy or content in one's skill set. Certainly establishing core values and living according to them is an important aspect of wisdom in a general, practical sense.[1] However, living well and being successful does not necessarily lead to Sophianic insight nor to a spiritual understanding of the ontological depths of Wisdom. Perhaps living in poverty and lacking many of the fundamental benefits of social life may be a goad for developing an understanding that surpasses normative attitudes toward success or happiness and can produce a profound wisdom-insight into human conditions. Perhaps suffering is a valid existential condition, as in Buddhism, for the arising of enlightened intuition. Perhaps renunciation derives from an insight that genuine wisdom requires total dedication and focus.

If expert knowledge does not produce enduring metaphysical insights, even among philosophers, perhaps it is because such insights arise through alternate, transrational means, conditions, or states that are neither normative nor even usual. Wisdom seems to require anomalous encounter, immersion, a shattering effect that breaks down the disciplinary contours of normative thinking and action. If that is the case, then neither practical nor theoretical wisdom is the basis for Sophianic insight. Alternately, we might artificially distinguish secular from sacred wisdom as is often done in esoteric traditions; but such traditions inevitably make the "sacred" into a doctrine based on authoritarian claims to insight usually not attained by the members of that tradition but only by the teachers.[2] Authoritarian doctrines of wisdom are not the basis for the development of a Sophianic understanding, open to every individual, though such doctrines can assist in a deeper metaphysical understanding of how others have assimilated wisdom into philosophical systems of belief.

Finally, there is a simple wisdom based on lived experience and born out of kindness toward others, including animals, that arises through genuine compassion and results in a nurturing care for the well-being, not of self, but others that may require sacrifice and dedication that can diminish self, requiring long hours of effort and daily demanding commitments. This includes caregiving of the sick, the elderly, the traumatized, all those in need of care but unable to care for themselves, a willingness to dedicate effort, time, and energy to the needs of others. And that may be the best beginning of true Sophiana understanding, a shared concern for the well-being of others not through ideas or elite membership but through the primary fact of shared, challenging existence, a willing participation in a lived-world inseparable from the well-being and struggles of others.

Wisdom in the deep spiritual sense is both practical and theoretical, but even more so it is ethical and moral in its recognition of the transpersonal ground that instills intelligibility in every creature. Ethical wisdom manifests as care and concern for the well-being of others, the moral impulse to treat others with respect and responsible love is a direct manifestation of that ground. True Wisdom does not arise from the mentality of the individual but is sourced from the soul's connection to Being and Mystery; the mentality of the individual shapes understanding but the source is Infinite in capacity and possible forms of expression. The shaping of Wisdom is reminiscent of Russian matryoshka dolls, nesting dolls with larger dolls containing the smaller ones, such that all forms dwell inside a single larger form. Just so is the soul's wisdom, a reflection of the scope of awareness and containment of embodied thought and practice, always capable of enlargement, knowledge garnered from experience, step by step, but contained in a greater Infinite. Each doll and each life has a unique face, not a repetition but an enlargement reshaped in accord with new understanding, and even the overall pattern can radically change, reshaping the entire configuration.

Spiritual Wisdom, in the feminine sense, is a value-ladened perception, a valuation of personhood over beliefs and ideas, a willingness to let differences be secondary over a shared concern for mutual well-being. We negotiate our differences through an ethos of mutual respect, and where that respect is lacking, we cultivate soul-centered compassion for those differences by "seeing through" the limits of a specific thought-world, including our own thought-world. We can negotiate without losing center, we can accept differences that cannot be reconciled, and we can maintain integrity in the face of critical aggression. But the goal is to seek an understanding that values the person regardless of differences, still pursing core values, but in a caring and kind way. Spiritual Wisdom is a creative path, one open to discovery and unique intuitions, there is a dynamic flow from the Infinite and when attuned to that presence, innovation and insight can flourish.

A NEW FEMININE WISDOM

I see the primary basis for the arising of Feminine Wisdom in care and concern for others, as being motivated to maintain a quality of life that is not based simply on success or happiness but upon the shared satisfaction of basic needs that do not privilege either wealth or social status. Nor is this wisdom some form of covert socialist agenda promoting "equality" at the expense of suppressing individual skills, talents, or accomplishments. By the satisfaction of basic needs, I mean not only food, shelter, basic services, and meaningful employment, but also the satisfaction of needs for love, family, and community, as well as for hope, aspiration, and meaningful work and goals that produce maturity and intelligent appreciation for diversity and difference. Basic needs must include emotional, aesthetic, spiritual needs, soul needs, not just external satisfaction but also inner satisfaction by enabling the cultivation of the good mind, good heart, and good soul.

In a complex world of multiple societies and diverse cultures, histories, and value systems, basic needs cannot be reduced to a simple list nor to fixed values undifferentiated from context and circumstances. The new Feminine Wisdom is adaptive, local, and *communitarian*—it arises through people working together to form networks of diverse skills that support the purposes and goals of that network. This wisdom is not about grand claims to truth, or abstract ideals, as much as it is about cooperation, shared responsibility, and the importance of good communication and trustworthy goals and lasting relationships. It is a shared Wisdom that arises out of a concern for the value of all life, even in its most simple forms, be it butterflies and bees, or natural habitats and ecological sustainability. Its most common form is a network of linked co-workers sharing responsibilities meant to sustain valued ways of life without emphasis on wealth or social class.

This emergent wisdom is transformative, a swelling wave of women (and men) working in concert to change the old patterns of wisdom through dedicated commitment to shared ideals. Patriarchy must fall because the old stone that formed those masculine images is no longer a viable building material; new wine requires new bottles; a new taste requires a more educated tongue. What is emerging is not monumental, nor grandiose, nor a declaration of a submerged collective will; what is emerging is local, interconnected across multiple media, to form large-scale communities dedicated to specific tasks that honor each individual in contributing to that task, each in their own way. Social service networks, animal care, ecological concerns, thematic social organizations, gender and racial equality, all represent this trend.

Expertise is recognized and honored within the context of

those larger, shared relations; cooperation seems paramount, and willingness to contribute seems valued above the degree or amount contributed (though exceptional contributions are certainly valued). What differentiates these new communities from past communities, even in the matrifocal context, is that they are not created by enforced or inherited cultural patterns transmitted through collective conformity. They arise far more spontaneously through an open invitation in which volunteer action and commitment sustain shared values dependent upon the long-term (or short-term) commitments of members.

These networks are not culturally informed as much as ideologically informed by service-based action and values aimed at sustainable goals that require community support. This aspect of Feminine Wisdom is its shared social context working with technologies that support participation beyond a given locale and open a pathway to membership in a "translocal" context extending all the way to global networks that can span the planet. There is a mesh between local needs and large communal resources that can address those needs insofar as members combine diverse social, economic, and pragmatic skills and abilities. In the new wisdom, *local* has taken on more diverse meanings because the data-stream can be not only local but national and global.

Another aspect of the new Feminine Wisdom is the importance of individual differences and the creative value of self-expression in the context of cultural complexity. There is no one Feminine Wisdom but a diversity of views, practices, and concerns held by or embodied by individuals in a stance that seeks cooperation and simultaneously challenges patterns of dominance, unreflective conformity, and hierarchies that privilege men over women. It is a call for equality without gender bias, a recognition of uniquely embodied skills, talents, and abilities that can apply to any area of life, regardless of gender or gender orientation. The collapse of gender identity as based on birth or sexual qualities is no longer a determinative in forming creative identities fully capable of attaining the highest goals and maximum expertise in any area of human activity. And this new freedom for self-construction has a deeper Wisdom purpose, to reveal the soul's capacity for creative life beyond the constraints of socially formed (usually masculine) attitudes toward sexuality, biology, or a limited traditionalization of social roles.

Changes leading to equality reflect an ethos deeply rooted in a global social need, to give full appreciation to women in all walks of life, in all professions, and in all areas of human endeavor. It is also a call for an end to sexual predation and male control over women's bodies; it is call for a recognition of the sacredness of life-bearing capacity whose importance need not be determinative in defining a feminine role. It is also a call to recognize that gender reversals and gender changes are no longer determined by biological origins. The new Feminine Wisdom requires personal choice, education, and commitment to values that support the diversity and unique aspirations of each and every person. Some may choose motherhood, but many other choices are possible, and all of those possibilities can result in exemplary accomplishment fully attuned with spiritual values that best reflect a feminine/womanist perspective. As a man writing about Feminine Wisdom, I can say I have the highest degree of respect and admiration for women whose courageous efforts are in fact changing the world in which we all live in ways that will far surpass the older masculine social paradigms.

The Sophiana aspect of this change is based in *soul knowledge*, in an innate capacity for continued growth and development whose origins are not simply dependent upon a current lifetime (or personality) but reflect a much longer trajectory of development. This does not mean to imply that the Sophianic perspective requires belief in reincarnation; however, for me, reincarnation is an intimate aspect of the great social changes taking place on a global basis.[3] In turn, this belief arises through a sentient ontology (see chapter 6) and the recognition that the cyclical nature of time reflects a growth process that requires periodic immersion in life experiences through multiple bodies, in diverse social contexts and eras. However, a similar point can be made without reference to reincarnation. The Sophiana Wisdom is deeply aligned with self-knowledge and soul awareness; what is required is a deep intuitive knowledge of self, or deep motives and aspirations that may arise independent of local context or social location.

These deep intuitions may spring up in dreams, imaginal moments of reflection, through a variety of artistic, literary, or meditative activities, as an image, a symbol, an idea, or vision of a possible mode of present and future being.[4] In order to act upon that intuition, there must be social and communal support that allows the soulful individual to find its best practice, its most satisfying mode of expression that solicits and actualizes identity in terms of the primary contents of those intuitions. And this expression is part of a larger creative process by which souls discover their inner potential for self-realization—not through an abstract model of transcendent spirituality, but through embodied praxis and dedicated commitment to its artful expression. Spirituality as the "art of transformation" requires social support and cultural alternatives that help to foster creative discovery, and to provide some ways to sustain a life based on that discovery.[5]

The new feminine spirituality as an open horizon of creative possibility and soul knowledge is intrinsic to the process of creative discovery. It offers a new kind of *salvation*, salvation through wisdom, through soul knowledge.[6] Soul knowledge references an intuitive awareness of soul purpose, as a need to know why motivation and action is directed toward certain goals. The allure of successful action is not based, in this case, on social recognition or social rewards but on a dedicated commitment to goals often less appreciated or marginal to mainstream attitudes toward success and accomplishment. Caring for the well-being of animals, helping to protect local environments, loving a needy child, giving support to those in pain, speaking up in the face of injustice, aggressive wars, or social prejudice are examples of soul knowledge where the response rises out of a deeply felt need for balance and reharmonization. The very sense of imbalance, of disharmony, of excess and overvaluation reflect a felt sense, a lived awareness, of spiritual disequilibrium.

The Sophianic soul feels, and feels deeply, the conditional circumstances under which others suffer, struggle, and seek redress of their existential condition. Mind may analyze, but soul expresses a heart-centered response to human conditions, a sense of empathy and concern that does not seek to explain why such disharmony exists, but rather to acknowledge the lived reality of its conditionality. To feel, to act, to respond meaningfully to the imbalance, to offer positive support in a context of need—to sense the vulnerability of the sick, the aged, the bewildered animal, the lost person, the homeless, the confused and betrayed, whose care and well-being are not irrelevant but central to a greater shared sense of a justice and equitable lived-world, is to acquire soul knowledge. And such knowledge arises through the very fact of confrontation with social, racial, and gender inequalities and intergenerational bias that is currently so prevalent.

This conditional factor of Feminine Wisdom is central to the motives that seek to redress that imbalance, and soul knowledge refers to a deeper sensitivity than any rational account of why or how such imbalance came to be. What matters is feeling and acknowledging the imbalance because the emergent wisdom is based on a heart-centered concern for a shared, just, harmonious world where suffering and imbalance is taken as a sign requiring social, responsible love. We all share the imbalance as well as the balance; soul knows the unequal scale in which self-serving egoism, predation, or aggression outweigh kindness and compassion. It is a felt reality, a deep centered perception that the chaotic and self-centered actions of others create only confusion, pain, and sorrow. The new wisdom arises on a willingness to take responsibility, to act, to engage in praxis, for the good of others without asserting dogmatic claims that define that good in a narrow, partisan fashion.

Feeling the imbalance requires action, not passive awareness, a creative response, a sense of agency meant to address and redress that disequilibrium. It is salvation through shared heart-centered social responsibility, a genuine care for the well-being of others. The new wisdom thrives on *agency*, a sensitive ability to act in ways that help redress imbalance and to restore a sense of cooperation and shared creative efforts. And this felt sense can and does arise because we have, in past circumstances, felt and lived that injustice as a teaching to heighten our awareness of the limiting and constraining impact of harmful circumstances. It is not merely karma of past lives, but the constraint of agency, a lack of opportunity, a loss of social harmony, a loss of partnership, repression and opposition meant to privilege select others, resulting in loss of social cohesion. The freedom to act requires an assessment of individual capacity, to find the right skill set to contribute to social change is a unique challenge; we join together and also honor what each person offers in support of mature collective transformation.

The new Feminine Wisdom is built in and through partnership while also genuinely honoring individual talent, ability, and unique skills and insights. A soulful approach to such Wisdom requires a heart free from jealousy, possessiveness, and tendencies toward control and dominance. Anger may spark resistance and confrontation, but in the end, anger is transitive, a medium of intense emotion whose creative expression must eventually transform into a new vision of creative responsibility. Blaming the guilty does not produce insight; berating the self-centered does not result in new self-knowledge. What is required is a skillful understanding, a heartfelt, soul-centered awareness that reaches more deeply into the very source of imbalance and heals that wound for new life and restoration. It is a touch that is shared, that communicates a sense of shared sorrow at limitation and a partnership in the healing of wounds so long held in bondage to old injuries, to a crippling sense of past history lived in imbalance. This soulful healing will take many generations; there is no quick redress, however powerful, that can resolve our social ills. The "new wisdom" is generational, it takes a long view, an understanding of a task passed on through multigenerational responsibility such that, even to the seventeenth generation, the task of healing is still viable, successful, and vital. This Wisdom is not transitory, but enduring, sustaining, and directed toward a world healed of all the harmful effects of past error, ignorance, and violent self-interests.

MANY MYSTICAL PATHWAYS

The theme of salvation is crucial to the Sophianic path, though it is not understood as a doctrine of the soul's future, but as a need of the soul's present, embodied life. Sophianic salvation is not based on commitment to a doctrine or a predetermined belief system; it is not a matter of belief but depends upon actual insight and maturity. This maturity can be based in a variety of worldviews and is not reducible to an explicit, necessary set of inflexible ideas. This theory of salvation is ancient, a salvation based on *direct visionary knowledge*, encounters, and mystical affirmations (gnosis) that result in a marked and notable wisdom, attested to by the recognition of others impacted by that visionary knowing. To understand this wisdom means to understand the nature of ignorance and not-knowing. The epistemic base of wisdom is the enlivened heart-mind opened to new dimensions of awareness and intuitive knowing, a knowing not based on collective social attitudes or traditional models of belief. This wisdom is not based on scripture or sacred texts as proof of its validity; the value and validity arises through human relationships, becomes evident in mutual interactions, and flows into the world through an application to real-world problems and challenges. It is not passive but creative and interactive; not esoteric or hidden, but open and available; not limited to certain persons but a gift and grace available to all. But it takes effort and determination, humility and surrender, to gain even a modicum of genuine insight into its cosmic and universal aspects.

The problem of *ignorance* is paramount in the sense that attaining this wisdom requires a willingness to look beyond the security of a predetermined belief system, be it spiritual, social, or material. Ignorance has many forms: inflexible commitment to a biased worldview; intransigent attitudes toward the possibilities of other ways of knowing; the overvaluation of one's own in-group over the knowledge and insights of others; attitudes of superiority based on privilege, wealth, race, training, or social status; a desire for dominance and control of others; anger and hostility as a means to assert a value system. The roots of ignorance are based in a lack of empathy, in self-centered thinking, and in the denial of alternate ways of life. Such ignorance is often sustained by fear; a fear of loss of center or lack of control, of not being dominant, of having to listen and attend to the concerns of other ways of thinking and acting.

Empathy is not simply caring about others or sensing their struggles but also requires us to overcome our own biases in terms of what others believe and value. Like a turtle protecting itself by pulling into its shell, ignorance seeks to protect its vital core through withdrawal, unresponsiveness, or uncaring and dismissive attitudes of mind. Or a person lashes out, strikes others, causes pain or harm through imbalanced acts and extreme attitudes cut off from the heart, emphasizing ideas or desires relevant only to the perpetrators. Ignorance often reflects soul loss, a loss whose cure requires reestablishing a soul-centered way of life supported by caring for others in a healthy-minded context of shared social responsibilities. Ignorance is a limitation of soul awareness, a blindness created by ignoring complexity and more nuanced ways of seeing and being.

To overcome ignorance and its accompanying sense of isolation, we need compassion, social maturity, and genuine wisdom that can find solutions able to impact and overcome the limitations of not-knowing and not-caring. Not-knowing and not-caring is a stage, a partial condition, capable of being transformed. The Sophianic turn is toward a shared light, an illumination whose gracious radiance reveals alternative actions, strategies, and insights to overcome the contracted shadows of ignorant actions and harmful attitudes of mind. This turn toward the mystical is not a turn away from social problems because this wisdom, while more than practical, is not lacking in practical applications. It is not simply theoretical but experiential and self-evident as a stance toward life that values the illumination of each individual as they contribute to new collective insights.

Such wisdom is a grounded realization applicable to the lived-worlds of others, however mysterious or profound the personal experience. The question is not "What was your experience?" but rather "What did you learn that might apply to shared social transformation?" Experiences come and go, high or low, profound or ordinary, but the outcome, the consequence, the import of encounter is valuable insofar as it offers insights and attitudes that help to promote human health, well-being, and maturity. The many mystical pathways of the present are not those of the past—the search for personal illumination gives way to the search for shared social transformation. A transformation based on a new understanding of how such illuminations can assist in creating a more creative, stable, open, feminized world.

This wisdom is non-ordinary because it finds its ground in the very nature of Being itself, in the direct encounter with creative fullness, through immersive awakening that supports diversity in outcomes and consequences. An Infinite ground cannot be reduced to a single path and truly requires a multitude of expressions and discoveries, in every area of life—in art, science, religion, education, politics, commerce, industry, and all the isms of everyday living. An Infinite ground refers to the depths of human experience in a non-ordinary context, through enhanced human insights, and a plausible embrace of psychic and spiritual modes of knowing. In this sense, an Infinite ground references dreams, visions, imagination, creative play, discovery, and innovation as applied to all areas of human interest and activity.

An Infinite ground does not simply reference spirituality or religion but is the permeable matrix for all forms of psycho-mental-emotive life. This ground does not have a distinctive discipline or area of study that best represents its depth and fullness. What best represents it is the totality of human thought and action throughout all time in every world and dimension, including all physical, psychic, and transpsychic domains. Knowing and understanding are relative terms, stages on a path toward greater maturity that is capable of overturning a former stage for new insight and discovery. In other words, an Infinite ground is the dynamic process basis of everything we possibly know, imagine, or speculate in all areas of human exploration. Call it an unending field of possibility and impossibility, of limited and unlimited, of natural and supernatural, of physical-spiritual-transcendent potentials.

There is a Mystery in not-knowing, an affirmation that seeks to acknowledge our limits in a way that does not impose closure on the possibilities of discovery. Not-knowing is good in the sense that it reflects self-awareness as a structure capable of deconstructing its own habits and attitudes of mind. At times, it may be necessary to give up whole patterns of thought and belief in order to accommodate a wider, more comprehensive perspective. But that new perspective is itself capable of change and radical alteration. We tend to believe that our thought-worlds are a necessary stability in the midst of the flux and flow of contemporary life and all its turbulence. However, what may appear as stable ground can easily become an anchor resisting change and confining us to shallow water and low tides; to let go means to sail freely into the depths where anchors cannot reach the bottom.

Not-knowing can be an index of our courage to learn; knowing our limits means recognizing the boundaries we must cross to enter new territory. And there are many territories to explore, far more than what we may know in a given local setting. There are a multitude of worldviews, and Feminine Wisdom seeks to value these differences as expressing our creative abilities to inhabit a multitude of spiritualities. Not-knowing is a kind of affirmation of what is possible without presuming any special insight about how knowing can occur to move us to new vistas of insight. Not-knowing includes soul knowledge, not as complete or fully optimized, but as a dynamic process in which new insights can bestow new understanding, even to the very core of our individual self-awareness. A pathway may be chosen, followed with dedication and full commitment, and produce a desired result without delegitimizing the pathways of others. This is intuitively understood because diversity is the very nature of the Infinite.

Is there a moral core? Yes, very distinctively; that core depends upon collective social well-being and patterns of maturity that promote and sustain healthy, well-integrated individuals, networks, and collective activities in a matrix of sustained harmony and creative relations. Love is at the core, it is a fundamental quality of the matrix of not-knowing because creative tensions are overcome through the application of insights that seek to modify, elaborate, and build upon positive, loving relations that enhance the quality of life. Love does not mean conformity, it means challenge and discovery, overcoming limits, passing beyond old patterns for a better way of life. Such love is transformative, a basis for wisdom, and a necessary quality that infuses our relations with positive, even if challenging, interactions. To love and be loved is a true wisdom maxim insofar as it leads away from stagnation that inhibits discovery or innovation. Moral wisdom is sustained by sympathy and caring about others, with discrimination concerning how our differences support or possibly inhibit spiritual development.

The link between mystical insights and salvation is the way in which such insights support a greater sense of wholeness. When we give up the partiality of our isolated self-awareness and become more cognizant of the fullness, the abundance in which and through which we dwell, then we can enter a state of shared illumination. It is not one enlightenment that matters but the entire spectrum of all possible enlightenments, a salvation through knowing that leads to shared attitudes and creative relations. Illumination is a form of emergence within that greater Wholeness, and its consequences are not limited to individual realizations. Entering that more expansive field, we become agents able to enact new modes of understanding that result in positive change through communal transformation. This is the core of many religious movements, where a shared sense of illumination lights the way for others to also enter into that understanding. Salvation then is not simply an individual mode of discovery but much more a shared sense of "going into the light" together, to activate core values and to realize, together, the spiritual source of those values. Salvation through knowledge reflects a cosmological process, the ways in which the Whole influences and fosters the development of each and every part, each and every person, each and every being.

THE GROUND OF ALL-KNOWING

The Sophianic knowledge is a special kind of knowing that is intuitive, spontaneous, and informed by ethical choices and commitments. This does not mean it lacks logic or structure; rather it indicates an openness to Being and Mystery that seeks to accommodate both individual and communal adaptation and discovery. My way, your way, and our way are three perspectives on a single continuum. Sophianic Wisdom is grounded in a communal sense of shared values that do not deny the uniqueness of an individual perspective. Dialogue is the proper praxis for communal interactions and refinement of ideas; however, the realization of such ideas often requires a deep inwardness that cannot be determined by consensus or required steps and stages.

The path to gnosis is an individual path supported by shared values and practices that must be adopted in accord with individual temperament. Core values of Sophiana Wisdom are rooted in a deep belief in the sentient universe as ensouled with life-force, vitality, and spirit capable of infinite manifestations and numerous pathways of knowing. And yet, there is the basic truth of unknowing, that is of seeing our own limits, of knowing the relative and partial nature of our own gnosis. Understanding the Infinite means "standing under" the horizon of all possible ways of knowing and recognizing the specificity and limits of our own committed path of learning. Feminine Wisdom teaches us that there is no final knowledge, only an ongoing creative process in which discovery and overturning of old values must proceed through stages of faith and development. Gnosis is not absolute but relative to the experiences and insights of the individual; however ultimate the vision, there is still more to learn.

Without doubt, some ways of knowing are more applicable to specific problems and challenges; these ways of knowing can merge in terms of ethical guidelines that direct creative energies to solving those problems. Core values can be in partnership with diverse points of view, they can harmonize and individuate and still fulfill their intent. The Sophiana of knowing challenges us to formulate the unique value set that corresponds to our own personal understanding of wisdom. And then to work toward a harmonization of those personal values with the values of others, standing firm in commitments and being flexible in their application. However, what I refer to is "deep knowing" based not on a set of ideas or principles inherited from others but based on discoveries made by delving into the depths of Being and Mystery as the ground of all-knowing. Such knowing is not simply a reiteration of human truths, but a consequence of a *passionate search for truth* resulting in direct participatory, spiritual encounters. These encounters are not limited to only those between discreet beings but arise out of the ocean of our becoming as truth-seekers immersed in a vast sea of possible profound knowings.

Such knowing has a grounding effect when it assimilates itself to the very sentience that provides life to all beings. Like a lightning rod channeling earth energy to the expansive heavens, this knowing, this gnosis, provides a release and a stability that acts as a conduit for that greater Mystery and Being.[7] We are each a lightning rod insofar as we are able to embody and manifest the deeper source; not simply in ideas or words or feelings, but as actual lived presence. This is the Mystery of salvation, this kind of knowing, because it liberates us from the intellectual fascination of complex ideas and opens a vista on the unitary basis of all-knowing that animates those ideas. Salvation in this sense is liberation from local knowledge for a broader and more comprehensive knowing, not ultimate but ever more expanding into unrealized potential.

I call it Feminine because it does not seek to embody itself abstractly or systemically but wholistically; it seeks a multitude of expressions and avoids closure in a single point of view. My thoughts and writing are nothing more than a single contribution to a much more profound awakening whose vessels and vehicles are so abundant and diverse as to be uncountable. The many are One but the One is also necessarily expressed through the Many without limiting its own inherent unity. Insofar as we can attune to that deeper unity as source of life and awareness, we are able to recognize and appreciate the tremendous diversity in possible manifestations. And unity is itself only an attribute, the true core is *life, awareness, sentience,* a living sense of a planetary wholeness in which Gaia thrives and evolves in a vast sentient universe of diverse other worlds.

In a living cosmos of sentient becoming, such knowledge, gnosis, is a gift and a reverent realization of the true nature of our shared becoming in a sacred life process. One of the responsibilities of sentience is to develop goals and outcomes best expressing the highest qualities of sentient awareness, manifest in intentional living, care for others, and care of the world at large. The environment is our responsibility, good ecology is a spiritual practice congruent with the higher goals of sentience. Knowing this truly is not based on theory but on direct participation in a sentient cosmos of beings whose health and flourishing require co-operative relations and creative discovery of a common life source. This life source has many names, God or Goddess, Dao or Qi, Spirit or Mystery, all designating a depth and fullness of divinity that overflows our theological constructions and surpasses our philosophical imagination.

There is no limiting the Infinite. Thus, Being and Mystery are Sophianic designations representing All Being and processes of becoming not yet fully understood. It is a spiritual truth that we can know the unity and wholeness of Being and yet not comprehend its purpose or intention. Our best intuitions arise from human minds, be they enlightened, mystical, or illumined, they are nevertheless finite in experiencing the Infinite. Such experiences reduced to words and sacred texts are a pale image of a distant sun whose brilliance and inner processes surpass all specific description. True gnosis is a creative act, an affirmation of unity and multiplicity as an integration of inner and outer aspects within a single emergent cosmos of creative self-becomings.

Salvation as a mystery is based in this paradox of knowing, entering the One; becoming an initiate through that knowing is a baptism, a sanction legitimizing a path, but not a realization of all that is yet possible. A Buddhist enlightenment, a Hindu liberation, a Chinese Daoist union with the Dao, Christian or Sufi or Kabbalistic mystics all legitimize their paths through attaining goals whose realization justify a practice. But those realizations do not exhaust the Infinite; they only specify and individuate templates for spiritual realizations consistent with those traditions. And millions of people have experiences outside of those traditions that also legitimize other paths or practices, even if spontaneous, based on a refined sensitivity for certain states and realizations.[8]

There is no hierarchy of paths that best represents the sum of all such realizations that actual human beings can attain, regardless of the many masculine claims for the superiority of a tradition or realization or a preferred hierarchical order. The Sophiana perspective is to recognize, celebrate, and value all life-enhancing traditions and practices that do not demean others in exalting that tradition, neither by gender, nor race, nor age, nor by any other discrimination that would deny our creative capacities for discovery. Sophia thrives on diversity and realizations that enhance the richness of the possible, the splendor of the impossible, and the mystery of the yet undiscovered. Even the poor in spirit shall inherit the mantle of impossible realizations, even the last can be first, even the mighty can fall.

Salvation is not a doctrine based on faith alone, but on a *knowing* based on firsthand experience through immersion and individual heart-centered commitment. Such knowing proceeds, in my experience, through stages, through rises and falls, through progression and regression. The path is not straight, but a winding way, with difficult trials, sudden surprises, successes, temptations, illusion, and misdirection. The goal is to proceed ahead, to stop when necessary, to rest and recover, but then to pull up stakes, pack, and move on in search of the promise that such knowledge is based in lived experience, not theory or abstractions. The life pilgrimage is ongoing; we can create a home, have a family, friends, and community, be grounded in one place, but the call for soul development goes far beyond the local without denying the value of the local. This call is universal, but heard by only a minority, within a majority deeply immersed in local being and resistance to becoming.

The illumination of the heart is a realization to be longed for, an aspiration whose embodiment takes a lifetime of effort no matter how dramatic the momentary event. I have had many moments of spiritual realization, some of an utterly transcendent type, but those experiences pass, leaving an imprint, the mark of an awakened Anthropos, as an illuminative taste of an Infinite capacity. Such knowledge is self-surpassing, it cannot be held and measured but must be incorporated and lived as a gift whose value cannot be weighed on a scale of ordinary concerns. Such knowledge is extraordinary, sacred, an indescribable taste of sweetness and light beyond description in any final sense. Salvation is a form of transformation, different for different persons. *Self-surpassing* does not mean the effacement of self but its enhancement, a greater becoming in which self becomes more fully informed by the Mysteries that make life valuable.

The salvation of the Sophianic Mystery is salvation from ignorance, a gnosis freed from the narrow confines of everyday material and physical life not by denying that life but by enhancing and expanding the everyday boundaries through psychic, spiritual, and transpersonal awakening. While such knowledge is self-surpassing, it is also world transforming; and this is as it should be, we wake from sleep to a bigger, more comprehensive world of concerns. Our horizons are lifted to new vistas and perspectives that take in the entirety of creation, all creatures, all processes of life as an amalgam of sacred energies seeking to enhance even further our inherited self-limitations. We are both creature and creator, both nature and spirit, both mind and body, both soul and spirit and the integration of our wholeness is inseparable from the wholeness of the world; insofar as we are spiritually aware, so too the world is awakened and transformed.

Our responsibilities in this process involve a caring guardianship of the precious gift of life for all living creatures. To live in peace, not war, health not sickness, thriving to create not destroy, nurturing creativity not negativity, and to demonstrate our adaptive strengths in overcoming the burdens of our past errors and in our willingness to serve the needs of others unable to care for themselves. What we inherit is what we co-create; the marks of war, violence, oppression, and illness mark our world; much work remains to be done and so doing, will require the utmost in Sophianic Wisdom. For our children to flourish, this wisdom must also flourish, as a primal source of respect, appreciation, and love for the well-being of all. Salvation is there but we are required to make the effort, find the discipline, and dedicate our energies to its manifestation. This is not an individual call only, but a shared awakening, a communal realization in which we can each contribute unique qualities to a collective discovery of shared potentials.

COMMUNITAS AND SELF-AWARENESS

Community is built on shared ideas, cooperative actions, and inspiring goals meant to stimulate energy and purpose. In this process, sacred teachings play an important role. Sacred teachings (hieros logos) tend to be established as guidelines for a community of believers or practitioners of a specific pathway. However, there is a creative tension between the understanding of an individual and the general consensus of the community, each has their place, and in the Sophiana view neither has precedence. Like children in a family, there are differences that truly matter, not only in gender and age and ethnicity, but also in terms of the relationship of the individual to the family or community.

Consensus reflects generally agreed upon interpretations usually passed over time through individuals with special knowledge or training in that interpretation (minister, rabbi, priest, teacher, guide, or leader). This transmission of knowledge is often given structure by collective attitudes and communal ideals that may differ from individual experience and response. The creative tension between the individual and the community circulates in accord with the truth content of a teaching as understood by multiple persons, trained or not. The Sophianic perspective recognizes the validity of both the individual and the community; based not on authority or training but on respect for differences and the importance of communitas. Sacred texts require respect and appreciation because they represent long traditions of belief and practice; however, individual choices are not determined by those texts, they represent possible choices, not necessary choices.

The life of the community, spiritually and socially, is a matrix of ideas, beliefs, and practices validated by the individual experiences of each member. *Communitas* is the felt sense of shared ideals, beliefs, and practices in a context of social relations in which the experience of the individual is supported and enhanced by other participants. For example, a Native sweat lodge, a communion service, chanting or praying together, a healing ceremony, a discussion group, can all create a sense of shared experience that reinforces the value and positive nature of that gathering. A Sophianic view supports both the integrity of each participant and the value of shared experience. However, not all experience is similar, and many subtle differences can accentuate the diversity of views within a single community. In turn, this leads to deeper problems and challenges.

The question arises as to the nature and determinative strength of communal and collective attitudes: How do those attitudes create or strengthen certain aspects of experience while possibly diminishing or denying the value of other aspects? There is a subconscious tendency to follow the norms of communal actions, beliefs, and behaviors, regardless of how they may contravene any deeper internal sense of authenticity or truth. Conformity can lead to inauthenticity through collective expectations representing the goals and intentions of action supported by a noncritical majority. By *noncritical* I mean a passive acceptance of collective attitudes and entrenched thinking that results in a more superficial, less meaningful interpretation. Even the most spiritual community faces this very problem.

In contrast to this tendency toward inauthentic co-participation, the Sophianic individual takes responsibility for cultivating a mature and critical sense of subjectivity.[9] This responsibility is an individual calling, one that requires testing ideas, beliefs, or practices against the most authentic basis of self-other relations, a weighing of internalized values and spiritual ideals held to be paramount in guiding of one's life. This is a path of courage and inner determination, not based on conformity but on integrity; it is a call to test the legitimacy of belief against the actuality of real human experience. Not the experiences of others, but against one's own inmost core experiences and encounters, those moments that have become a defining base for the soul's evolution toward wisdom. It is not "all-knowing" wisdom, not a façade wrapped around an authoritarian stance, but a tempered sense of one's own limits in contrast to what one knows with some sense of enduring and meaningful truth—through humility rather than grandeur.

It is the task of the individual to challenge the collective (and the communal) if and when that collective loses the very sense of legitimacy that makes it worthy of positive regard. And yet, communal support can be a key factor in validating one's own experience, helping to refine one's understanding of what the experience means in a larger social context. There is an interplay between the individual and the community that can facilitate growth and development for both; the individual as a stimulus for unique insights and the community as a stable resource for sharing those insights. There is an ethos of cooperation if the community permits some degree of contestation; if not, then the individual must choose, integrity or conformity? Challenge is a necessary aspect of spiritual development, not only when overcoming inner attitudes but also in confronting attitudes in others that impede or misalign with communal goals or teachings.

Wisdom in this communal sense can be a source of salvation, an awakening to untapped potentials through the medium of gifted and insightful individuals. Like an inspired speaker whose words and enhanced state can lift the community, the shared sense of co-participation can be a resource for even greater inspiration. The Sophiana of this relation between the individual and the community rests on the foundation of shared sentience; as sentient individuals we all participate in the life-force of our collective being, we resonate with an undercurrent of vitality common to and shared by all. Sentience is our resource, our well of soul that draws sustenance from the very depths of Being and Mystery. The shared task is to continue the process of refinement and transformation, not to fall into fixed patterns of belief and action but to work through those patterns for the emergence of new insights.

Our in-dwelling harmony, as a current or heart pulse of shared awareness, has deep currents swelling up from an unfathomable source. It surges through the collective, into diverse communities and finds unique expressive individual channels as authentic lights to illumine emergent horizons of becoming. We can overflow with the abundance of that current, spilling life source into diverse networks of world building or we can contract, cut connections, and shrink into the knot that represents our resistance to change and transformation. Sophia teaches us not to cut the knot, but to unravel it carefully, and re-strand its colored threads into new patterns with others. This does not require giving up our center, but it does require sharing that center as an opening to deeper communitas. It also means being open to discovery that might shift and change the center without denying its value. The balance is between enduring principles and new modes of expression and action that support the development of those principles.

There is no bottom to the collective; it does not rest on some mythic foundation, but instead it is a conjunction of processes whose embodiment is found in the actual forms of nature, in flora, fauna, and species. By *nature* I mean actual living nature, the deep earth elemental processes that sustain life and support the possibility of species development. As a dynamic process, the collective is not static, only more massive in its turning over; its cycles are much more incorporative than those of the individual seeker. For me, the fullness of the collective includes all of nature, all of cosmos, and all species, and not simply human experiences. Species evolution is inseparable from its sentient base, shared across all species making humanity one among many, not unique, but distinctive with potential for greater self-awareness.

This means that the origins of the collective are no different than the origins of nature and cosmos; we are not unique, but we are participant in a collective process, and we have our own history and patterns of becoming. In that nature-based process, we have co-created a subjective sphere of psychic signs, images, and symbols whose (cultural) meaning lies below the horizon of everyday awareness, like most of the processes in nature. The community acts as an attractor for certain signs, symbols, and analogies whose meanings reverberate with sympathies from deeper processes. Sophia represents one of those signs, a feminine image of a divine process, one of tolerance, discovery, and understanding of the diverse and complex nature of those processes. But even Sophia is a veil over a Mystery, a sacred image whose radiance stems from the deep, beyond form and image. Her image and qualities continue to evolve as new aspects and nuances emerge through collective refinement.

Self-awareness is inseparable from this creative process, in community, in the collective, in nature, and in and through its sacred dynamics. Individuation is part of that process; integrity is the luster that gives specific form its enduring character. Each person, in search of wisdom, faces the challenge to grow into maturity, resonant with multiple communities, in order to impact the collective in moving forward to an ever-greater shared sense of responsibility for the well-being of all—all species, all worlds, not just humanity, but all beings. Sophia's wisdom is all-inclusive, specialized and generalized, unique and collective, communal and individual, an inner dynamic of creative discovery and actual realizations. Our self-awareness is developmental and has no final end or form; it continues to evolve in an ever-creative universe of tremendous complexity.

Therefore, the collective does not determine our future, nor does the communal represent our best insights; inevitably it is the illumined actions of each person that contribute to the evolution of the Whole. Sophia, as Feminine Wisdom, calls us to maturity in the name of a cosmogenesis directly linked to our local, immediate place and setting. It is where we are now, today, that matters in terms of this realization—every situation is an opportunity for wisdom, no special place is needed, and no ritual context is necessary. What matters is the luminous heart ever ready to serve and respond: to know when to go forth and when to draw back, when to rest and when to act, when to give and when to accept. This is how community is built, one person at a time, together. Local leads to global and global leads to transplanetary and in this process of development, the local is not diminished but transformed.

Positive communitas supports this process of individuation while also providing a social context for nurturing a healthy sense of membership without denying uniqueness. More complexly, we are members of multiple communities and our sense of communitas extends through a variety of social and communal settings.[10] The Sophiana perspective on these relationships is to foster a sense of presence that enhances the quality of interactions and builds trust and appreciation for all members. Variety offers opportunity and appreciation supports discovery, even when divergent and eccentric. The basis of communitas is trust and mutual support, particularly in trying times and crisis; conformity is not the key, what is needed is emotional support and a willingness to listen. The transformation of the local is through communitas, a shared recognition of change as an index of enhanced awareness in an increasingly complex world of shared interests.[11] Communities intersect, the borders become more transparent, and resistance to change reveals the hard points that prioritize stability over flow.

The heart must be open to receive the impulses of spirit in the context of shared concerns. Those impulses, as Sophiana wisdom, can sustain the bond of friendship and community even in the face of disagreement and debate. It is not simply a matter of obedience nor of surrender, but of integrity based in loving concern for others that allows for and supports differences. One may break away and another may return, but in this process of growth and development, the Sophia of salvation seeks to sustain each and every stage of development. This salvation, this grace of wisdom, is born out of our ability to stay with the process of discovery through all its cycles and stages as we are drawn with others to enact our deepest values for the good of the Whole. This is the Sophiana of self-awareness and authentic communitas.

5

Mystery of
Deep Union

HIEROS GAMOS

There are three unions I want to address, all of which form a single harmony when balanced and enacted in concert. The three unions in a discreet sense are male and female, body and mind, God and soul. The topic here is *hieros gamos*, sacred marriage, in which these three relations each play a critical role in determining the depth and fullness of a complete union. Alchemically, the hieros gamos symbolizes the integration of the divided psyche into Wholeness, a transmutation to golden light, a realization of preexisting harmonies made actual and visible through practice, commitment, and many cycles of refinement. Wholeness in this sense is not an analogue for personal development only, it necessarily includes others, and more profoundly, all others, not simply the integration of individual psychic elements. The Mystery of hieros gamos is found in a union that does not dissolve the parts but distinguishes and harmonizes difference into a larger field of knowing. The *tertium quid* of this unity is the "undefined third" that unites the distinct parts, in this case, a sacred Presence, Spirit, and Mystery that animates and harmonizes two into one through a third.[1]

Every union of two results in a third as an emergent field representing the interplay between the two; unity is attained through a complex process of harmonizing discreet aspects into a greater wholeness as a state of awareness extending beyond self. Even the deeper and more mature Self is a part-whole relation, Brahman-Atman, conjoined in a unitary bond that erases borders and boundaries, yet whose elements are distinguishable. The "sacred marriage" symbolizes a process of development through stages leading to a new sense of integral co-participation in a harmonious cosmos of spiritually aware others. The third aspect is the invisible Presence that sanctifies the integration of differences, not through mergence or erasure, but through the dynamic interplay of each partner's unique, distinctive attributes and abilities.

Within the push and pull of our relations there is a principle of attraction that often initiates the process of co-discovery, not always conscious and often subliminal to the everyday conscious mind. Subliminal activities represent not only the underlying processes of psychic life but also reflect the ontological depths of soulful being. That depth is Sophianic, a wisdom-depth whose life vitality flows into the receptive psyche as inspiration and guidance, soulfully offering possible avenues of development. Attraction can be spiritual, an alluring sense of inherent beauty hidden behind a mask of diffidence or uncertainty, a beauty not yet fully come into the world. Body attracts mind and mind attracts body with a healthy sense of appreciation for the necessity of each. Body and mind are already married, intrinsically, deep down, such that soul remains a hidden third uniting body-mind.

I am this body, I am this mind, I am a soul, I am not divided;

harmony is the healthy integration of elements, each contributing to a sense of wholeness in which soul becomes a vital presence enlivening all that mind and body are. There are multiple layers of vital life, like sheaths, one within the other, supporting organic processes, glandular cycles, moods and emotions, memories, dreams, and imagining. And mind is also layered—conscious, subconscious, hyperconscious, thoughts, intuitions, metacognitions—all contributing to the complexity of an embodied mind. The hieros gamos of body-mind is a foundational aspect of being in the world, it is not an arbitrary relation, and it does not require asceticism or sexual repression to fully realize its inherent spiritual capacities.

Mind is not trapped in body, contra Gnostic or ascetic teachings; mind is the natural psychic aspect of bodily life and body gives foundational structure to mind. The natural body-mind is the primal vehicle of illumination for Praxis Sophiana, a wisdom that celebrates all the beauty and power of eros of body and mind mixed in the crucible of soul. The attractive power is eros, an initiation whose kiss is light and unforgettable, a breath of ecstasy on the cheek, a tear of joy. Eros seeks union, fully embodied, fully mindful. Eros is life breath, but eros arises through spirit, through the deepest sources that give both body and mind their integral unity. Spirit is unity, a single reality within all differences. Wisdom recognizes the vital healing that spirit brings to every healthy relationship, a marriage that sustains the many cycles of union and separation necessary for soul's development as a preparation for a higher merging with the sacred ground of Being.

The archetypal union of male and female reflects the very nature of the life process, that life springs from the pleasures of union, from those heartfelt moments of deep connections freed from all the dross and damage of sexual predation and abuse. The spiritual union is between equals, each distinct, neither subordinate, yet each able to play a diversity of roles in relationship to the pleasures and needs of the moment. The final ecstasy is a merging of twin impulses bonded in the overflowing field of a third presence, the gift and grace of Spirit, uplifting both into the light that lights up the world. This marriage, this soulful union, this merging that leads to a new horizon of spiritual insight is a gift because we do not create the outcome, only receive it with thankfulness in the very moment of its passing. The fading light reflects the passing of shared ecstasy for the sobriety of individuation; we are not the other, but we are less without her, without him.

This union is multilevel, it connects through body, feeling, mind, heart, and soul, and it connects in the most complete sense to the very foundations of Being and Mystery. It is also a kind of knowing, one that requires a sensitive appreciation for the subtle and energetic, for the ways in which the neural impulses activate altered perceptions, opening the horizon on our shared awareness. When we open to this horizon, we discover how the creative energies act to release deep feelings of joy and luminous moments of insight. If we cross over into the unbound expanse, into the larger matrix where knowing is also sharing, we can reach the soul of others, their deeper identity, their long-term sense of self. This openness is a gift, a form of ecstatic insight, allowing us to experience the deeper nature of the self-other relationship, an eros of communion, merged with divinity. This intimacy is formative for the hieros gamos, a forging of shared experiences meant to reveal how souls resonate with life and vitality. It is a gift of the most precious kind, a thankful consequence of genuine, soulful sharing.

Our gratitude is not directed toward only the other but also toward the very undercurrents that created the male-female, female-male differentiations, in all their varied roles and expressions. Hieros gamos (sacred marriage) includes those diverse relations in gender change, reorientation, transexual or hermaphroditic, as expressions of diversity in the most explicit sense. Souls, not just bodies, seek union, and it is soul life that seeks expression in gender orientation; having lived before, in past lives, we are perhaps all transgendered. Sophia teaches us that she too is male as well as female, sprung from the head of Zeus, she shines forth in a multitude of forms. I am thankful for this diversity, for wisdom's many faces, across the entire range of all human faces, who is she not? She is all, in all, through all, All-Being in all forms, a living Presence animating the soulful union of every pair and couple.

THE CHRIST-SOPHIA UNION

The relation between Christ and Sophia is varied and there are many different accounts, some built around Mary Magdalene as a true knower of the Christ teachings. These texts teach that Mary Magdalene was one of the most advanced students of Jesus and questioned him deeply and interpreted many sacred writings correctly and profoundly.[2] This tradition also includes the Sophia narrative as part of an even more ancient Mystery tradition, in which Sophia is one of the twenty-four Aeons of creation, a seeker of light beyond the Pleroma.[3] What these texts reveal is a tradition within Christianity in which the feminine played a more important, even central, role than usually recognized by the masculine hierarchies of the church. The symbolism of the Divine Feminine as an equal, not only as a partner, but as a creative spiritual source, a full representation of divinity equal to Christ is an emerging Sophiana teaching today.

The hieros gamos relation as a creative partnership in which each person represents fully and actually the divine source expresses a new ontological realization. The core of that realization is that the feminine sacred, the Sophia, is fully expressive of divinity in and through the mode of being female, in a way that is distinct from the Christ, and yet as equal, as fully representing feminine characteristics of that same sacred. Each represents the other insofar as each carries within a sense of the unique and distinct nature of the male-female relation. This affirmation of equality refines the Christ teachings; it honors partnership as a spiritual norm, a sense that without such equality, maleness is lacking fulfillment through an ingrained social bias against female equality. And further, the feminine perspective, in all its diversity, offers not only equality but in its own way, a superior point of view because it honors those differences without denying the value of the masculine.

This unified female-male symbolism, as an *anima-animus* harmony, resides in the heart of every wisdom seeker; the marriage as a sacred event dramatizes the attraction and difference between the two, in search of integration and wholeness. Just as mind and body form a whole, so too do our masculine and feminine characteristics contribute to that whole. The introjected alternate gendered parent (father for women, mother for men) reflects the light and shadow of our multigenerational struggle to bring parity and right relations to male-female subjectivities. The spiritual task is one of recognizing that an introjected parent, of either gender, often projected onto opposite gendered others, is not a basis for the realization of the wisdom teaching on male-female balance. Each person must undergo the challenge of reconciling parental models, and collective attitudes toward gender relations, as a sacred work aiming toward integration and equality, without erasing differences.

Sophia is not Christ and Christ is not Sophia; they each express spiritual agency through unique embodied modes of being and yet both can be equally empowered souls filled with the light of understanding. Light conforms to the vessel it illumines, red or gold vessels shine with red or gold light; water takes the shape of the vessel that holds it; human beings give character to the indwelling rise of inner illumination. A masculine realization is not the same as a feminine realization, even when they share intimately a single divine source. The source is qualitatively Infinite, therefore capable of innumerable variations, including all those among a single gender—there is no reason to believe that one person's realization is the same as another, and yet those realizations may cluster to form recognizable patterns and outcomes. Further, certain characteristics of experience may surpass gender differences without denying the value of those differences.

Parental models may encourage or mislead in this process of discovery; what matters is turning within and preparing the heart for a deeper union. Gender models based on long traditions of bias obscure the Mystery of this union. Patriarchy cannot offer the correct model insofar as it embraces masculine superiority; it fails completely when it subordinates the feminine, there is no justification for such suppression. Sophia teaches patience but also action, resistance is a spiritual discipline when applied to the problems of gender discrimination. A test of this model is to hold up a feminine example of equal status for every male teacher, the Christ, the Buddha, the Avatar, all have their counterpart feminine forms, the Sophia, the Tara, the great female saints of India.

Deep down, however, the sense of equality must be found in the heart of the believer; this is not a matter of simple acknowledgment, but one of discovery, by which the feminine character is sacralized as truly equal with the very best examples of spiritual realization. Equal does not mean identical, it means equal in merit, accomplishment, and realization, equal in representing and expressing sacred ideals, equal as examples of the very best qualities of illumination. But not the same, rather, unique, individuated, distinctive, and offering variation, diverse views, and multiple points of view, all the while sharing an inner sense of genuine revelation. This is the beauty of Spirit, its incredible eros and diversity in expressing sacred qualities, not as a repetition or imitation, but as a remarkable, unique expression for each and every being. We are blessed to have such diversity and the lack of recognition of its value and importance is a form of spiritual blindness.

The Sophia-Christ relation is best understood in the light of this equality that sustains differences; each brings something that amplifies and enhances the other, neither is subordinate, and both are strengthened by a complementary sharing of insights. Thus, there is no one interpretation of those characteristics that differentiate; each seeker must find the qualities that best exemplify the relationship. To what degree does the divine Christ live within you? How manifest is Sophia in your inner life? These are the twin spiritual questions that do not require belief in any doctrine that would define those characteristics dogmatically when, in fact, they are life-forces ever shifting to adapt to the capacities and character of the seeker. I use the names Sophia and Christ as exemplars, not as necessary signs to the hieros gamos, but only as conventional designation given new meaning.

Other names can be given, Sita and Ram, Isis and Osiris, Freya and Odin, Hera and Zeus, Asherah and Yahweh, all representing a divine couple, as with the ancient Ogdoad of Hermetic traditions, eight God and Goddess couples. The Sophia-Christ paradigm is simply more pragmatic in terms of the widespread popularity of Christianity. And yet for the Western psyche, it is perhaps the most representative relation symbolizing the hieros gamos as a spiritual union honoring both genders as sacred persons fully able to embody a deep spiritual conjunction—and yet each expressing unique characteristics of their gender orientation. Christ is not Sophia nor is

Sophia Christ, yet each complements the other. This sacred quality of differences is the very source of creativity, and the emergence of wisdom celebrates the distinctiveness that allows for discovery through individuation. It reveals the profound depths of what is possible through actual examples, displaying the Infinite through unending subtle distinctions.

The Sophia-Christ mystery is a mystery of redemption and transformation. It is not a redemption of the female by the male but a co-redemption that uplifts the male through deep appreciation of the female in partnership with a female recognition of the value and contribution of the male. Each contributes to this redemption, a salvation from the sins of pride and arrogance that would elevate one gender over the other or seek to justify the subordination of one beneath the other. It is also a redemption from the isolation of only one kind, one ideal in the form of one gender; spiritual maturity requires a harmony that overflows into a multitude of forms, shared relations creating a plurality of ideal types. The sacred Anthropos is dual gendered, an integration of feminine-masculine characteristics whose Protean forms can hold innumerable images of the sacred human without privileging one gender. This is a great spiritual mystery, the plenipotent capacity of Infinite forms melded into the human being as a spiritual ideal without limiting that form to any one image or manifestation. The alchemical marriage creates that image in all its diversity, giving birth to a child-spirit whose gender is all-containing at the deep psychonoetic, biological level.

Evidence suggests that all embryos start as female (phenotypically) and are then capable of diverse gender adaptations; symbolically this represents core alterity, where differentiation is not only biological but cultural and spiritual as well.[4] A feminine baseline as a phenotype for actual becoming prioritizes the feminine as a creative starting point for such differentiation, with the male as a later development, equally potent but not as primal. The masculine myth of superiority is a myth of dominance, not a myth of sacred origin. Sophia springs from the head of Zeus not as an afterthought but as a profound *forethought*, as the original impulse to understanding as a feminine gesture toward future becoming. Adam is created from the embryo of Eve. Christ discovers Sophia and is uplifted by that discovery, inspired, and enters into dialogue in order to explore diverse interpretations of the ancient sacred teachings. In a deep sense, priority belongs to the feminine as source and basis of life, stimulated by male interactions and harmonized through the hieros gamos, sustained over a lifetime of cohabitation. The feminine mystery touches every human being at the very beginning, as a core imprint representing the life spark. The evolution of that spark requires continual diversification and responsiveness enhanced through male-female relations without falling into culturally narrow attitudes or succumbing to the influence of male authoritarian claims.

The Christ-Sophia relationship reflects a spiritual union of the best qualities of spiritual development through both male and female stages of realization. But there is the Third Presence, the uniting gift of Spirit, or source and ground, providing the correct nurturance for the most balanced integration. Just as each gender has its own pathways to maturity and wisdom, so too the union of those pathways requires an opening into Being and Mystery that truly enhances and vivifies the depth and complexity of that union. Spirit acts to guide this process as a natural progression toward light in the ascension model and a sinking into depth, roots in the soil, in the descent model. Adam descends with bright thoughts down through the spheres into the arms of Eve who provides the warmth and passion as a holding ground for life and birth.[5] The soul's union with the embryo is also an alchemical marriage by which soul takes on incarnate life and embraces a gender orientation harmonized with bodily attributes. And yet, soul life encompasses both genders, an anima-animus union whose influences correspond to life choices and attitudes toward gender and becoming. The ideal is differentiated in accord with the inmost amalgamation of feminine-masculine aspects, correctly balanced in the model of the Sophia-Christ relationship.

The actual characteristics of this union are distinctive in terms of how the union is actualized in an individual case; my own Sophia-Christ union is a unique synthesis growing out of a lifetime of spiritual inquiry. But that synthesis is not a necessary pathway for others, nor does it best represent the ideal. Each person faces the challenge of this integration, in whatever terms best reflect a pathway that most inspires choice and action. What is common, intrinsic to this alchemy, is the presence of Spirit guiding both individual and collective evolution toward synthesis and differentiation. The Third Presence is the true guide, the blessing that sanctifies the marriage, the light that illumines the Christ-Sophia relationship. Without that light, without the blessing, the work is stillborn, an imitation and not an actualization; the true marriage is creative, alive, active, working to fulfill the promise, seeking to give birth to the works of Spirit however humble or simple.

This union is not apocalyptic, not a heavenly drama, but a down-to-earth relationship meant to instill appreciation and a positive regard for others as a gift to be shared with all. It is seen in the faces of those who live with compassion and care for the well-being of others and whose thoughts are not always for their own good. The witness is the thankfulness of those who have been served and received that compassion without any need for recompense. Examples are often found among those who are not seen or recognized for their gifts—the caretakers, the helpers, those dedicated to services that are often difficult and very demanding. The soulful integration of the feminine-masculine aspects is an alchemical work of a lifetime, more than one, and its accomplishment is an unending process that leads to new stages of insight. Holy wisdom needs both the feminine and the masculine to accomplish the work of transformation, without both the attainment is less complete.

BEYOND DARK AND LIGHT

The relationship between duality and unity is complex, having much to do with transmitted mental attitudes based usually on male oppositional logic. Duality is not a blunt fact, but a perception based on categorization, while some facts may support this perception, for example magnetic poles of positive and negative charge, the majority of such perceptions follow convention rather than facts. Hot and cold, high and low, black and white are all relative terms that each belong to a spectrum of gradations, changing by degree the temperature, color, or measure that gives no special priority to specific fixed points on the spectrum. A circle has 360 degrees, and any two degrees may represent the circle as adequately as any two points in juxtaposition; in the circle of life, all such categories are relative to the observer. The observer is both a subject and an object. It is a false polarity to imagine that subject and object are distinct; they are each a point on the spectrum of consciousness, more a relationship than a content.

The same can be said for theodicy, the perception of good and evil, not as predetermined attributes, but as relative perception on a scale or spectrum of possible actions and behaviors. Relative good and relative evil may have more absolute forms, but that judgment is not a simple duality, it is a complex mix of ideas, beliefs, and issues that temper and shape the judgment. The same can be said for the very terms *absolute* and *relative*, not as logical categories, but as actual perceptions matched to experiences that qualify what absolute or relative means to the individual. The circle gives us the best view if we honor every degree of change and do not falsely imagine that polarities are somehow more relevant or important, they are not. Duality is a matter of prejudice, a kind of myopic seeing that fails to distinguish the degrees of difference that actually constitute the world of lived experience. We are conditioned into duality because it is an easy, even lazy way to make distinctions.

The metaphorical reference to light as a medium of consciousness is not opposed to dark, which may be a healing presence as well, and more salient, as an analogy mapped to subtle experience. Gnosis is like entering the light, not overcoming darkness, rather attaining a profound illumination, a clarity and lucidity that opens a new horizon of perception. Darkness may represent rest, quietude, silence, a place for moon glow and night flowers, a tranquility that sustains peace and deep restfulness. Both may be metaphors for spiritual growth and development; neither is in opposition as both are natural circumstances reflecting cosmic order and cycles of nature. The problem of duality is found in the assertion of an agonistic, masculine attitude that polar differences are contrary—a false attitude greatly responsible for suffering in the world. The implication is one of conflict, black against white, male against female, mind against body, not neutral but biased by an assumption of inherent irreducible tension and conflict. The Dao of dualism is all too often missing, the concept that dynamic relations express distinct phases across a wide spectrum of changing conditions, a nonlineal transformation that recognizes the positive value of differences.

The better analogy is the spiral, cycles that expand or contract in relationship to stages of life. The phases within the spiral reflect life rhythms, times of wakefulness and times of sleep, times to plant and to sow, to break down and build up, to weep and to laugh, to think and to imagine (Ecclesiastes 3:1–10). The stream of experience is not divided by contrast alone, but by shades and degrees of difference, wakeful, lucid, daydreaming, distracted, or deep in thought, sleepy, actively imagining, or subtly aware of the mind and feelings of others. The Sophiana of understanding, of sacred insight, proceeds by degrees, by shades and nuances, by distinctions and associations free of a strict, overbearing masculine dialectic. This requires thinking wholistically, by ramifications connected in patterns and gestalts, embedded in the cycles and rhythms of lived experience.

This does not mean that the dialectic is not useful or appropriate in certain circumstances; however, it is not the methodology of Sophianic perception. Knowledge, as sacred wisdom, as a basis for life decisions and insight into the very structures of consciousness and cosmos, requires a different kind of thinking, less bound by dialectic method and more pattern based, more wholistic, more a shared dialogical interaction. What is the basis of this patterned way of thinking and believing? It begins with the very idea of Wholeness, that cosmos and consciousness is a single, intimate, complex set of relationships in which every element and being plays a role in contributing to the processes of the constantly transforming Whole. Every person, every creature, every element plays a part, from the most subtle and minute to the grand structures of cosmology.

The Sophiana perspective embraces this wholeness as a unitary, dynamic complex vast beyond articulation and subtle in ways that we barely comprehend. It includes the physical, energetic, psychic, paranormal, mystical, mythic, supernatural, and transpersonal as concomitants of the Whole relative to the persons and communities that hold those concepts to be valid and real. This overall gestalt is not reducible to the individual, but every individual contributes to its complexity and participates in its processes. The cosmology of becoming is a long-term process of many cycles, and in these cycles we explore, interact, discuss, and attempt alternate ways of life.

Self-knowledge is also part of the pattern, not dialectic, but associative and centric, built around internalized habits of mind and emotion, acted out in relationships, and epitomized in creative efforts. The deep "logic of self" is wholistic; it encompasses all of our life experiences, remembered or subliminal, thought or dreamt, imagined or projected. Such logic is more *dialogical* than dialectic, more an internal conversation than strict juxtapositions of logical opposites. This dialogue includes the mythic and imaginative, a conversation with Sophia, words heard in a dream, lucid thoughts without a context, all striving to communicate insights beyond the border of logical discourse. We can have rational discourse and we can value that discourse, but its formal logic creates an abstraction from the actual dynamics of interior associations and the creative play of free thought and active imagination.

The mind at work, and more so, the soul at work, proceed by the pathways of learned experience building meaning in stages or cycles that require continual refinement, an alchemy of interior dialogues leading to lucid insights about motives and goals and aspirations. Sophia embraces the whole, but the whole exceeds our grasp; this is a foundational claim, we are working our way toward the discovery of value and meaning in how we live, or manage our relationships, or accomplish our ideals. But our knowledge is limited, our insights only travel part of the way, our intuitions illumine a corner, an aspect, a shard of meaning that must be fitted to the whole of our shared understanding. It is a slow process punctuated by sudden bursts and the occasional leap, only to fall back into our patterns and habits. Stages and cycles bring us back to core issues, seen a bit differently, with more perspective, or more grappling with how those issues can be refined to produce better insight.

Such thinking does not proceed in categories of opposition, but through a process of weighing a variety of meanings in relationship to the intuitions of the heart. They say that after death in ancient Egypt, the heart was weighed against a feather of Maat, Goddess of truth and harmony, because every action and intent was recorded by the pen as a record of the soul's thoughts, words, and deeds.[6] The pen or feather outweighs the heavy-handedness of injustice, prejudice, bias, discrimination, lies, perversions, and misrepresentations and further, inscribes on the heart the codes of spirit waiting to be discovered. This is not a matter of simple black and white but includes all the shades of meaning that relate to the integrity of soul's purpose. We seek wisdom, Sophia's grace, insight that is able to penetrate the confusion that would mislead and that offers us a path guided by a deeply held spiritual purpose. This is a Mystery, the true purpose of soul's life in a cosmos of divine attributes, a mystery requiring our most sincere attention.

Like the scales of a musical composition, the right combination of notes creates the motif that represents a soul's capacity for beauty, harmony, and justice. There are not just two notes, but a plurality of notes, sharps and flats all necessary for a composition that creatively expresses soul desire and gives inspiration and new breath to soul's development. Further, our song is in concert with the songs of others, diverse in style and meaning, but part of an even greater harmony of Sophia's making, spirit born. We rise to a level most expressive of our soul development when we honestly express our heart song; we join in harmony with those whose scales resonate with our own, offering new variations in theme and purpose. Together we co-create the music of the spheres, and in isolation our song may fall on deaf ears; may those who can hear join our song. Every singer has value no matter how simple or exquisite their song, and as songs evolve, becoming more complex, new meanings emerge.

The hieros gamos of soul's relationship to Spirit, to God or Goddess, to the Infinite Unknown, is already active, "a marriage made in heaven," in the sense that our preexistent participation in cosmic harmony is an unbreakable union. We are already intimately part of that greater unity however opaque or distant it may seem in the present. We may feel isolated, alienated, alone, fearful, anxious, cut off, and desolate, but those feelings are not an index of our soul's full capacity. We have deeper roots in the matrix of all-becoming; we can grow into those roots, draw nurture and health from them, grow strong and vibrant. But we must free ourselves from closure and contraction based on limited views and false notions; our identity is cosmically constructed, not simply biological or cultural, but much, much more. To know this requires an opening to cosmic vistas, which we inhabit as self-aware souls participant in a vaster process of becoming that includes all beings, multiple realms of existence, and a transpersonal horizon that overlights the totality of All That Is.

The aspiration of soul is toward this light, an open horizon of infinite extent, a thirst for the nectar of immortality—not because we are immortal, but because immortality is a quality that gives life freely and always. Death is only a change in the cycle, a transition, another perspective, an alternate view imbued with the same hope for more life, wisdom, and understanding. Death is part of the cycle of life enduring, not an end, but a stage leading to new life. The constricted psyche caught the shadows and sorrows of experience, cultural confusion, and historical events can easily lose sight of this greater horizon and feel an insignificance in purpose and direction. But these clouds of delusion and ignorance pass when the pure light of spiritual awakening stimulates the heart and opens our mind to "that peace which passes all understanding" (Phillipians 4:7). This peace is already there, waiting discovery through inner dedication to spiritual awakening, through partnership and shared desires for illumined transformation.

There is balance and harmony in partial knowing, it is not necessary to know all or to be all; one only needs a dedicated heart, honest self-appraisal, and a dedicated will directed toward the good of others. Such is Sophia's wisdom, a teaching whose purpose is to offer genuine insight to those whose understanding is still in development, still striving to grasp what is yet beyond comprehension. This wisdom of not-knowing is a gift of spirit, it embodies an acceptance that beyond light and dark there are many more shades of becoming and Being yet to be assimilated or comprehended. As limited beings, however illumined or not, however grand an enlightenment may be, there is yet more, much more, to be learned, not only about the foundations of Being and awareness but also how the world is made and unmade in processes of wisdom and discovery applied to real-world challenges, solar expansion, and cosmic awakening to vaster fields of knowing.[7]

Beyond the dialectic there is an infinite universe of beings and domains awaiting discovery and exploration, such that inner and outer must merge, incorporate, and assimilate whole new fields of learning. The alchemical marriage carries us beyond our local, known reality, and reveals that we are intrinsically united with a much vaster cosmos in which dialogue and multiple points of view will become the primary medium for understanding. Beyond the dialectic there is a multiverse expectant with anticipation, awaiting our world-awakening so we too may enter into conversation across the full spectrum of our cosmically shared relations. How many shades there are—beyond counting, hundreds, thousands, millions, each marking a place in the full spectrum of all possible realizations. Spirit animates all, every shade has presence, even more so if the carrier of that shade is awake and self-aware.

THE FULLNESS OF THE ALL

There was an image of the Goddess Isis, veiled and sitting upon a throne, in the ancient city of Sais in Egypt with the following logion (sacred text): "I am all that has been and is and shall be / and no mortal has ever lifted my veil."[8] This text is both a promise and a warning. The promise is that all that has been, all that is, and all that shall be is under the guardianship of feminine divinity, all permeating and omnipresent. The warning is that human knowledge is limited and cannot explain all mysteries, particularly the mystery of divinity, nor the sacredness of nature imbued by that divinity. The fullness of the All overflows; it is not constrained by myth, theology, or science, and has a depth and complexity that extends into the most minute particle and expands through a vast array of complex constructions to the full totality of the multiverse itself.

Myth has embodied explanation in stories, images, and art meant to epitomize the power and sacredness of divinity but without offering explanations for the deeper working of nature and cosmic phenomena. Both theology and science have tried to lift the veil, articulating theories meant to explain the origins and processes of nature and cosmos. The Sophiana perspective is that all these voices offer insight in different modes that align with specific ways of thinking, be it theology, science, or myth. And yet none of them are complete, nor are they sufficient as texts meant to explain cosmological processes in relationship to human evolution and the inherent sentience of all cosmic life. Further, dreams also reveal the sacred in even more complex forms and dramas, the veiled Isis is itself a dream metaphor, an image of feminine divinity graphically portrayed to illustrate queenship, nobility, and mystery, an inscrutable presence whose image is multifold.

Many disciplines have contributed to this attempt at unveiling, but the fullness exceeds the grasp of any discipline or area of research that does not also accommodate a genuinely spiritual view of nature and cosmos. By a spiritual view I do not mean a specific religious or traditional perspective, I mean a stance that accepts the plausibility of divinity as intrinsic to nature and human becoming, through stages of discovery and insight. Such a view would not polarize body and mind, or soul and body, but rather see the intimate unity and wholeness of our world embodiment as an intrinsic feature of larger cosmic processes. The articulation of those processes might be artistic, poetic, scientific, theological, literary, mythic, or imaginative without violating the sacredness that imbues all those articulations. Fullness overflows and is not constrained by theory or research except by the parameters of the disciplines that seek to validate their views. How many ways can the Infinite be explained? There is no one best view for All That Is; multiple views are illustrated by multiple religions, multiple scientific approaches, multiple humanitarian ideals, multiple value systems, and multiple persons. There is something in the very nature of the fullness that accommodates all of our differences without demanding a singular account of what is higher or best; it is a human (male) tendency to make such evaluations, often to the detriment of others.

At the core of this teaching is a reverence for nature, for creatures and habitats, for life in all its many forms. Nature is sacred and should be treated as such, protected and sustained, as life expressions of the possibilities inherent in divinity. The beauty of nature is possibly one of the greatest expressions of divinity, how life can evolve in the context of a planetary home in an incredible diversity of niches and ecologies all meant to sustain specific life-forms. Be it mountains or swamps, deserts or tundra, hidden valleys or plunging waterfalls, there is something remarkably sacred in the beauty and wholeness of these ecologies because they promote life. Even life in the most simple and basic form deserves our reverence, as life evolves from the simple to the complex, carrying with it the simple forms of origin. Nature in all her adornments is a sacred image of the whole, a feminine archetype of creative becoming whose aura touches every life-form and every process of nature with a subtle caress of spirit, animating the entirety. This presence is not in the foreground but stands within and throughout the whole as an inherent vitality at every level of organization. Only through the mix of the visible, partially visible, and the invisible, is wholeness made complete and real, some of its most sacred aspects are a hidden, veiled mystery awaiting discovery.

One of the signs of this beauty (kallos) is the implicit symmetry of nature, its fractal patterns reflecting principles of order and harmony. From butterfly wings to pinecones, from honeycombs to sunflowers, from seashells to peacock tails, from spiderwebs to snowflakes, from planetary alignments to galactic spirals, nature abounds in symmetrical configurations revealing visible fractal patterns.[9] However, these symmetries are not identical but *approximate* among the various types of symmetry, such as bilateral (a human face), radial (a starfish), or strip symmetries (stripes on a coral snake). There is symmetry with variation or subtle difference, two eyes, but not exactly the same, revealing adaptive characteristics influenced by many subtle causes. And yet this pervasive symmetry is a visible attestation of harmony in nature, variable and idiosyncratic, but revealing an aesthetic principle of balance and beauty. Nature in aesthetic expression demonstrates both creativity and order, variability and consistency, adaptation and individuality; these are attributes that support cosmic order as well. Fractal patterns, from blood vessels to lightning bolts, from crystals to pineapples, reveal self-similar symmetries across a wide scale of recursive types, in which parts are similar to the whole, as seen in cumulus clouds or the fractal coast of Norway.[10]

These recursive typologies reflect the processes of nature as creative and yet *self-similar*, demonstrating stability through cycles of repetition and change through variation. It also demonstrates that complexity can arise out of simple, dynamic principles, such as reiteration, repetition, feedback, and compression.[11] Nature is both simple and complex, chaotic and ordered, variable and fixed. The Sophiana perspective on these principles seeks to recognize the full range of the processes involved in creating, sustaining, and rescinding visible nature, in both the local sense and in the solar-cosmic sense. The All is not limited by reference to the overall totality but also includes *processes within that totality* that contribute, even in the most minute sense, to the ongoing cycles of harmonic being and becoming. This includes the human psyche as well, the patterns of repetition and reformulation, the archetypes of recursive cultural patterning that inform our collective and individual awareness.

The feminine archetype itself is a fundamental recursive principle, an anima of creation, whose contribution cuts across a vast multitude of species, animal and plant, reflecting generative, nurturing, and reproductive capacities. The alchemical marriage, the hieros gamos, highlights the necessity of the balancing principle of the masculine, the required animus archetype, as a complementary symmetry also generative, nurturing, and productive. Each contributes, within our soul awareness, to inner balance and integration; marriage is an image of cosmos, a fractal of a much larger cosmological process by which species thrive and coexist. Beauty requires refinement and partnership, a purity that honors the whole, the parts, and the processes as the basis of all self-surpassing insight. Beauty calls us to be more aware of the complexity of wholeness, its processes, and its outcomes in a profound diversity and symmetry of expressions.

The fullness of the All exceeds our view of what constitutes the true nature of divinity. The uncovering of the All takes us far beyond written words and sacred texts, beyond male theologies, even if those texts and theologies help to guide our search. The web of life, its multiple layers and interconnections, reveals the miracle of the body-soul-mind paradigm. Personal existence is not isolated to only our limited field of sensory perceptions; it also includes our psychic capacities, our paranormal abilities, our discovery of transpersonal horizons that encompass the cosmos as a whole. Sophia teaches that we are soulfully linked, have subtle intuitive resonance with many others, including animals and plants, as part of our shared wholeness. The individual is a nexus, a knot in the web, a living center in the multidimensional matrix of creation whose development and awareness can open to a much vaster sense of co-participation and connection, with others, with nature, with cosmos.

Divinity is not simply an Anthropos, a human image of the holy, but much, much more; just as Sophia is only one image of the Infinite, so too all images together do not exhaust what divinity is or can become.[12] The Mystery of this plentitude is its unending capacity for forthcoming through intimate connection with all creatures; each being is a possible source of emergence and discovery based on relatedness to others. Following the patterns of nature, we can unveil by degrees, fractal nuances and new meanings, and when possible, make a leap into new ways of thinking and perceiving. From the Sophia perspective, this discovery is communal, shared, a dialogue with others through the medium of a third presence. The All is that presence, in Hermetic teachings, *Hen to Pān*, "the One that is All."[13] But that One has complexity throughout its entirety, it has many, a multitude, a vast array of differences all expressing possibilities within a shared unity of becoming and being.

An analogy often used for this sacred source is that of space (in Sanskrit *ākāsha*), that is, an all-containing, primal Ur-space that includes all that exists within its total expanse as a vast, open cosmic field. This idea has been popularized in some quantum physics theory as the "ground-state" or zero-point field that sustains, supports, and correlates all that appears.[14] All processes are energized by this field, extending in a nonlocal sense to connect distant elements through intimate connections. This field is often conceptualized as an information field in the sense that impressions transmitted within it are retained in the field, from the smallest subparticles to atoms, elements, organs, and a vast array of macrostructures. This all-containing space as a quantum vacuum field is inseparable from the activities, objects, and beings that inhabit the field as it acts to sustain correlations and transmit information. Such quantum space is a metaphor for spiritual unity, for an energetic sense of cosmic process that imbues even the most distant particle with complementary, parallel behaviors and reactions. "Spooky action at a distance" (Einstein) implies coherence in the deepest sense.

Mind-to-mind, heart-to-heart communication, telepathy, and other paranormal abilities are also participant in this unified and interconnected field. We are all connected at the most elemental level of being, inhabiting and embodying information, knowledge, wisdom as an inseparable aspect of an all-encompassing cosmic totality.[15] And yet, that field is itself a foundational attribute of an even deeper sacred source whose capacities surpass and enliven the Whole within, through, and beyond any conceptions of that field. Space, ākāsha, remains a metaphor representing the All-Containing not as source but as a medium of connection; the deeper connection lies in Spirit, in the depths of Being, as a transpersonal reference to what cannot be contained. The reality exceeds our capacity to comprehend in the full sense, our limited perceptions narrow the field, and yet, step by step we can move beyond those limitations.[16]

From the Sophiana perspective, the All-Containing provides a context for unity, connection, and relatedness across all fields of knowledge. The relationship between knowers is primary, what we know, believe, commit to, is a recognition of the sacredness of life and its sources beyond any containment in theories that fail to fully honor that sacredness. Whatever form or variant it may take, that recognition rests on reverence, acknowledging limits, accepting the partiality of our beliefs and thoughts, and fully appreciating the transpersonal horizon as extending far beyond our present understanding. Sophia teaches wisdom and humility, knowing and accepting limits, valuing what supports life and health, social communion, and collective harmony. Our goal is gradual development sparked by luminous moments of insight and spiritual realization, as a setting for the inevitable next stage of development.

There is excitement in discovery, a way forward that does not have all the answers but does proceed through the most appropriate questions. The unfathomable All is the very source of this excitement and of the calm acceptance of our limits; it is natural to have limits, no tree grows forever, and no flower blooms without ceasing; we accept partiality as a form of Wisdom, and we give thanks for our capacity to move beyond those limits without denying the incompleteness of what emerges. Through discovery we can enter into new vistas of perception and thinking, new beliefs, and more subtle understanding; we can become pilgrims on a hidden path where rest is when and where we choose to catch our breath. The path of becoming has its heights and depths and the pilgrim road is a winding way; we have a vista for inspiration, and we have a valley and sacred groves for rest; in this way we proceed step by step, breath by breath.

ECSTASY AND REVELATION

If wisdom is a form of knowledge, what kind of knowledge best describes its contents? There is much written in mystical literature about illumination, enlightenment, and higher states of unity and oneness. However, ecstasy and revelation are not the same kinds of experience; *ecstasy* refers to states and personal instances of transformation, whereas *revelation* is about contents and knowledge unveiled through sacred encounter. Both are aspects of the process of discovery, but neither ends in some terminal state of awareness—in this sense, there is no end to the path. Sophia teaches that there is no one ideal higher state, only an array of states described and experienced differently according to the training, commitment, and teachings followed by the seeker.

Not all seekers are equal, some are less able and some are more able to make progress based on innate abilities, past history, and circumstances that promote that development. Masculine spirituality has promoted a variety of teleological goals, end states that represent the All, often arranged in hierarchical order as stages and steps on the path. The ten stages (*bhūmi* or *vihāras*) of the Bodhisattva, the eight limbs (*aṣṭāṅga*) of Indian yoga, the eight stages of Daoist immortality (*xiān*), or the various stages in Sufism, Western occult teachings, and in many Native Indigenous pathways, all reflect the tendency to organize experience in terms of specific steps required to reach the goals of a spiritual practice. This is a natural formation based often in a mix of real experiences and theories about those experiences, with strong tendencies toward dogmatic male assertions on the necessity of those stages.

While I certainty agree that it is a typical procedure to organize both practices and teachings in accord with a series of stages or steps, such arrangement is more a reflection of routinizing the practice than it is of analyzing the phenomenal stages for each individual. Usually in such a staged approach personal experience is mapped against an array of organizational stages and states and evaluated in accord with the standards of excellence and expectation represented by the tradition. This is of course one way to proceed, but it is by no means the only way or even the best way; it is a way among many others. Sophia teaches alterity, diversity in practice and in states and stages; Feminine Wisdom (not under the control of masculine paradigms of development) proceeds through creative freedom to recognize a vast diversity of possible paths and practices. This deconstruction of hierarchy is not based on delegitimizing those more structured and traditional paths but on recognizing many alternatives beyond those paths and practices.

There are stages and states, there are steps to take, but the outcomes of the practices engaged must also include the spontaneity and unexpected results that can be a profound guide on the path. For example, there are dream teachings, unsolicited visions, intuitive insights, sudden mystical encounters, crisis events that result in radical shifts in states and awareness, deeply emotional bonds that result in powerful affective perceptions, or artistic activities that produce altered states. The masculine critique that these examples do not equal the "highest insights" is a profound fallacy, a dogma that has no evidence based on the real experience of persons outside of a specific tradition. The masculine bias has been to promote an exclusive path that does not recognize the validity of other less structured paths—the Sophiana teaching is "know them by the fruits of their actions, not by their stage or realizations."

The hieros gamos of the soul's union with God is a mystery, not a known fact, and every such union has its own contents and outcomes; the record of the soul's mergence can be idiosyncratic, highly unusual, and uniquely individuated. The attainment of such unity is an archetype without precedence in any one form, a journey whose path is broken or smooth according to circumstances.* We are each a pilgrim on a journey toward a height or depth that is not fully charted and has much that is marked as "unknown" and with indicators that "here be dragons." It is not a safe and known path, but a challenge to overcome past bias, spiritual control, and dominance by paradigms that reinforce authority. Sophia is one way, not "the" way, only one path among many; the teaching refers to those in search of guidance beyond the norms of traditional masculine authority.

Opening the way forward means not denying the practices of the past nor dismissing masculine religious traditions. However, those traditions are far from complete and they do not in any one case best represent human spiritual potential for all persons. Spirituality without tradition is possible and, in some ways, better aligned with science, humanitarianism, and social reforms seeking to address collective imbalance, gender bias, racial discrimination, and better ecological practices. The Sophiana of higher states is not based on the authority of any one realization; it is not a path based on holding up a masculine ideal as the common goals of all spiritual longing. Sophiana teaches wisdom as an appreciation of differences able to see the spectrum of each tradition, the strengths, weaknesses, vulnerabilities, and purpose. In that appreciative evaluation, Sophia teaches us to see the limitations of each perspective without denying the value that each has for its practitioners.

Sophia teaches ecstasy without particularity, the possibility of spiritual illumination in a development arc not predicted or described by others. She teaches an open horizon in which authority is given up for authenticity, for actual realizations, then interpreted with new freedom, not following a predicted path but receptive to

---

*William James (1936) wrote about this over a hundred years ago; see also Lee Irwin, "Supernal Dreaming."

multiple interpretive views. Dreams are clearly a medium for such revelations, content-based encounters, rich in associations and following no known path but motivated by deep sentience aimed at personal transformation.* Spontaneous states initiated by art, dance, drumming, spiritual practices, and creative heart-centered activities may produce unexpected results of the most profound sort, based on the inner life and dispositions of the practitioner.

The path is not predictable; it can lead one astray as any path, can be difficult and incomprehensible, and that is the very ground of discovery. We must apply our creative capacities to understanding what manifests as something more than traditionalized ideas or beliefs; there is much more that is not accounted for and a depth of complexity far exceeding most spiritual teachings. Liberated from the doctrine of masculine control, we face the chaotic boundary of the unknown awaiting realization, means and methods stretching out into unexplored territories of spiritual existence no longer confined to known maps and pathways. This takes courage, inner determination, and humility to recognize how limited our understanding is of that vaster All in which we dwell.

Structure gives comfort to those in need of an external authority that directs and guides their values and practices. This is a typical aspect of masculine spirituality, one with little tolerance for spontaneity and unpredictable behaviors. The "wild freedom" of a more feminized approach finds support in a community of caring others who can respond and advise without demanding conformity to external ideals. A heart-centered spirituality seeks no harm to others, has an open horizon of the possible, and a sense of shared communion with others also in search of the undiscovered realizations. Presence has its own authority, a different stamp of validity, a sense

---

*See Lee Irwin, *Dreams Beyond Time*, where I discuss the spiritual importance and metaphysics of dreams in detail.

of offering guidance or insight based on living spirit manifest in and through a glance, a gesture, and response arising out of a deep inner source. This inwardness that touches authenticity, that calls up living spirit as a manifestation of inner accomplishment, may appear very simple, nonintellectual, down-to-earth or it may be highly intellectual, ideational, and cross-disciplinary in perspective. Revelation teaches us many skills and gives abilities that are often not understood even when clearly manifest, like healing, clairvoyance, telepathic knowledge, and so on. The powers of the saints demonstrate this, but they do not demonstrate that only by being a member of a tradition is such manifestation possible. Spontaneous spirituality has its own pathways, and the unpredictable is not mapped.[17]

The Sophiana concept of gnosis applies to these diverse states and insights. However, gnosis is more than a content; it is also a participatory event, a process encounter by which the seeker becomes aware of a living relationship to the larger cosmos.[18] It is not an idea or a theory, but a direct experience that gives "knowing" a new meaning, a lived sense of immediacy that there is indeed a responsive, living cosmos of depth and purpose. This encounter can take an immense variety of forms, all leading to an affirmation that sacredness is an inherent feature of life and that holiness represents a manifestation of living presence that shines forth from the depths of Being and Mystery. It is a light colored by the predispositions and attitudes of the seer; pure light is a metaphor for a sense of immersive participation in that living presence, filtered by the mind and heart of the participant.

Gnosis is not one thing; it is a spectrum of living energies across a vast interiority touching the hearts and minds of living creatures open to the Mystery. In those who are closed to such mystery, it is there, hidden in the depths of everyday awareness, a life source animating intelligence and feeling. The all-penetrating, subtle sense of Sophia, wisdom as illumination, is there, active, alive, a spark and intuition lifting awareness to new vistas through the media of healthy, normal thought. Love brings it forth, a sharing, an intimate interaction increasing the felt sense of mutual participation; kindness manifests it, generosity can display it, compassion refines it, and patience sustains it. This inner light illumines the entire mind and soul with a living sense of the animate cosmos and its participation in a shared, universal process of growth. This growth proceeds in cycles, such that new illuminations reveal new horizons yet unseen by past generations, beyond even the most profound realizations. This is the core aspect of salvation, an inner transformation leading to new lifeways and alternate paths.

There can be ecstasy, very profound immersive experiences, a flood tide of light that fully saturates and surpasses the boundaries of individual awareness. This is Light filled with sentience, living presence, a vast sea extending and lifting the soul to complete oneness and attunement with Source. In my own experiences, this ocean has no boundaries and demands nothing, it simply holds the soul as a precious life-form, an entity inseparable from the caring concern of presence that gives it life and inspiration. Sophia's depth is not measurable by degrees of experience or encounter; there is always more, the yet undiscovered depths, hidden treasures obscured by soul's limitations, however brilliant the light may shine. Revelation is there as well, new contents, new ways of thinking, new perceptions additive to past experience and indicating future vistas; there is no compulsion, only invitation. The content is rich and complex, verging on incomprehensibility and yet offering clarity and greater perspective. This is Sophia's way, giving inspiration and extending what is beyond the known horizon. Such is the Mystery, always extending beyond our grasp, yet calling us out beyond our own limits, an echo of what is possible and yet unrealized.

6

Mystery of the World Soul

Psyche Kosmou

The theory of the World Soul (*Psychè Kósmou* or *Anima Mundi*) was developed among the Greeks and articulated in Plato's *Timaeus* (35A) as a philosophical description of the animating presence in and throughout nature and cosmos. The theory has a long history in alchemy, Hermeticism, Christianity, Renaissance esotericism, Romantic poetry, and among later modern philosophers and esotericists.[1] In general, the theory is diverse but expresses a core idea that there is a subtle, soulful influence that pervades nature and cosmos, animating the whole. The theory often corresponds with *panpsychism* as "soul throughout all" even to the smallest particle and encompassing the universe in its entirety.[2] A significant feature of this theory is the aspect of soulfulness as fundamental to the overall theory, not energy, not contemporary consciousness but soul (*psyche, anima*) as life-giving presence.

For me, this soulful reference expresses an inherent interactive capacity that I call *sentience*, a responsive, adaptive, and reactive sense of relationship between entities. Sentience is a developmental capacity, a dynamic process-based tendency directed toward increasing complexity. As sentience develops, through relationships with others, through differentiation and assimilation, it forms patterns of greater complexity, patterns that can be self-surpassing in terms of organization and understanding. The very idea of a World Soul is one such pattern, one that is evolving in the minds of diverse persons into an increasingly complex theory integral to ecological, spiritual, and psychic developmental trends. The core of the idea of World Soul is shared sentience on a global scale, all life participates in that shared reality.

A crucial point to understand is that a concept of the World Soul has its roots and values in actual beings, in the hearts and minds of those who hold the theory as vital and meaningful. The theory points not toward an ontological substance or energy separate from living beings, nor to some "super field" that is somehow distinct from the beings who participate in it, knowingly or not. The development of the idea comes from a powerful sense of "living nature" as something more than a mechanistic assembly of discreet parts or processes. Instead, World Soul offers an archetype representing an enduring and imperishable co-sentience inherent in nature and becoming. Change and transformation are natural features of this shared process, as are continuity and reiteration; however, those changes are *causal*, leading to consequences that continue to promote life and awareness without loss. Sophia teaches that *nature nurtures*, sustains life, through cycles of death and disintegration, resulting in new emergence, rebirth, and a new blossoming forth, as in solar cycles of winter, spring, summer, and fall.

The World Soul is the guardian spirit of this process of life, death, and renewal; it is the animate sense that life endures, through all the dramas of psychic revolution, and results in a continuation of every life stream. Loss is possible, what perishes can only be sustained by the proper balance and harmony; if we lose harmony, if ecosystems collapse, if imbalanced minds dominate, then we can expect loss with little recovery. Nature urges us to stay in balance, to not lose the gravitas that is necessary for the propagation of positive ideals and spiritual goals. Sophia teaches groundedness, stability with creative flair, complexity evolving toward greater integration. This is not simply a spiritual value but an essential expression of the dynamic process of ongoing creation, an unending transformation, one whose purposes align with our shared intentions. If we choose badly, then the consequence results in disequilibrium and loss of balance.

In this creative process, self-surpassing is a natural tendency, an inner urgency toward greater understanding and insight not only into self but also into nature, culture, and history. Sentience is a dynamic, interactive capacity able to assimilate and absorb information, experience, and interactive relations in such a way that enables our ability to overturn old ideas and habits for emergent attitudes and beliefs. This is not science, nor philosophy, but an aesthetic of spiritual development, a tendency toward refinement, psychic growth, and an expansive mental horizon. The World Soul is a symphonic construct, an amalgamation of psychic and spiritual aspects intimate with physical and material processes in a cosmos of evolving co-sentience; it represents the soulful interaction between the transpersonal, personal, and impersonal, between spirit, nature, and cosmos. Soul mediates, this is its primary function, to provide a medium for lived experience to imprint developmental effects through relatedness to others, to objects, to the world at large.

World Soul does this on a cosmic scale; it mediates the interactive field of all our relations in an *ecosophic* manner, aimed at preserving balance, harmony, and integrity in a process of growth and development.[3] Human will and practices impact this process through agent-centered causality; we can preserve or destroy, nurture or impoverish, support or disavow these processes in ways that can amplify or impede development. The choice is ours to make, and not choosing has its own negative outcomes; every gesture that supports the balance and harmony of nature and society offers hope, indifference supports chaos, and every abuse degrades us all. Sophia teaches commitment to maintaining balance, sustaining local ecologies of mind and culture that encourage growth without damage or destruction. The best examples are seen in the integrity of our daily actions, in our loving relations, in patterns and attitudes that support the Whole; such integrity provides a sustained ground for World Soul development.

THE VITAL LIFE-FORCE

If sentience is a pervasive quality, then *pansentience* describes the total field of all sentient beings and all sentient processes. In my view, this means that at the least complex level of organization there is sentience, that is, primal characteristics that express life in terms of the most basic attributes, as "original conditions" in the ongoing creation process. In the most basic sense, three characteristics of sentience stand out—attraction, neutrality, and repulsion—all active in a matrix of lively relations. With increasing degrees of interaction, new wholes are formed; a molecule of water formed from elements of hydrogen and oxygen (attraction) increases complexity, therefore increasing sentience. So it is throughout all of nature, as elements combine and separate, engage and resist engagement, complexity develops and as complexity combines more aspects, sentience increases. Throughout all of nature, from elements to minerals, to plants, animals, and human beings, complexity creates novel aspects of sentience related to environment, shared interactions, and complex organizational structures. All is alive with vital life-force, sentience spilling over into adaptive forms, responsive to change and species interactions; nature adapts, sheds its husks, and offers new transformative images able to break free of the limitations of strictly material form.[4]

The vital life-force, the *aqua vitae*, or water of life, symbolizes the distillation of nature into spirit, the sublimation of the coarse into the refined, the gross into the subtle. This is a metaphor that moves inward, toward the less tangible without denying the intimacy that links material and spiritual into a single continuum. The medium of that continuum is the soul, *psyche*, as a psychonoetic process-awareness in which sentience is refined, spiritualized, and made adaptive to increasingly subtle complexity. Our spiritual understanding is not moving toward simplicity, however important simplicity may be as a virtue, but toward greater complexity as religious traditions, sciences, humanities, arts, all contribute to our sense of what is sacred and valuable. The world itself, nature and cosmos, is not simple; it is highly complex, currently beyond our comprehension; the more we understand about the working of nature, the more we understand our own complexity.

We are not simple; our bodies, minds, emotions, neural activities, and organ functions are profoundly complex; our awareness has threshold conditions that mediate our subtle perceptions, subconscious or hyperconscious, sensory or psychic, intuitive or rational—all contribute to that complexity. Human sentience is an amalgam of attributes integrating psychonoetic influences into a sense of personhood impacted by gender, race, culture, education, social location, and a host of innumerable factors. Sentience urges us toward ever-greater awareness based on innate capacities and circumstantial providence. Becoming more aware is a choice, an urge we can deny (or repress) without risk to our overall development. Through the processes of spiritual alchemy, we each contribute a modicum of insight to the whole that supports our continued growth.

The distillation of our sentient awareness is grounded in our vitality, and that vitality is linked in depth to spirit, to a sacred well of pure water, aqua vitae, whose alchemical influences require attention and practice. Imagine the well as soul-depth, an inner capacity to absorb and transmute the waters of life, to draw up from this well a purifying presence, to wash away imperfections through the application of principles. It is not a magical process, transformation takes effort and self-discipline; it requires the creative work of discovery and adaptation. Believing is one thing but assimilating belief into practice and practice into results requires inner clarity and intentional motivation. The gift of life, the greatest gift possible, has a self-sustaining capacity, a resistance to death and extinction. But life as creative discovery requires dedication to principles of life that affirm existence as an opportunity for development and continued positive growth.

Among these principles, the World Soul represents a wholistic field of sentient awareness that supports this positive affirmation; it is a primal source inherent in the entirety, the yeast in the dough, the mother in the cider, the sugar in the grape juice. The fermentation process converts the aqua vitae into an intoxicating substance, to pure alcohol, spirit, whose absorption requires self-discipline and careful processing to avoid excess and abuse. Spiritual abuse is not uncommon; it is the consequence of power and presence whose impact leads to self-inflation and excess. What is needed is ecstasy and not excess, balance, harmony in process directed toward sobriety with humor and joy. The World Soul is not a guiding media, but more a context that supports life in all its forms, even though inherently there is always a tendency toward health, integration, and discovery.

We can distinguish between Spirit and World Soul; *Spirit* refers to an abiding presence whose pervasive influence acts to enhance human capacities and provide inspiration and guidance. World Soul is itself rich in spirit as an inherent presence, but the formation of that presence occurs through archetypal patterns, psychic structures, conditional manifestations of order and organization unique to a planetary history. *World Soul* references the chronotypes of human existence through cultural, religious, and scientific thinking, through actual patterns of thought, social organization, cultural values, and aspirational goals motiving behavior. By *chronotype* I mean responsive patterns of behavior, developed over time in specific circumstances, social conditions, and species interactions. These patterns—mental, emotional, and spiritual— can be biological, psychological, social, cultural, or transpersonal. The vital life source, spiritual in origin, evolves through specific human experiences, through interactive relations, through interspecies encounters, and attitudes toward nature and cosmos.

These developments become consolidated as traditionalized patterns (sociocultural practices) that form psychonoetic structures in contrast to other contradicting or challenging or emergent patterns, forming tensive, subtle psychodynamic relations whose evolution requires collective adaptations. Cultural contestations map to individual attitudes, real persons enacting specific patterns in the face of global and collective changes. The World Soul is the record and habitation of all these patterns, something more than a "collective unconscious," as it sustains the *ontological value* of the patterns as originating in a soulful, spiritual depth. The World Soul is an ontological matrix, a global linkage of patterns-in-being, reflecting the consequences of soul-making through vital shared life patterns on a planetary scale. The evolution of sentience, as a complex field of interactions, is coalescent with our spiritual depth and intelligence in an increasing global context. The new Feminine Wisdom is such a pattern, an emergent sense of spiritual development less determined by authoritative attitudes and more free-flowing and spontaneous.

Vital psychic life is not simply an energetic concept; it is also a source concept for mind, soul, and intelligence. Spirit is not energy; it is life source, the very stuff of sentience, whose evolutions lead to creatures and self-conscious awareness. To be alive, to have sentience, implies intelligence even at the simplest level of organization. Brute awareness can be slowly developed through increasing complexity, thus very complex beings are more highly sentient and possibly more highly intelligent based on life choices and beliefs.[5] The nature of complexity is expressed through shared or integrated information, unlike memory storage of bits without connection (for example, pictures in a computer), intelligence functions through connection, association, the integration of tacit information in which a memory is related to many other events and has a highly complex field of meaningful associations. Complexity is a process of information sharing, increased associations and sentient connections, able to link the parts to a greater whole. This is true of the World Soul as an ever-increasing field of complexity in which information is shared and exchanged in dynamic patterns of meaning, through the agency of actual individuals. We cannot take the individual out of the picture; every individual is a grounding point in the larger World Soul field, even when individual views radically diverge and conflict.

Convergent and divergent patterns coexist in varying degrees of assimilation, as the World Soul undergoes its own evolutionary trajectory, given vitality and sustainability through the life choices of each creature as additive to the whole. The Sophianic teaching here is that we each can support an evolution toward a more integrated totality that sustains and values our diversity and complexity. This complex mergence is not an erasure of differences but a celebration of how differences contribute to positive wholeness, an outcome supportive of human growth and further development. Rejection, war, terror, disease, famine, abuse, domination, or cruelty act to impede and repress this developmental trend toward wholeness. We can fail, fall back into regressive patterns, try to maintain old standards that block and inhibit shared development; we can have a stunted World Soul. The emergent process of vitality enlivening life through creative agency can plateau, or decline, based on collective attitudes and choices.

Soul does not dominate or guide the process unless it has genuine attunement to life source, to genuine spiritual depths able to overcome shallow attitudes and superficial thinking and harmful acts. We are each an agent of change; there is no super-force that predetermines our possible evolution, only the inherent gift of life and its profound abundance given to us as acolytes of grace through inner attunement to source. If we can conserve vitality and direct it to positive ends, with others, including those with diverse views and attitudes, then we can find common ground for a sustainable world. In such a case, the World Soul can contribute to this evolution through the continued assimilation of Spirit as a guiding, inherent presence, instantiated in and through the illumined heart of each dedicated seeker. In this sense, gnosis is shared knowledge, not privileged or secret, but open, luminous, and vital.

The vitality of the life source cannot simply overcome age, decline, illness, or organic diminishment. We all age, grow older, face some degree of decline in the natural process of our existential conditions. Sustained health and well-being require balance and inner harmony, even in the face of death, illness, or decline. There is a vitality of the soul, which we can distinguish from the strictly physical attributes of aging; the health of the soul does not depend on physical determinants, it depends, in a deep connective sense, on spiritual development. Maturity does not lead to immortality, even if soul lives on after death; maturity of soul is a dynamic assembly of attitudes and insights relevant to the life choices of each individual. Continued existence does not necessarily imply immortality, only continuity through sustained vitality, with all the limits of awareness carried forth into new circumstances. Death is transition, a change sustained and shaped by World Soul development.

Within the World Soul, life can exist beyond the death of the body; there are spiritual forms of existence that are part of that greater Whole. The World Soul is a subtle field of life whose provenance is an intimate aspect of all life-forms on this world from the very beginning. Over time, we have all evolved together to form an increasingly complex, multidimensional reality inhabited by life-forms gross, subtle, and etheric. While body grows older and health declines, mind and spirit can remain vital and at death transition to new vitality through rediscovered multidimensional existence. The World Soul functions through cycles, patterns of life, reiterated and refined in accordance with the efforts and self-discipline of individual commitment and actual lived values (and not just abstract ideas, beliefs, or wishes). The World Soul is a unifying process, not a fixed substance nor an unchanging absolute; instead, from the Sophiana perspective, the World Soul is an evolving entity co-created by the entire global population through millennial stages of growth.

ANIMATED AND AWARE

What is the relationship of Sophia to the World Soul? Often the image of the Anima Mundi is a feminine figure with a crown of stars, robed or naked, standing above the visible cosmos and holding a golden chain that links to the lower solar system, its planets, elements, and world structures. The image is astrological in origin illustrating cosmic order and harmony imbued with a creative feminine nurturance that supports life and evolution. This is not Sophia but a World Soul image, linked to alchemy, cosmology, and the astrological cycles of nature. Sophia, as an Aeon, or sacred entity or primordial archetype whose formation preceded visible creation, is usually portrayed as a winged figure, an angelic form, whose intelligence and questioning mind sought out answers of the most profound type, requiring foreknowledge and prescience of the highest order.[6] It is important to note that Sophia as Wisdom is not strictly identified with nature or cosmos but moves within and throughout nature as an animating intelligence whose origins and source are beyond the physical and psychic domains. Nor is Sophia exclusively identified with sentience, as life vitality or responsiveness; her origin is deeper than any sentient forms of life even though she once again manifests as an animating intelligence in even the simplest life-forms.

Sophia as an angelic entity has no one form, and while her wings symbolize etheric and heavenly aspects, she is not reducible to any external image.* Her angelic nature signifies our human capacity to see into the subtle realm, in vision, dreams, and intuition, as Wisdom takes a multitude of forms relevant to our seeking. Wisdom moves beyond form and into formless insights,

---

*For more on the Earth Angel, see Tom Cheetham, *Green Man, Earth Angel*.

beyond images into startling intuitions of truth, grounded in our capacity for deeply penetrating realizations beyond all form and matter. There is a vast transpersonal horizon through which Wisdom shines her luminous glow into all our thoughts, questions, and seeking.[7] There is no end to the possible revelations of Wisdom and her manifestations are not reducible to codes of behavior or soulful virtues. Wisdom applies to all situations, to all circumstances requiring intelligence and forethought, to any condition, in any domain, where understanding is possible. Wisdom is the subtle, adaptive power of insight applicable in any context that requires attention seeking to break through the mold of less aware thinking. It reflects a contentless activity of heart, mind, and soul absorbing and transmitting life-source intelligence through authentic dedication to its core principles.

All creatures "animated and aware" bear the potential for discovery in circumstances most conducive to their lived environment and positive interactions with other beings. Awareness is the medium of Wisdom, not just mental activity or thought, but the integrated information of all our senses, our intuitions, our internal self-consciousness, our dreams and imaginings. Wisdom is an inherent constant, similar to *prajna* in Buddhism, that indwells and inhabits all of our perceptions.[8] Such Wisdom is transconceptual, a gnosis that illumines the very ground of being, revealing the underlying unity and coherence of creation, a lucid intuition that has gone beyond the constraints of conceptual thought. The meditative state for this gnosis is a calm, focused, deeply stable mind unburdened by worry, anxiety, or distracting habits of mind or emotion.

Unlike Buddhism, the goal is not perception of "emptiness" (*shūnya*) as a primordial foundation of all that appears; rather Sophianic Wisdom teaches the spontaneous realization of how the deep sources of life apply to living circumstances as expressive, creative becoming. This is Wisdom beyond absolutes, Wisdom that thrives through the process dynamics of creative expression, evolution, and emergence. Being animate and aware has no end state in enlightenment; instead it thrives through growth and development to acquire new understanding of nature and cosmos, as well as human capacity and inner potentials. I do not deny the reality of either enlightenment or emptiness but offer an alternative ontology: Wisdom is not simply based in ground state acknowledgment of an ontological condition (*shūnya*). Having recognized that claim as valid for Buddhism, Sophianic Wisdom makes another claim, that the realization of Wisdom applies to more than the preexistence of an underlying ontological constant, it references process and change as implicit in cosmogenic discovery, as a necessity leading to wisdom through embodied experience, and life as something far greater than conditional suffering (*dukkha*).

Creation is much more than suffering (or sinful existence), it is a celebration of life and its value as expressed through existential commitments that rejoice in life, embodiment, pregnancy, birth, and cycles of growth to greater maturity *in this world*. Sophianic teaching is directed toward this world, its beauty, value, miraculous nature, its sacredness and wholeness. Wisdom celebrates this as an ontological fact worthy of continued efforts to evolve and develop, not to transcend but to transform. Enlightenment is an alternate path in its renunciation of the world, monastic virtues, and male-dominant discourse dismissing worldly life and feminine values while exclaiming a transcendental model as an ultimate goal. That is not a basis for Sophianic Wisdom.

Sophia emphasizes harmony with feminine values, the celebration of life, of communal relations, offering multiple points of view and the acceptance of differences; it confirms a process view, emergent, and forthcoming as creative occasions not yet realized.

And this Wisdom goes all the way down into the animate vitality of other creatures, into deep sentience, into a World Soul orientation, not based on avoiding harm to others for the self-serving rewards of karma, but loving creatures, valuing their worth, their beauty, and life-force as worthy of partnership and as intrinsically valuable and necessary. And it goes into the plant world, to the animation of every biological species, every plant, every element as also participating in being animate and aware. Sophia embraces affirmation, not denial, and supports suffering as a transitional mode to new integrations and positive, loving relations.

This is a sacred fact, the existential heart of creation, that values everything, all creatures as though we were in a garden from which we are not cast out because we have awakened to its sacredness and have become caretakers to assist with its growth, beauty, and luster. The Sophiana call is for awakening to the value and beauty of life in all forms, life as joyful and reverent, deeply appreciating every ecology, every biosphere that propagates unique lifeforms. We are called to world affirmation, not world denial, to nurture what we are given and to value through love and kindness the fact of life in every form it manifests. Suffering is a fact but not the definition of life nor its core condition. We must not cage the tiger nor confine the "wild animal" but overcome these tendencies for control for a new management that preserves and supports the freedom of every creature, accommodating their needs and not just our own. The heart of life is joy and affirmation of beauty and the value of the goodness and compassion found through the illumined body-mind-soul.

The World Soul is the co-creative field within which this Wisdom manifests through a vast multitude of creative agents whose aim is to restore the world to harmony and balance. The World Soul expresses a multidimensional *process* not a content, a means by which intelligence and kindness come to fruition through global cooperation, ecological practice, and a deep sense of reverence for the precious gift of life. The World Soul is an evolutionary expression of our global development, in stages of manifestation, representing the potential and future possibilities of responsible human love coupled with attitudes that support shared positive growth. The World Soul can contract, become a more static condition reflecting human resistance to change and new modes of growth. As in the individual, soul is malleable, subject to the conditional influences of life choices, value formation, and actions based on self-centered desires or on compassion and care for others. Our collective choices matter, attitudes of mind shared by many persons create multiple subfields within the larger domain of World Soul development.

Sophia teaches an ethos of partnership and cooperation without denying differences in approach, practice, or hoped for outcomes. To again cite the French Catholic theologian Teilhard de Chardin, "union differentiates," it does not merge and erase but gives particular character to individual choice and actions.[9] These differences matter because they reflect complexity, demonstrating how information can particulate, be adapted and used in varying circumstances with diverse nuances. There is no simple merging, rather an unveiling, a glance into a more profound horizon of complex meanings whose subtlety requires adaptation and new methods of cooperation. Unity opens the vista of the possible by incorporation of the impossible made more accessible through stages of transformation. The universe is a wonder of complexity where Wisdom requires utmost attention to what emerges in order to capture that emergence in new forms of embodiment.

Explicitly, the Wisdom needed for this positive World Soul development is rooted in feminine values for the preservation of life and its nurture through life-sustaining practices. The Sophianic perspective is emphatically feminine in compensation for overly emphatic masculine attitudes that lack the subtle nuance of cooperation and equality in partnership. Sophia values each individual, gathers the entire world into her embrace, as the nurturing presence inherent in all sentient intelligences, as the primal ground for the expression of diversity, and as the abiding illuminative source for the many stages of spiritual development. There is no limit to her forms and teachings, old paths and new paths participate in her gift of life; what is, what is coming to be, and what will be in the future, are all participant in multiple degrees of Wisdom. Sophia has an infinite content in an unending process of self-surpassing discovery, urging us to awaken the World Soul to its most profound possibilities through individual actions and choices.

This Wisdom is in each of us, hidden in our habits of mind and resonant in soul, as a thirst for greater understanding, a felt sense of breaking free from bondage and overcoming our own ignorance. The task is collective and not just individual, it requires a cooperative, nurturing ethos on a global scale motivated to preserve distinctions while working toward harmony and balance in overall policies and practices. There are a multitude of paths whose members must make the effort to allow Wisdom to guide interactions with others for the most positive outcomes. Our burden is to overcome the shadows of hatred, racism, blind prejudice, and spiritual arrogance or unhearing and uncaring indifference—all of which are real and active in that same World Soul. Only through great effort and focus can we overcome our limitations and irrational propagation of models of dominance or superiority no longer meaningful in an emerging World Soul context of health, balance, and shared harmony. We are all animate and alive, and now we must make the right choices for the right reason that life may propagate in all its amazing variety.

ELEMENTAL AND ASTRAL BEING

The evolving concept of the World Soul, in its historical development, has long included other entities besides currently living human beings and other organic life-forms. Not only does World Soul include postmortem human beings, the ghosts of the living, but also other entities such as spirits, angels, devas, immortals, gods, goddesses, and so on, including animal spirits and mythic entities as well. The question arises not about the existence of such entities, but about the fact of human belief in and experiences of such entities. Shamanic traditions have long believed in spirit entities, often in animal form, as populating the cosmologies of a vast number of Indigenous belief systems. Angelic lore is pervasive in Judaism, Christianity, and Islam, derived from even earlier traditions in Zoroastrian, Gnostic, Persian, and Egyptian religious worldviews. In Islam, the theory of the *ʿAlam al-mithāl* ("realm of images") was formulated to address the "intermediary" domains of angelic and astral beings so popular in Neoplatonic thought.[10]

In Western esoteric traditions, the World Soul is populated by diverse strata, as creatively articulated by Dante, in which there is a sense of hierarchical order in the postmortem afterlife, through various lower to higher angelic realms (the nine angelic choirs), culminating in the *primum mobile* ("prime mover") often symbolized by the Throne of God. These structures as imaginal, as visionary recitals of the possible heavenly, cosmic order, reflect attempts by earlier traditions to organize the complexity of heaven (and hell) as a way to give an overall sense of order to human existence in a cosmic context. We can find similar structures in

Hinduism, Buddhism, Taoism, Shinto, and so on, each with their unique vocabulary and structures. However, from the Sophianic World Soul perspective, we can, in partial accord with Sufi teachings on the ʿĀlam al-mithāl, postulate an intermediary imaginal realm, as mentally imaged in complex psychic symbols reflecting shared thoughts and beliefs about cosmos and nature.[11] Rather than debate cosmological order and structure, heavenly or otherwise, the Sophiana approach is to see all such structures as mediated symbolic forms reflecting images of ontological possibilities.

Entities of all types are one thing, and cosmic order is quite another thing. Rather than debate any fixed forms, I take the Sophiana perspective that these heavenly imaginings are psychic constructs within the developing World Soul that contribute to our collective history as archetypal images of possible transphysical order. It is also quite possible that these multiple orders may coexist, reflecting the complexity of psychonoetic post-death existence. Perhaps there are many diverse realms of afterlife and various domains within the cosmic order that reflect specific belief systems. Perhaps that order is a reflection of those beliefs, as psychic constructs within a much larger cosmic scale of possibility. Perhaps the Bardos (Tibetan afterlife realms) of post-physical life are like specific frequency waves, specific modular zones in which life continues in a unique spectra of shared life with others; and perhaps, powerful nonhuman spirit entities are part of the complex, multidimensional order.

The theory of the ʿĀlam al-mithāl has been debated concerning the degree to which that domain is a mirror of human thought or belief, in contrast to it being a domain of preexistent archetypal images (divine ideas) foundational to the creation of human life. The Jewish scriptures presuppose an angelic order before the creation of humanity, a not uncommon theme in other Abrahamic traditions like Christianity and Islam. Is the idea of a messiah or savior figure or that of a master a preexistent idea-image? It certainly is an archetypal theme in terms of human existence, but does the heavenly cosmos contain pre-physical domains of beings and/or ideals that precede actual physical creation processes? In other words, cosmological structures may be imagined that both precede and extend beyond strictly physical, incarnational life.

The most obvious aspect of possible post-physical life is the universal belief in afterlife existence found in almost all religious and spiritual traditions as well as in modern research on the topic.[12] The Sophianic view on this complexity is to affirm post-life theories as part of the natural cycle of life-death-rebirth, without necessarily subscribing to any specific formal view. Uncertainty and not knowing play a role here, without denying possibility, we can affirm the positive nature of life after death without knowing or explaining how that occurs or what the teleological results are of such a process of rebirth. There is no doubt that a large multitude of persons believe they have contact and interaction with those who have died, without understanding the exact nature of that communication. Nevertheless, for that majority there is a positive sense of genuine communication and recognition of souls in a post-death state, also reinforced by the ever-increasing collection of near-death experiences that tend to also reinforce afterlife theories.[13]

In terms of World Soul theory, the afterlife becomes not a domain as much as a medium for such communication, usually through dreams, visions, and intuitive encounters. Here we see the imaginal realm as a medium for communication between beings, regardless of the specific properties of their physical or etheric existence. Sophia teaches that we do not understand the afterlife, not clearly, even though we may well communicate with postmortem individuals. There is Mystery there, deep and profound, yet to be fathomed, part of a much larger picture that as yet remains unclear and whose boundaries we do not comprehend. The World Soul is a matrix of life-forces and vital beings whose communication is facilitated through ordinary and extraordinary means such as visions, telepathic interactions, and other forms of paranormal exchange. Further, such entities can manifest in the ordinary world, breaking through material boundaries as uncanny examples of postmortem life or nonhuman "spirits" of various types.

A common element in the World Soul matrix is a belief in spirits, or nonphysical entities whose roles range from interference, to observation and assistance, depending upon the nature of the spirit. In a Sophiana view, spirits of all forms are part of the matrix of human experience and there is no current means for proving or disproving their existence. I take spirits as a given feature of all spiritual worldviews, without making any attempt to explain their origin or ontological status. I know many people who claim to have vivid interactions with spirit beings of various types; I have myself had frequent encounters with such beings, usually positive in nature. I have also had a few limited encounters with entities of a stark and disturbing nature, demonstrating the possibility of entities capable of harming others, sometimes apparently created by human thought and beliefs. These "thought forms" as collective representations (demons or angels) are active in the World Soul context with some degree of autonomy, supported by collective mass beliefs, while other entities seem fully autonomous and possibly preexistent to human thoughts or ideologies.

There is a rich plenum of possible life-forms of a nonphysical nature whose appearance, actions, and effects are sensed and felt directly by psychic human perceivers. Spirit guides, masters, and teachers can all be experienced in vivid forms of encounter, arrayed with mythic aspects, and linked to beliefs in aliens, otherworldly beings, and a wide diversity of spiritual domains. All of this circulates in the World Soul reinforced by entertainment media, novels, and a multitude of supernatural writings and publications—all expressing the religious, spiritual, and literary imaginal.[14] This imaginal is an intermediary realm of creative possibility in which entities can impact, motivate, and on occasion, terrorize living human actors. Many women have been mediums, and in fact, mediumship has been a consistent feature of a feminine view that accepts interactions with the postmortem as a natural expression of psychic intuition. Women seem to have a unique ability for postmortem communication, deepening that unseen domain within the World Soul.

The World Soul is not a subject for scientific research; it is a liminal concept whose function is to act as a unifying matrix for species development in which mental and spiritual attitudes create the binding energies of the matrix. I take the position that such a concept has ontological validity by breaking out of the mold of materialism and by recognizing the value and importance of psychic and soulful life—for both women and men. The Sophiana teaching is not based on science but on soul, on the reality of psychonoetic experience and the value of direct encounter in a transphysical sense. Sophia embodies the Wisdom that accrues over a lifetime of such encounter and experience, as a lifting of the veil that allows us to peer into a much more expansive cosmos where postmortem others, spiritual entities, and other less well comprehended beings are creatively active within a more complex, sentient reality. Through soul we can acknowledge the greater, vaster horizon, which is the true domain of Wisdom, and through such acknowledgment, we develop our own soul capacities. A contracted world reflects contracted souls, and a narrow vision cannot apprehend the actual complexity of transphysical existence. Our challenge is to acknowledge our limits but not to be defined by them; having seen the boundary, we must make the effort to extend beyond those limits in search of even deeper Wisdom.

There can be psychic sciences, as often articulated in various esoteric traditions, but such a science requires an integration of mature Wisdom with the discipline of dedicated research and positive methodologies based in an ethos that acknowledges the importance of integrating physical, psychic, and transphysical aspects of reality. The imbalance of an overly material view is a contraction, while insistence on the absolute nature of the spiritual easily becomes an unhealthy inflation. The World Soul encompasses all positions in the spectrum of belief, whatever the basis of those beliefs, and works toward the sentient integration of enduring truths that sustain positive species development. The decision of what survives and what is maximized or diminished in that process is based on human actions, policies, and structural forms; we are the agents of change for better or for worse. Soul knowledge extends into the cosmic domains and our challenge is to comprehend how our beliefs may shape (or not) what appears.

What we commit to, what we emphasize and passionately support, becomes the media of World Soul development; inherently, the tendency toward integration, balance, and harmony is fundamental to the process because sustainability requires cooperation and partnership. Positive, mature growth is not self-centered, not based in flagrant ideologies of oppression or reward for the few. The actual development for an enduring future requires an unselfish approach, one that values the other as much as the self and works with passion to create just and nurturing social orders that benefit the whole and not the few. Wisdom asks for cooperation, respect for others, and more than tolerance—Sophia teaches reverence not just pragmatism, and patience not a rush to an unstable future. She asks for love with intelligence, actions with compassion, and kindness with integrity. The cultivation of virtue is key to this process; it is the luster that illumines the World Soul.

AEONS AND HOLY SPIRITUALS

In the creative process of development, archetypes are co-created by human actors through encounters with the sacred that result in forms and figures of great power and presence. Spiritual leaders have helped to shape these forms: the Christ, the Buddha, Lao-Tzu, Muhammad, Saint Teresa of Avila, Sri Anandamayi Ma, Sufi master Rabia Basri, Hasid Hannah Rachel Verbermacher, and many more, all representing supreme examples whose wisdom and intelligence have become models for millions of human beings. Figures such as Mother Mary or Mary Magdalene have become archetypes within the Christian tradition as preeminent feminine figures representing illumination and often miraculous powers, sources of visionary encounter, and unprecedented examples of healing and recovery. These divinely imbued individuals, be they embodied human beings or subtle forms of a transphysical nature, reflect the interior light of the awakened soul, a radiance so powerful that it breaks through the forms and limitations of ordinary thought and intent.

These figures represent the transpersonal nature of our creative becoming, epitomized as male or female figures, saturated with an aura of sacred presence, and overflowing with the unpredictable grace of Spirit and Mystery. However, these forms and figures are not reducible to simply human examples. The human vessel is not the same as the light and spirit that fills that vessel with the overflowing fullness of the All. The vessel is a limitation on an Infinite capacity; like a magnifying glass that focuses sunlight on a specific place and time, but whose source covers the entire solar system, so too these "Holy Spirituals" are each a lens through which the hidden capacities of spirit are manifest in specific forms. By *Holy Spiritual* I mean a recognizable sacred form, entity, or being, whose radiance is evident to the observer as manifesting a genuine transpersonal presence, a sense of the holy transmitted directly to the mind and heart of the observer.

In older spiritual literature, these forms were often called Aeons, partly in relationship to their ancient long-term existence (eon), and partly as noumenal intelligences representing specific ideas or, often, virtues. Such Aeons were named Silence, Peace, Mystery, Thought, Love, Beauty, and so on. They are formulations that represent a complex of ideas and feelings, universal in nature, and imbued with qualities unique to the name or form taken. They also have a sense of personhood, a sense of autonomy or identity-in-itself, a kind of self-sustaining energy that reflects qualities of mind and intelligence. They often reflect intentional relationships, a responsive center whose contents spill over into a relationship with another, like a god or goddess figure whose qualities are assimilated by or react with their believers and devotees. The impact of encounter is powerful and memorable, leaving a lasting impression, imprinting the perceiver with a sense of awe or wonder. Holy Spirituals are primary expressions of the sacred in human (and sometimes animal) form.

In my own experience I have had what I call "holy-spiritual encounters" in which a very luminous being appeared and interacted with me, giving me instructions, often nonverbal, and leaving a profound impression of the sacredness of the encounter, similar to what Rudolf Otto called the *"mysterium tremendum"* (tremendous mystery) of the sacred.[15] These are not necessarily identifiable gods or goddesses, nor angels or devas, nor ordinary spirits, but very powerful archetypal forms resident within the evolving cosmos as transpersonal agents, as Aeons or emissaries of the sacred. Their deeper nature may be more fundamental than their form, as primal expressions of sacred realization, such as the master or saint archetype or guide or teacher, taking unique forms in the context of encounter. What is communicated is a sense of the sacred, the import of a direct encounter with depths of awareness beyond the ordinary and not reducible to strictly traditional examples.*

Thus an Aeon is something more than an archetype, if by archetype we mean a human pattern created over time, formed through role identities (father, mother, child, male or female), and specific role types (trickster, guide, king, queen, shaman). Mythic archetypes, such as specific gods and goddesses, angels or devas, or spirit types like fairies, Little People, water spirits, animal and plant spirits and so on, are also archetypal in terms of belief systems that sustain theories of interaction and communication with such entities. By *archetypal* I do not mean the entity, but refer to a complex sacred pattern, a type of interpersonal encounter with the entity. These interactions are archetypal in the sense that they reveal certain relational patterns that are reduplicated across different cultural contexts. For example, contact with "beings of light" in NDE usually results in a pattern of affirmation and support for the visionary, regardless of cultural context. This moves us toward the Aeonic aspect, toward an interaction with the sacred that takes on a visible form but refers to a higher ontological construction that is something more than an image from the collective unconscious.

The ontological value is crucial because it implicates a higher domain or source for such encounters beyond the strictly human historical context. The term *Holy Spiritual* is a contemporary way

---

*See Lee Irwin, *Sophos Ontology*, for more on post-traditional encounter with the sacred.

to discuss this issue of higher ontological sources that may well coexist with human and other species. Like Aeons, Holy Spirituals are potential entities whose manifestations relate to critical or exceptional human conditions and who provide contact and possible guidance from a sacred source through profound encounters or manifestations. While Aeons tend to be a complex of qualities, such as Wisdom or Peace or Silence, Holy Spirituals tend to appear in human forms, as agents or manifestations communicating oracular information, often in symbolic form. The distinction is subtle and Holy Spirituals may well have Aeonic aspects.

Holy Spirituals may take on archetypal qualities but their source and origin points to something more than a specific cultural historical context; they have a universal quality, a form that conveys a sense of sacred power instilling reverence, awe, gratitude, and deep appreciation for the encounter. Nor am I referring to "spirits" in a more general sense, of which there may well be a multitude, of many types and kinds, but limited to a more local expression of power or ability. By Holy Spiritual I reference the highest kind of sacred encounter, for example, an encounter with the Holy Mother Spirit, with Sophia as the living presence of Wisdom, as a divine image of profound grace and power. Every Goddess is an archetypal form of Holy Spiritual.

I believe the source of such a form is transcultural, deeply ontological, and rooted in the primal sentient that animated the entire cosmos and instills life and vitality in all beings. This is not a psychological claim nor a psycho-social observation, but an ontological and metaphysical assertion that there exists in a deep and profound sense a sacred depth capable of forming emissaries of luminous form and ethical qualities able to guide and assist human relationships and decision-making. Such an entity is beyond the angelic insofar as the angelic references a specific cultural pattern or belief system. What appears as an angel may be simply a form taken on to better communicate the belief pattern of the observer; beneath that form is the Holy Spiritual entity whose nature and capacities remain unknown but whose source is Life itself.

The Sophianic theory of the Holy Spiritual is not limited to any one form nor any particular number or account of qualities or representations. The Holy Spiritual is a marker in an infinite space of possible forms and manifestations that cannot be fully described; the very nature of the Holy Spiritual is based on the question of the transhuman potentials of a sacred cosmos. Rather than offer some speculative theory, Sophia teaches acceptance and patience in terms of the transpersonal aspects of human and other species existence. Holy Spirituals exist in terms of actual human experiences, in most cultures worldwide, and they represent profound encounters with the sacred, however framed in those cultural settings.

Holy Spirituals are imbued with ontological significance that illustrates the sacred foundations of the creative process, both in terms of the imaginal and the actual. Our collective coming-to-be has manifested in concert with these images and appearances in terms of the most sacred persons within (and without of) our global spiritual heritages. As persons, as spiritual exemplars, and as transpersonal entities, Holy Spirituals resonate with the power and presence of the sacred as something far more than the emotional and intelligible reactions that such an encounter solicits. They reflect Mystery and Being in ways that are not reducible to obvious theological or psychological metatheories meant to explain such phenomena. They are not explainable, nor are they comprehensible as humanly created phenomena. Sophia as a Holy Spiritual is a Mystery of great import reduced to an image that cannot contain that Mystery.

Even as God-manifestations, like Avatars, Holy Spirituals carry a depth and fullness that truly transcends the strictly human and opens a vista on horizons of existence we do not yet understand. The fusion of god-man and god-woman is not a comprehensible union, more an enigma that cannot not be adequately described, let alone explained. The Sophiana perspective is to recognize, confirm, and support such a manifestation, with healthy reverence and respect, as a sign that the human condition is metamorphic, able to move from ordinary to extraordinary to superordinate manifestations. Our human-transhuman potential reflects the innate capacities of sentience as it evolves toward ever-more complex forms and conditions that surpass older forms and images. Sophia teaches respect and appreciation but does not seek to emphasize such forms as anything other than divine possibility seen through the lens of actual manifestation.

What was and what will be may well take a leap through the imaginal into new forms and capacities not yet well understood in terms of what Wisdom has yet to reveal. The Imaginal is the active domain of the impossible, the creative ground through which inner abilities may evolve and transmute in accord with our intelligible insights. In this circumstance, Wisdom is the intelligible ability to foresee and, in an oracular sense, predict the forms and likely types of manifestations that may well exceed traditionalized or universalized images and ideas. The theory of Holy Spirituals is one such prediction, Wisdom is itself a Holy Spiritual, a transarchetypal Aeonic entity whose deep ontological source is irreducible to fixed cultural forms, past experience, or historical formations, and whose nature is aligned with the rich potentials of all possible sacred manifestations.

The concept of the World Soul is another vivid example of a Holy Spiritual. It is an image-idea whose nature reflects sacred depths and whose global nature as a shared, worldwide soul field is imbued with life energies from every species on this planet. It is also an image of nature and cosmos as a unitary symbol of a much more expansive psycho-cosmology than our local solar system. Metaphorically, the World Soul images a sacred universe of infinite extent, in which a local cosmos is ensouled through the reality of the many living species who each contribute to World Soul development. There is no one image of the World Soul. It has many possible images and many nuances; its roots are biological, ecological, ontological, psychological, and spiritual. It is a metaphysical concept imbued with Imaginal capacities meant to hold the collective spiritual and psychic life of all beings, living and postmortem, and all spirit forms. Sophia teaches acceptance and critical self-reflection, a Wisdom capable of imagination and creative vision as well as down-to-earth practical abilities and explanations.

A Holy Spiritual is capable of evolution, change, being reshaped and reimagined in new contexts that support contact and exchange between actual human habitation and a divine ground that inspires creative discovery and powerful manifestations. We see this in the reimaging of the sacred feminine, reconstituting the significance into new modes of authentic womanly realizations.[16] Our partnership with the sacred is an ethical call for spiritual cooperation that respects and supports a wide range of spiritual views and types, including all feminine archetypes, without demanding conformity to any one view or type. Wisdom is adaptive based on moral commitments to shared global development; the World Soul is a feminine ground that thrives on sustainable relations between all species and promotes social harmony and nonviolent practices. Form is variable while intent is shaped by clarity of purpose; the goal is to live in a mature, healthy, balanced world, one that is soulful and wise. We each contribute through our daily efforts to World Soul development and in this process, Holy Spiritual encounters, waking or dreaming, are a guide to possible ways forward.

7

Mystery of Rebirth

METEMPSYCHOSIS

The metaphysics of rebirth are traceable to the Greek theory of *metempsychosis*, or change in soul habitation, that is, the transmigration or relocation of soul from one body to another. Having discussed this topic in detail in a previous publication, here I will only mention those aspects of the theory relevant to Sophianic Wisdom.[1] For me, the Sophiana perspective affirms reincarnation as foundational theory relevant to long-term soul life and as relevant to various development theories individually and collectively. However, "rebirth" has many nuances and meanings beyond the theory of multiple physical lives; the concept reflects radical changes, conversions, awakenings, and discoveries that can reshape a life path or our understanding of the world. A literal interpretation is not necessary within the Sophiana of its many implied meanings.*

In general, rebirth reflects the cyclical processes of nature, such as the rebirth of seasons in the spring, or lunar cycles, or stages of

---

*See for example Carl Jung, "Concerning Rebirth."

the life cycle, such as marriage or divorce, child birthing, or the after-effects of a serious illness or of a partner's death. Rebirth as part of the life cycle pivots around the central theme of the discovery of new meaning or significance that results in change and adaptations based on an ending that results in new discovery. On a deeper level, it signifies a shift in psychic disposition, an opening to new horizons of insight guided by a different way of thinking or acting. As an overall concept it suggests a development track, a transformation of soul as it becomes more self-aware, mature, and wise. It is not a one-time thing but more frequently a cyclical process by which we discover greater nuance, meaning, and values that can be integrated and refined into a renewed lifestyle or spur growth on a spiritual path. Rebirth is a process, not an event, a series of stages that can lead to greater insight and ability, if we choose to embody what emerges in those moments of insight. Sometimes this occurs without effort based on life events but usually it is a consequence of a dedicated search for greater meaning and purpose.

A theme that is inseparable from rebirth is the necessity of loss. Inevitably, it is loss that often triggers the rebirth process—be it loss of a job, a partner, a living condition, or loss of faith or purpose or direction—the loss is often a precursor and a catalyst that initiates a new cycle of reconfiguration. Further, a loss of perspective can obscure the cycle because the individual does not grasp the value of such loss, seeing it as only a deficit when in fact it offers an opportunity for redirection. That does not mean that such loss is not painful and earthshaking; it is often a trial and challenge to face the aftermath of any form of radical loss. We can descend into patterns of grief and deep regret, into melancholy and loss of purpose or direction as a result of a beloved partner no longer present, a child lost, the end of a valued relationship. Such loss requires time and patience for healing even while the memory and sense of what was is still vibrant and recurrent; we carry the past with us and in order to move into the future we must realign and reconstitute direction and purpose.

Sophia teaches compassion for all loss, encouraging us to examine how we might learn from such loss in order to face loss in the future. The grounding practice is not detachment or emotional repression of feelings; we have to face loss with courage and openness to our feelings, feelings that are themselves cyclical. Loss is a recurrent pattern in the fabric of our maturation, extending to loss of culture, loss of older values, loss of ancestral knowledge, loss of the heritages of human history. Where there is so much loss, there is also much need for rebirth and rediscovery. What is imprinted into the warp and weft of our individual and collective past is also carried in our soul life, in the intimate and delicate impressions we carry from other lives and circumstances. And perhaps, there is a more detailed record psychically resonant in our being, together through the very ground of sentience, imprinted into Being Itself.

Because loss requires compassion and an understanding of patterns, rather than detachment, it requires us to dig more deeply into the patterns we form with others in a variety of circumstances, with family, friends, jobs, in social work, and so on. Compassion teaches sympathy for the loss of others, a heartfelt awareness that resonates with the difficulty and challenges that so many face, often in a context of indifference, dismissal, or denial of the impact of such loss. Being-With invokes a sense of responsibility for the well-being of others, not just self, and our ability to support others in their losses is a mark of Wisdom. We can still cherish past relations and circumstance even while moving forward into new possibilities, and we bring a lifetime of experience to help us better understand the meaning of such loss. Loss is painful, and overcoming loss requires enduring efforts.

We carry our losses with us, and yet, they should not be determinative of our future choices; we may choose to give up a pattern in order to make new patterns, such as in divorce or gender change or a radical shift in employment or creative activity. As creative agents of change we can choose new ways of life, even in the face of loss, particularly when others offer a compassionate attitude that supports new choices. Rebirth is not easy nor by any means predetermined, choice always plays a role; there is no such thing as karma without choice, after all, karma is the product of choice. As mature beings, we have to recognize the consequences of our actions, particularly their impact on others, and how those choices may or may not facilitate rebirth in the most positive sense.

Rebirth as a theme has many implications, personally and socially, as we undergo collective changes and confrontations. Rebirth is like shedding an old layer of thinking or belief, such that "new wine in new bottles" means that the old patterns of containment can no longer hold emergent insights and new ideas. We are each a vessel of spirit, within which the effervescence of possible discovery acts to open a horizon to new vistas unseen by more conventional collective views. And radical confrontations can and do shift the collective, not always positively, giving birth to regressive and resistant attitudes closed to emergent horizons. Rebirth can result in less awareness, a closure of possibility, a renunciation of former states no longer valued because of the instability fostered by discovery. Finding a new path is not easy or without challenges; a once open person can choose to realign with older patterns because it holds a promise of safety or known boundaries. Those that seek an enduring Wisdom must be willing to undergo the uncertainty of the liminal condition, an in-between state, open but challenged to find a new stable ground.

CREATIVE SELF-BECOMING

The pattern of self-development, in stages and cycles, is a movement toward greater maturity and hopefully, greater Wisdom. Much has been written about the process of individuation as a psychological arc that promotes growth through greater self-awareness. Disidentification with the collective attitudes and patterns of behavior helps to differentiate the person from mass consciousness. By the term *person* I mean a discreet individual with notable traits, abilities, talents, and varying degrees of self-knowledge that help to sustain a specific point of view; a person is someone whose life experience has resulted in the formation of an enduring identity beyond the social persona. By *persona*, I mean the outer face, the public image of self as recognizable in terms of discreet roles and relationships, relevant to specific social location. The persona is the identity we wear in a given social context, often not the most authentic self; the person is the deeper identity, often veiled.

The inner person is the more subjective identity, the lived core of being-in-the-world where one's choices and actions are determined by personal decisions rooted in a sense of authentic individuality, rather than in conformity to collective or social norms or expectations. Wisdom teaches us to cultivate the inner person as an authentic basis for action and thought, a sense of lived identity open to the diverse influences of inwardness—dreams, imaginings, aspirations, hopes, ideals, higher values. In this process of individuation, as a spiritual practice and not simply as a psychological pattern, Sophia teaches the importance of our intersubjective relations. Social cooperation, partnership, co-creative relations, working together, and good family relations all matter as much as, if not more than, individuation. It is one thing to have a point of view, an individuated sense of purpose and direction, but it is quite another thing to have loving human (and animal) relations that often require self-sacrifice and subordination of personal goals or ideals.

Higher Wisdom is not simply about individuation, it is also about understanding the matrix of all our relationships, of understanding the fit between our values and aspiration and the values of others, who may hold very different points of view. On a global scale, individuation can offer a creative perspective, but that perspective must find partnership with others to flourish; we do not flourish in isolation. In the pattern of death and rebirth, we discover how new circumstances, new life conditions, can act to relativize former lives and perspectives. Dogmatism is an anchor whose weight and hold are relative to a belief, to a social consensus whose dominance is only valuable in the context of specific mass assent. As mass consciousness evolves and develops, through both individuation and cooperation, authority has become less able to stamp that collective with limited constructs meant to control mass attitudes. Differentiation is the key to evolutionary development, the particularization of attitudes fused with a value-oriented sense of partnership creates a context for differences while maintaining a sense of shared purpose and direction.

Social transformation is contingent upon our ability to rally with others the energy and purpose that inspires communal action as a cauldron of creative elements able to nourish a wide spectrum of differences. The future is not about conformity nor collective dominance; it is about creative self-becoming in a more feminized matrix of diverse relationships directed toward the transformation of social life. Sophia teaches us that we must work together without denying our differences, to cultivate respect and appreciation for those differences and yet, to merge our creative energies into circumstances that will produce benefit for all members of a given community. The task is to give energy, time, and effort to those communities that do not subordinate individual points of view but seek to integrate those points of view into a shared heritage worthy of future development.

Creativity plays a central role in this process because existing social structures are too often biased and inflexible in terms of past traditions. The theme of death and rebirth encourages a recognition of the life cycle of a social ideal whose termination requires courage and a new vision of what is yet to come. If social life is evolutionary, then in stages we can shed the inadequate, prejudicial, and limited attitudes of the past. This overcoming implies radical transformation, a death that inevitably occurs in stages; revolution is part of the pattern but so too is constitution and resolution. Death and rebirth occur in cycles and the stages each have their own unique psycho-social-spiritual aspects. Reincarnation as a social phenomenon includes past values as an important aspect of what emerges; we do not simply leave the past behind but carry it with us in a subtle, psychic sense.

Creativity is based on our freedom to imagine alternatives; it encourages an open horizon on the possible and urges us to participate in communal efforts to revalorize our collective well-being. This includes discovering the value of past traditions that can amplify and enhance current development. Mental attitudes that reject the value of differences and insist on a privileged point of view based in conformity to a select group ideal that denies the rights and equality of others cannot flourish in the face of genuine individuation and a shared ethic of cooperation. Old biases will eventually die out because diversity encourages creative thought and action through the synthesis and syncretism of diverse points of view. Starting over is just another phase of this long-term process, cultivating "beginner's mind" (*shoshin*) is the correct state for such development—a Japanese Zen teaching that we need to bring an open and uncluttered regard to each and every intent or action, a sense of manifold possibilities, a primal receptivity, and not a restricted expertise.[2]

Self-becoming proceeds through humility and unknowing as fundamental to the human situation; we may have expertise, skills, talent, and knowledge, but those attributes are not definitive of our deepest intersubjective potentials. This is why death is necessary, as a termination of a pattern and as an opening for new emergence and discovery, for a release, a complete letting go for a new cycle. And yet, we still carry with us the samskaras (deep impressions) of our ingrained mental habits and attitudes, the consequences of our choices but reconfigured in a new context, a new body, and new situation.* There is both letting go and carrying forward, release and sustained tendencies, mixed with our attractions, desires, and aspirations toward what is emerging. This is the paradox of self-becoming: we are really never a completely blank slate; the palimpsest of the soul carries within us earlier stages, hidden marks inscribed beneath new writings that exclaim the present but cannot escape the past.

This is why *unknowing* is a positive virtue—it calls for a surrender of expertise, of what we think we know, for an open horizon through which what we do not know can emerge more clearly. There is so much we do not know, so much hidden from our material attitudes, our mythic preoccupations, our philosophical attitudes, our spiritual ideals and beliefs that blind us to the multiverse in which what appears and what Is are not the same. Sophia does not teach encyclopedic knowledge, but clarity of mind and heart that allows Mystery to inscribe its truths directly on our soul's receptivity. This Wisdom is not based on information or data or facts; it is something quite other, a living sense of the fullness in which we all dwell as co-participants seeking to enhance our participation in the depths

---

*Stephen Phillips, *Yoga, Karma, and Rebirth*, 81–88, gives a good overview of samskaras.

and heights of All That Is. This gnosis is not an archaic link to past mythologies but a vibrant affirmation that death is not an end, only a transformation whose purpose is the full exploration of our species potential in a cosmic context of a vast multitude of possible worlds and patterns of becoming. But this vastness is not easily accessible, not something to be assimilated as an idea or a symbol; it must be learned through unlearning, through death and rebirth.

It would be simpler if we were able to be honest about our limitations—if we could get past our inflated sense of accomplishments (or a deflated sense of lacking them) and move forward with inner dignity in terms of our unknowing. It is all too common that people do not see their actual state of development but instead cultivate an overly expanded or shrunken image that hides the real person from view. This is not just a shadow aspect but a constantly reinforced tendency to exaggerate self-perceptions based on culturally ingrained tendencies where so-called heroic imagery, mastery, or expertise overrides a living sense of stages of growth, not based on accomplishments, but on the attainment of insights (prajna) arising from mature wisdom. This does not require metaphysics nor esoteric teachings; it is truth in plain sight, requiring disidentification from the accumulation of experience for a vivid participation in spiritual presence that flows in and through everything.

Death cannot awaken us to this presence except in the rarest of cases; instead, we continue on, through death, as the patterns shift and realign held by our unwillingness to let go. The grip of attachment is a powerful tendency that requires genuine effort to overcome. Spiritual practices (Praxis Sophiana) can help in this process, can create an open space within which it is possible to let go and to discover, to be reborn in a subtle sense, reanimated by new insights arising from previously unseen horizons. This takes many cycles, punctuated by sudden bursts or leaps that then require years of refinement and integration; step by step and stage by stage we can progress by letting go and then rediscovering. Death is an intermediary stage, one that can be creative or simply a time of recurrent patterns expressing the last life, caught in the turmoil of generational confusion. Death is not release or some form of ideal uplift; instead it is often a theater where we play out our life actions in a more etheric context, repeating all too frequently, our past errors and biases.

The processes of individuation and cooperation are contingent on our ability to self-surpass. Individuation has no final state or end; it is a process of moderation and insight that brings personhood into harmony with the spiritual ground of our shared becoming. Beyond the archetypes of cyclical human development there lies a vast territory for psychic discovery not reducible to past traditions or patterns. There is no plateau for individuation, no final peak experience, only the highs and lows of development that may result in peak moments that must then pass into the long-term patterns of maturation and development.[3] The psychology of Being as an ontological process points us toward the direct cognition of Being Itself, not simply for us, or in us, but *as it is* in the actuality of its own existence. But that existence includes all possible existents, all beings, all creatures, great and small, all ecologies, conditions, all cosmic world horizons. And entry into that knowing is through soul, through enduring self-identity beyond a given life cycle, not as a reductive "knowledge of Self" but as a life process enduring through many revolutions in which concepts of self change, evolve, mutate, and collapse in relationship to new discoveries, insights, and developmental perspectives.

The self as an archetype is often explained as an image of completeness or wholeness and yet we do not know what such wholeness might include, certainly something more than psychological maturity. The ontological value of Wholeness includes development beyond the known parameters of current conceptions of health or well-being, such values point toward a more expansive, paranormal, psychically evolved humanity free from the clutter of superficial imaginings. In the death and rebirth cycle, we can discover our true freedom to evolve beyond inherited patterns of thought or systems of belief based more in supposition than in direct realization. But realization requires a naked sense of trust in that deep potential, an innocence of heart-mind-soul that can allow the forthcoming of what is hidden and unrevealed. Expertise has its place, mastery is an important aspect of the process, and knowledge is a bedrock upon which the world itself is created and sustained.

But Wisdom is something more than this; it is a natural flowing forth out of the deep energies of embodied life, informing mind and heart with truthful insights about the very nature of the process of being and becoming. This process requires death and rebirth. And this is true through the direct influence of Being in that cyclical process as it infuses into mind and heart inspirations for new patterns of growth and development. Our partnership with others, as infused with Being Itself, with Mystery as a cosmological context, establishes the norm of cooperation as a means for the actualization of that Wisdom. Not through individual discovery alone but through communal and global efforts can that Wisdom flourish in a multitude of forms that each speak to the needs and aspirations of that community. As individuals, families, communities, and cooperatives, we grow into Wisdom recognizing the necessity of death and rebirth as intrinsic to the evolutionary pattern. Our forthcoming is communal even while our realizations are individual.

MORE THAN FULLY HUMAN

Insofar as soul life has a trajectory beyond physical embodiment, as a form of identity continuity, the theory of reincarnation suggests multiple forms of existence, in different genders, including possible animal lives and even nonphysical forms of life as spirits.[4] Postmortem life is certainly a form of existence that requires no physical body and yet, based on tens of thousands of reports, postmortem individuals tend to take recognizable bodily forms. These spirit-bodies, or astral forms, are similar to other spirit forms, such as animal guides, angels, devas, sprites, fairies, elves, including aliens and other UFO related beings, all part of a spectrum of possible forms and identities. Astral bodies represent a genre of types hardly explored or recognized, including the memory construction of past-life forms, even though most postmortem persons generally appear younger and healthier than when they died. No doubt imagination plays a role in the construction of these various entities, as we can imagine a vast array of possible forms or beings and these imaginings may map to what is actually seen and heard.

The discrimination between actual entities and imagined entities cannot be well defined; further the role of *imagination* may play a crucial role in what is possible to be seen insofar as what we imagine may be a template that allows for the manifestation of an entity. I can imagine an angel and my ability to so imagine may provide a passive template for an entity that appears angel-like in form, while the actual nature of that entity may be something quite other. This is always the challenge of the psychic world, to distinguish between what we imagine, what we see, and what Is. There is no easy way to make the necessary discernment and many traditions have created conventional images meant to represent a transphysical domain of beings who can interact with embodied humans. Some theories of reincarnation recognize the possibilities of soul taking forms other than human, as animals or spirits of various kinds, whereas other traditions draw stricter boundaries and claim every species only reincarnates in that same species, but in different genders.[5]

There are many diverse models for reincarnation and the likelihood of human-to-human rebirth is only one of the possible trajectories, though it is perhaps the most common theory. The central question concerns the nature of the soul as the incarnating entity; in a strict sense, by *soul* I mean that entity that survives death, maintains cognitive functions, and sustains a sense of identity continuity with at least one former life. By *identity continuity* I mean the person carries a sense of who they are and has some sense of a former physical life, including possible multiple past lives. I do not posit any length of duration to this entity, certainly not immortality (though that is possible) nor any specific sense of a goal or outcome to the incarnational process. I personally believe that the origins of soul extend far back into the past, perhaps into a more collective sense of shared consciousness that has evolved into a more individuated realization of soul resulting in unique formations of personal identity. An important feature of this process is maintaining cognitive functions—thought, memory, imagination, intuition—as carried forward into the transphysical context. Evidence from near-death experients, as noted earlier in chapter 6, has suggested that such cognitive functions are *enhanced* after death, not diminished or weakened.[6]

Surviving death is the critical marker for any metaphysics of soul; it is perhaps the very best and most neutral determinant for identifying a post-physical identity. If a human identity survives death, then that survival opens a horizon on afterlife theories unburdened by theological speculation, which is why near-death experients, mediumship, visionary encounter, and reports of the dying matter as empirical evidence. The records on survival are extensive and human beings clearly and without doubt believe that they have encountered the dead in every culture and every historical period in overwhelming affirmations of certainty. This belief is not a speculative idea as much as the result of lived experience, often validated by information known only to the postmortem.[7] In terms of Wisdom, the theory of soul survival has long been a part of the Sophianic traditions, usually formulated as a type of reincarnation theory, in which former actions, beliefs, and attitudes impact future life events and encounters in unpredictable ways. However, in the earlier context of those theories, the teachings instigated an attitude of worldly detachment (as in Asian religious traditions) and an "escape from the weary round of births" as articulated in the ancient Orphic tradition.[8]

However, the new Feminine Wisdom teaches worldly engagement, commitment to world transformation, and incarnation as a creative, purposeful act directed toward shared, cooperative world making. Surviving death is not about escape but discovery, learning anew how to face and overcome the challenges of incarnate life, through multiple attempts, from diverse perspectives, in order to gain increasing insights into cosmological Wholeness and Being. It is about more than survival, the emphasis falls not on surviving but on *thriving*, on growth and development, rather than on weary repetitions and contracted self-preoccupations. Dullness in life is an attitudinal fixation, a stuckness in patterns that resist change, an unwillingness to take risks that may in fact terminate a way of life. Life requires enthusiasm, joy, vitality, humor, commitment, and passion for the transformation of the world into a place of beauty and truth.

Reincarnation is a soul process of cyclical refinement, without soul there is no incarnation; soul is the enduring entity that undergoes the challenges of each cycle or rebirth. A human body is not something we "put on" as incarnate beings; body is what soul becomes when incarnate. The body-mind unity is an integral synthesis of soul qualities, manifesting as mind and feeling, infused throughout the entire structure of our embodied, extended, embedded, and enacted awareness.* It is not two but one, body-mind enhances soul, makes it substantive and sensual in the most positive sense; embodiment is the place of discovery that allows us to exercise, extend, and enact our co-participation in a living, psychophysical cosmos, not just as etheric beings, but as living souls fully incarnate and embodied.

Wisdom teaches us respect for bodily life, for the miracle of embodiment and the sacredness of having the embodied perspective. The Whole is an embodied Whole where a universe of planetary worlds provides the physical and material means for fully actualizing our psychic and spiritual capacities. We are not immaterial beings, even in astral form, as even there we image the material aspects of bodily incarnation; the very idea of "heaven" as having form and structure imitates worldly life, either as a celestial city or a paradise of pastoral beauty. The incarnate world is the center of creation, not some lower level, but the very heart and soul of becoming as embodied life seeks to maximize our deepest potentials. We need physical life to actually reach maturity; we need the challenges and limitations as a means within which we can form and develop new structures and patterns of becoming.

Death is liberation from the old patterns; it opens a new horizon for opportunity if we have the wisdom necessary to choose the best circumstances for a more illumined way of life. Death is not an automatism, a blind consequence, but an opportunity for rebirth and renewal; I embrace death as a passage to new life, not knowing the outcome but trusting the process. The intent is to align with what is forthcoming based on key values lived in this life that are meant to establish patterns of transformation leading to a positive next life. Death of the old does not mean erasure, no trace left

---

*For more on the 4E theory of embodied, embedded, extended, and enacted cognitive awareness, see Albert Newen and Leon De Bruin, *Oxford Handbook of 4E Cognitions*.

behind, rather it means a *sublimation of effects* able to offer subtle influences in future choices. The inscription of values and intentions on soul carry forward; death of the body is not death of the soul, but soul remade in an image of what was and what might become. We are each the makers of our own soul qualities, what we become has much to do with what we were and what we choose to believe and enact.

While the soul itself may be an expression of sentience, or Being and Mystery, what we create through soul is the embodiment of specific patterns, intentions, and qualities. We do not create soul, but we do make soul into the shape, form, or quality that directly expresses our nature as embodied beings, our life choices, our relationships, our social realities, and our lived circumstances. We are given the gift of soul, psyche, to shape a being that best expresses who we think we are or might become, not through inflation or contraction, but through balance, harmony, and dedicated reverence for the sacredness of the process. Soul life, like physical life, is sacred, and the passionate bond between soul, mind, body, and feeling is the mark of that sacredness; our relationships resonate with soul and incarnate life offers us unending opportunity for rebirth and renewal. Death requires both surrender and courage, allowing the process and shaping a new future. I am a body, but I am more than body, and I am thankful for both.

Further, our soul life is entangled with many other souls; we do not simply die in isolation, but in a social and relational context. Death and rebirth are each complex social phenomena, in which souls are linked through multiple lives into collective patterns barely apprehended in a current life.* If survival is an accurate account of human life, then our relationships with others also survive in the

---

*For example, see Jesse Stern, *Edgar Cayce's Mysteries of Reincarnation*, 170–89.

form of latent psychic connections with others also reborn. I once had a powerful recognition of a young woman I perceived as a former daughter in a past life; I have also had other such recognition of relationships stemming from past-life experiences together. The web of all our relations is complex in terms of what we forget and what we remember, a sudden recognition or déjà vu experience may indicate persons or places once known or lived in the past, a sense of intense familiarity coupled with intuitive feelings appropriate to that place or person.

Wisdom teaches us to be alert for such intimations as they may spring from a deeper soul source than the ordinary conscious mind; soul knowledge has a depth and fullness far beyond the mental impressions of a current life. Such intuitions must be disentangled from projections and false imaginings; the best lived evidence is a sudden, powerful presentment breaking through everyday thinking with shocking clarity and at times detailed awareness. The most powerful realizations I have known came with no presuppositions or forethought, rather the intuition springs forth, as Wisdom teaches, suddenly with its own sense of legitimacy. This intuitive sense is also complex in the recognition that it comes with associated feelings and perceptions unique to the place or person; it is not simply information but a charter of a past moment replete with its own feelings, beliefs, and attitudes. It is as though a subpersonality, created in a former life, suddenly surfaces to momentarily dominate perceptions as that former person in relationship to a present moment. And then, it fades away in the face of rationalizing the experience—was it real, imagined, a fantasy?—all leading attention away from the actual experience. Soul life is far more complex than what is currently imagined.

TRANSPERSONAL EMBODIMENTS

While the core of these Wisdom teachings is rooted in embodiment, in physical life and development, there is also the question of out-of-body (OBE) and various spirit forms of life in relationship to actual lived experience. Human beings do in fact experience OBE states across multiple cultures, some of which have institutionalized the practice, as in shamanism.[9] These many accounts bear witness to a real phenomenon, a "subtle body" or a sense of identity that can depart from the physical body and yet retain full cognitive functions as well as a capacity for action and choice. The form of the subtle body often, but not always, duplicates the form of the physical body, though various shamanic traditions may train adepts to take animal spirit forms. Such experiences often occur spontaneously and are similar to a lucid flying dream, as a common dream type.[10]

The theme of OBE further complicates afterlife narratives in which the postmortem appears in transphysical form similar to embodied appearance, often younger and healthy. There appears to be a spectrum of forms, from literal physical form, to variable subtle forms such as OBE and astral forms, to more refined forms such as spirits and angels as strictly nonphysical entities. It also seems plausible that human beings can transmute awareness from the strictly physical to more subtle and etheric forms depending on ability and training—many esoteric traditions claim to teach exactly such abilities.[11] Crisis events, accidents, sudden tragic or unexpected shock can jolt the body in such a way as to dislocate an aspect of self into its astral form. The body-mind, while stable, is also malleable, capable of unique perceptual dislocations based on training and other psychic influences or unique psychic abilities.

While there is considerable debate about the nature of OBE and its relationship to esoteric ideas of astral projection and other forms of subtle body awareness, nevertheless, from the perspective of lived experience, it seems as though a subtle body has actually separated from the physical body. I have had numerous experiences of this phenomena and vivid moments of specifically separating from the physical body, journeying about, and then returning to the body (which is usually resting but not necessarily asleep).[12] From the Wisdom perspective, subtle body events reflect a kind of *autopoiesis*, "self-making," that enhances awareness and extends the range of perceptions into alternate domains of experience. Ontologically we can question the relationships between subtle body experience and soul life, particularly afterlife and postmortem existence, which also seem to support a subtle body form.

While there is no general consensus on the relationship between soul and the subtle body, I do not believe that OBE or subtle body separation is an indication of soul leaving the body. I would describe it more as an aspect-projection while the actual departure of soul from body would result in death. In my own experiences, subtle body awareness does not seem like soul awareness—it seems more like an extension of soul-like qualities (including mental cognitions) projected into unique experiential domains, an enhancement of acute cognitive perceptions made more lucid through detachment from the body. In such a state I am completely able to think, reflect, and analyze my experience while it occurs; there is no disconnect from cognitive processes and there is a vivid, lived sense of an alternate reality as something far more profound than imaginal.

Another source of this type of phenomena is NDE, near-death experience, in which a person experiences a deathlike state, one in which there are no biological markers for life in the body, while simultaneously there is awareness in often subtle body form.[13] The many accounts of these experiences map to an awareness of being in a form similar to the body but not identical with it, or possibly of being aware without any bodily form, as in my own NDE. These experiences amplify the soulful aspects of almost dying but then returning to bodied life with new perspective and understanding. There is transpersonal Wisdom in such experience, an awakening to transphysical awareness that no longer depends upon bodily sensory perceptions. There is a sense of opening a horizon on transworld existence that is knowable, interactive, and populated by many other entities also capable of cognitive interactions.

My view is that NDE is also a soul aspect projection, that is, an extension of individual consciousness into an alternate state similar to postmortem life, but one that is incomplete in the sense that the individual recovers embodied life and does not die. Death would be a final separation of soul from body and the collapse of body into a reduced material-energetic form, lacking self-awareness (but not necessarily lacking some degree of sentience). The value of such experience, either as OBE projection or NDE, is the enhancement of awareness in a multimode context of perception, beyond strictly physical sensation, and more akin to vivid subtle body expression linked to a World Soul realm. In this case, the World Soul domain takes on ontological aspects that reference Being and Mystery as formative for subtle body experience in a transdimensional context. There is something that is also imaginal insofar as even in a subtle body state, there is active imagination, an ability to create imagery in a World Soul context that could then lead to future embodied forms.

What we experience in OBE or NDE is not simply projection but a synthesis, a unique integration of soul-aspect projection and creative discovery, participant in an unveiling of new context for growth and development, thus autopoiesis. However, it is important to understand that this "self-making" through altered states and subtle body awareness does not occur *de novo* ("from the beginning, anew") but has deep causality inseparable from our attitudes, beliefs, and worldview (however partial). What we experience is an enactment that extends our lived-world perceptions into another domain of experience itself shaped in some degree by beliefs and shared ideas or values. Simply stated, subtle body perception is an extension of our current world into a more enhanced world inseparable from what we imagine the world to be. There is a fusion of the imaginal and the actual as a creative synthesis, just as in embodied life we imagine what we later create, an institution, a center, a place of prayer and meditation. Imagination is a crucial aspect of subtle body development.

People who deny OBE or subtle body as anything other than phenomena based on a material cause (such as brain activity or neurophysiology response) reflect their own worldview more than the actual complex nature of the phenomena. One needs multiple experiences over a lifetime of exploration to truly grasp the complexity involved. The imaginal aspects alone are poorly understood and often conflated with phenomenal descriptions that lack all manner of nuance. There is a social and cultural aspect to such experience; there is a historical context and a psychic development aspect; there are also religious and anthropological influences that shape the experience; the experience cannot be reduced to pure phenomena nor is it possible to give a full description of the possible psychic contents. These phenomena are complex because mind is an inseparable feature of what manifests, and it follows a necessary path that may well begin with an imaged possibility that then manifests as actual ability.

Wisdom teaches a counterpoint, that learning about such phenomena requires humility rather than knowing or expertise, and acceptance of our limits in terms of what we think we comprehend in the face of ancient aspects of human experience. OBE, NDE, astral travel, soul projection, and afterlife encounters are all very old phenomena, by no means contemporary and have influenced religious and spiritual traditions worldwide. The Sophianic view is to recognize, affirm, and remain open to such phenomena without closure into a reductive theory that only empowers the theorist and does not illumine the phenomena. Theory is necessary and good, but it is only a window on very deep complexity; we still strive for comprehension far beyond any closure in a defining theory.

That we experience such phenomena is without question, and many people value that experience as life-changing; however, we do not comprehend the phenomena as much as respect and support further investigation of what the phenomena may imply psychologically, spiritually, and metaphysically. There is a profound ontology at work, one that eludes our immediate grasp; even when we have the direct experience, it still remains something of a mystery. As someone with a lifetime of such experiences I can say that I fully honor each experience and do not seek to enclose it in any specific theory other than to note its revelatory quality and its capacity to enhance the field of our awareness both individually and collectively. The subtle body appears as a bridge to other states and other domains of experience, perhaps imaged in unique ways but giving witness to a more complex reality beyond ordinary sensory life. The new Wisdom honors the phenomena, respects its manifestations, and does not seek to enclose it in premature and limited theories of cause or origin.

In turn this leads to an even more complex phenomenon, the existence of spirit beings of any kind or form, covering a wide spectrum of types and entities, all of which may seem utterly real in the moment of encounter. Angel encounters, spirit animals, fairies, guides, and masters, or aliens of a completely etheric or subtle body nature, seem to be common encounter types replete in the history of all world religions. Such encounters are not simply fantasies or imaginings but reflect actual vivid experiences of interactive encounter of a life-changing and profound nature.[14] Without debating the ontological status, I take such encounters to be real to those who experience them. Wisdom teaches us to respect the experience of others, and to acknowledge our own, as valid sources of possible insight (or not) whose content and quality must be tested in the actuality of daily life, not stored away as inexplicable encounters.

Wisdom requires a certain degree of fidelity to actual experience, not to theory or ideas about experience, but fidelity to the specifics of real encounter. We can bracket our attitudes toward the experience as we attempt to record and reflect on it in order to come to some degree of insight into its value and significance. The real test is the application of those insights to daily life and living—how does the experience relate to and enhance genuine insight regarding a valued way of life? Does it throw light on our development progress, illumine our relationships, enhance our understanding of nature and cosmos as well as society and history? How does my out-of-body or subtle body experience relate to these encountered by others? What about my existence between lives, what do I experience or remember in terms of something more than other postmortem souls?

Angel encounters are fairly common in Western religious traditions, particularly at death, as are devas and spirits (*shen*) in more Eastern traditions, shamans frequently talk about animal guides, and many folk traditions have tales of Little People, fairies, and the *sidhe* (or the *Tuatha Dé Danann*). In dreams and visions, as well as in dying, we can encounter a wide range of possible entities, some more mythic than others, but often conveying a sense of the numinous or sacred, a latent power or presence animating the entire dream. All of these entities, including many god and goddess traditions, reflect the human capacity for *sacred encounter*, for a participant sense of the value and import of such encounter as something more than the result of belief or ideation. Without doubt imagination plays a role as it does in all human cognitions, thus in itself imagination is no explanation, simply a context for examination. What matters is the lesson learned, the impact that carries over into waking life as a form of guidance and a felt sense of direction and purpose.

Rebirth in this context is part of the process by which we can encounter altered dimensions of awareness and contact with other beings. If death is transition, part of that process involves existence in an in-between state, as a creative domain of postmortem awareness. In that domain there are many other entities who vary in degrees of insight and spiritual knowledge. The postmortem are no more wise than in life and nonhuman spirits have their limitations; even "beings of light" seem to have perspective and beliefs. The creative interplay between postmortem beings in a World Soul context includes all these entities as relative expressions of wisdom, whereas even in that state, higher insights can flourish based on opening to transpersonal aspects beyond any specific entity. Reincarnation includes being between lives and in that state we can discover further opportunities for development beyond immediate contact with other entities.

The means by which Wisdom communicates insights are various and complex, inseparable from culture, language, religious beliefs, and social context and nuanced by disposition and character. The lesson learned goes far beyond the experience, like an arrow shot into its target, the hit is in the impact it makes on the recipient, the impression carried over into actual life issues, not on the arrow or the shooting. If the impact opens our eyes to a new context, to intimations of immortality and to a sacred basis operative behind the scenes of ordinary life, so much the better, but the curative effect is most effective when applied to the ongoing transmutation, to an alchemy of soul that leads to true insight, better judgment, and mature thought and action. What matters is what we do with the gifts we are given, rather than on their sources or cause. For the new Wisdom, such encounters are valid forms of experience, but the key question is not the encounter, but the outcome in terms of quality of life, maturity, and grounded understanding.

SIMPLICITY AND PURITY OF MIND

Reincarnation is a fascinating topic and reflects a plausible theory of continued survival after death and then rebirth in new form and circumstances without bringing closure to the topic of soul life or teleological goals. As an open-ended process, rebirth suggests ongoing opportunities for growth and development beyond the struggles of a given lifetime. Rebirth theory in Feminine Wisdom does not predict any goal or end to the process but simply urges us to accept the possibility of life after death and multiple future existences shaped by past choices and present conditions. The process view looks more to the past than to the future, insofar as we may remember past lives without being able to predict future lives. If a given lifetime is the consequence of multiple past-life actions and choices, then the present becomes the focal point for future development in which such past knowledge may play only a minor role.

Possibly we do not remember past lives because it frees us from the burden of history, liberating us from past bad choices, harmful actions, and hurtful situations not conducive to our present development. As a metaphysical principle, not remembering may be a psychic means for fostering better opportunity for new growth and discovery. The burden of past-life memories might be overwhelming or troublesome in terms of our relationships and goals. In my own case I have many past-life memories, and some of them have been quite challenging to integrate into my present conscious attitudes; knowledge of another person's past lives is also somewhat burdensome, like a lens placed over a relationship that changes the view and focus. Past-life memory is only ancillary knowledge and freedom from such memory may be a gift, one that allows for a more open horizon of possibilities.

Therefore, I do not regard belief in reincarnation as a necessary belief, only a plausible theory that may be more persuasive through the recovery of past-life experience. Wisdom in the present is the key attribute meant to guide our decisions and relations and cultivating that Wisdom does not require any past-life knowledge nor belief in reincarnation. In the present, even the current Dalai Lama (14th), whose entire identity is based on being the same soul reincarnated repeatedly as the Dalai Lama, does not remember his past lives— but this in no way impedes his actions or decisions.* Even though reincarnation is something added, that does not mean that it is not a primary aspect of Sophianic knowledge; in the larger cycles of nature and cosmos, death and resuscitation are intrinsic to the life pattern. Cycles reflect nature much more accurately than a lineal pattern, where lineal time is replete with cycles that make its measure possible.

Rebirth is a cosmic theme not simply a human phenomenon, and the very universe itself may proceed through cycles of death and rebirth; many cultures have noted the primacy of the life-death-rebirth cycle.[15] Reincarnation is a subtheme within the larger pattern of cycles that constitute cosmological processes on a scale far vaster than the life of the individual soul. And yet, the life of the soul is intrinsic to the very nature of the sentient cosmos, thus inseparable

---

*See Dalai Lama, "Reincarnation," on the website His Holiness, The 14th Dalai Lama of Tibet.

from the cycles that provide a living context for growth and development. We can take solace in the fact of forgetting, or not remembering, our actions and decisions in the past, but that not-knowing does not liberate us from the consequences of those actions. Perhaps it is easier to adapt and respond to what arises without the burden of its causality, simply facing what arises and then responding with courage and self-honesty.

The problem of causality is too complex to engage in this synopsis of Wisdom, it is a large topic that is not reducible to simplistic ideas of karma or destiny. What is often missed is the fact that causal consequences do not proceed from individual sources, but engage a wide range of sources, often collective and reiterative within the larger cycles of nature. We hardly see the consequence of action no matter how vividly we experience the outcome; we are carried by waves of the past in ways barely discernible. We struggle to stay afloat, manage our voyage, keep our balance, engage our skills—all in the context of powerful shaping influences beyond our immediate awareness. Wisdom teaches centeredness, creative stability, and adaptive skill in the face of change; our not-knowing must proceed in partnership with our partial knowing; we seek to harmonize the known in the context of the unknown; we mediate change through a mix of facts and suppositions.

Causality escapes our grasp; we work within the limits of the known but with a purpose to better understand what is not yet known. In this process rebirth offers opportunity for new discovery in the face of old habits; the slate is wiped clean so we can reinscribe new directives for better understanding. But still, we live on the surface because in the depths the old inscriptions still matter, still have effects, can still cause reaction and response. Therefore, Wisdom teaches an ever-deepening path of self-discovery in the context of world understanding; we must delve beneath the surface life to find meaning more securely grounded in the very fabric of space-time, through insight into natural cycles, cosmic processes, and self-development. Reincarnation is a developmental theme and an ontological expression of natural cycles, and its relationship to human experience requires a deep and thorough investigation.

Rebirth is an *expressive function* of our cyclical patterns of growth and development. We can hold on to a given worldview or set of beliefs, but those beliefs are all subject to change in the larger scale of world events and dynamic processes of encounter and cultural exchange. Wisdom teaches integrity as well as humility, a sense of purpose and direction dedicated to responsible ideals and values. Grounding in a deep-rooted sense requires an inner stability free from collective doubt and harmful or skeptical emotions; we grow through trust, faith in core values, responsible love, and determination to actualize a better way of life. Rebirth in that context requires both stability and creativity, a sense of individuation open to new insights; rebirth is a pattern of *refinement*, an alchemy of soul whose practice requires attention to changing and reshaping our values in accord with developing insights.[16]

The Wisdom view is not fixed but developmental, evolving through stages and states meant to reveal not-yet comprehended aspects of our being-in-the-world. We are veiled by our own lack of knowing; veil upon veil, we are hidden from our own potential and possibilities of knowing. As a veil is removed, something more shines through the density of our current knowledge and reveals additional depths awaiting our participation. This refinement is ongoing; it has no culmination other than the limits of an individual realization, a stage where refinement becomes a steady state, a sense of completion congruent with a specific spiritual path. But there is yet more refinement possible, beyond a given realization or enlightenment, and that realization requires death and rebirth. They say that enlightenment requires no rebirth; however, no rebirth does not mean the end of existence, it implies a more radically altered state beyond the body, perhaps total absorption in Being-as-Mystery, or continued existence in some altered spiritual form. Enlightenment is not terminal but transitional.

Embodied in the world and embedded in social and cultural life means adaptation to the processes of unveiling and in that process, simplicity is highly valued. We do not need to make any decision with regard to higher states or processes of enlightenment; we need only to attain a greater degree of maturity and Wisdom that guides our thoughts and relations. The future is open, and the possibilities of illumination are not enclosed by religious or spiritual traditions; regardless of authoritarian claims, there is no predetermined end to growth and development, particularly on a global scale. Simplicity requires an indeterminate view, one that accepts the given and known and remains open to future developments not seen by current teachings or individual states. Feminine Wisdom holds open the horizon of what is yet possible without surrendering a sense of integrity in what is known; this means being centered and open.

Alternative knowledge covers a broad spectrum of possible views, a rich cornucopia of fruitful insights that range across the entire continuum of what is knowable and valuable—yet not enclosed by possibilities yet to be discovered. In simplicity we can recognize the limits of even the most profound insights, an infinite horizon allows for creative discoveries far beyond what we assess as crucial to our current way of life. Simplicity is not lacking in intelligence nor profound insight, it reflects an open horizon toward the possible, improbable, and impossible. As emergent beings, our journey is far from complete and our Wisdom is limited by the horizons that define our experiences. New horizons open new possibilities for new understanding that can challenge and overturn former horizons and belief systems. Simplicity stays open without claiming to know or understand what may or may not emerge.

Finally, we come to purity of mind—that is, to a condition in which the participant is no longer imbued with the falsehoods of knowledge or expertise. All knowing is limited, even if profound and insightful, and purity of mind requires us to accept the value of not-knowing as a legitimate stance toward everything we know and experience. Not-knowing acts as a buffer between our actual knowledge base and a sense of inflation based on knowing that tends to epitomize our insights as an unimpeachable source of truth. As knowledge is relative to experience and maturity, knowing (including gnosis) does not indicate a final end or completeness, always there is something more that can alter, shift, and modify what we think of as an unchanging certainty. Closure into a stance of inflexible certainty is not an indication of maturity, only an unnecessarily rigid posture asserting authority within a circumscribed domain of limited expertise. Often this posture is a stance aimed at controlling the thoughts and actions of others in service to an ideology that benefits the subscribers and empowers only a limited class of leaders or experts.

A more flexible attitude recognizes the alterity at work among human beings, where diversity, multiplicity, and divergent views are normative and part of the process of discovery, with all its ups, downs, and uncertainties. Purity of mind relates to the open state, perhaps more innocent and clearer, that allows what appears without overly celebrating its worth or value. Over time, through multiple rebirths, value will retain its worth, what appears will be sustained if its value is high enough and if its worth impacts more than a privileged few. Purity accepts what appears but sees it as passing phenomena whose import will manifest, to some degree, over time. Patience is part of this process of discovery, seeing and then waiting to see what evolves. Refinement requires multiple lives, new birth, and multiple rebirths to reach a genuine purity capable of reverence and clarity, without emphasis on one's own attainments.

This does not mean that Wisdom is strictly individual, but it does mean that worth and value can be learned and embodied by dedication and self-discipline that does not depend on expertise and esoteric knowledge. Wisdom is refined through life experience dedicated to understanding ever more deeply the formative currents and eddies of social life in the context of personal cycles of discovery, not as experts or masters or guides, but as authentic individuals living in accord with values professed to be true. Speak golden words and then do more than what you speak. With purity of mind, we can let go of our own accomplishments and learning; without sacrificing integrity or understanding, we can allow the future to shine its light into the yet unseen potential awaiting further discovery.

Purity of mind reflects a way of knowing, a Wisdom-based intuitive understanding of how mind and cosmos interact, how thought and action image the world in order to create or express meaning. A pure mind is a good mind, a healthy mind, a mind and soul dedicated to the realization of potential based on nonharmful values that seek to support positive, creative growth. A pure mind is not based in skepticism and doubt but proceeds through conviction and commitment to those values that support positive, loving relations and communal well-being. A pure mind is receptive to the feminine view, to Sophia as a symbol of a Wisdom paradigm whose diverse roots extend into nature and cosmos and encompass the worth of all beings without prejudice. A pure mind is decisive without being authoritarian and able to make judgments without bias that seeks to benefit from such judgment.

The pure mind is quiet, open, receptive, and stable—recognizing the not-known as the doorway to innovation and rebirth. The pure mind is constantly reborn through decades and cycles of dedicated effort in refinement and appreciation of the indwelling sacred, the very source of Wisdom. The pure mind is humble in the sense of recognizing limitations within one's self and yet living with integrity and honesty, fostering trust, love, and appreciation. The pure mind is a work of a lifetime and cannot be acquired through any particular altered state; the pure mind is a ground state elevated to conscious awareness as illumined knowing, with limits but without regrets. The pure mind is friendly, joyful, relaxed, and open to the greater horizons known by others; the pure mind is at its depth, communal and yet individual. Wisdom teaches us to cultivate such a mind and to know that our attainments are relative to the attainments of others; there is no final goal, only process and discovery in a cyclical universe of infinite scope. Selah! Salam! Peace!

The Masculine Logos

This work has offered a view of Wisdom as seen through the lens of a more feminized epistemology as a way of knowing whose value system is markedly different from many current views of Wisdom based on specific masculine codes of behavior or predetermined beliefs or fixed moral codes. The new masculine logos evolves through partnership with variable feminine views as a soulful relationship based in equality and shared values while prioritizing the value of all our relationships. The process of knowing comes not through expertise or specialized knowledge, be it scientific, humanistic, or religious, but instead it is based on self-knowledge and full attention to the boundaries of that knowledge. It is a partnered wisdom, shared and co-developed.

The key issue in this emergent hieros logos is being in relationship, that is, not as an isolated logos based on self-reflection and masculine values, but instead, developing values shaped through the priority of male-female-family thinking and belief. This partnership in thought and belief reflects a spiritual practice, not simply pragmatism or a current intellectual fashion. An enduring partnership requires continual commitment to the relative status of engaged partners; equal does not mean identical or the same, it means differentiating our differences and respecting them without abandoning integrity. Each person has a right to their views but in a context of mutual debate and discussion, respect, and gratitude, there needs to be a sense of compromise and cooperation directed toward a more integral partnership. Those rights are grounded in moral attitudes and practices that seek to do no harm to others while also fostering equal rights and social harmony.

Both love and respect are foundational to such relationships, a responsible love and honest respect that extends to all our relations, not just to privileged others. The love of ideas is not that kind of love, adept intellectual ability is not the marker of the emergent masculine logos. This refined and reborn logos thrives on positive, cooperative relationships as a responsible agent seeking to foster that love in others through exemplary behavior and honest self-appraisal. Such exemplary behavior does not require any sacrifice of intellectual interest or ability; what is required is to direct those interests and abilities toward a better way of shared life. This sharing requires intellectual integrity and critical thinking, subjective acuity, and psychic insight into the minds and hearts of others. It is not based on a specific ideology or some form of mass consensus but an individuated understanding in relationship to the unique character and abilities of each person. Partnership respects differences.

Our concerns, aspirations, ideals, and so on reflect our spiritual practices and our developing worldview; such differentiation does not collapse into indistinct mass beliefs but forms unique orientations amidst a complex array of other worldviews. Diversity should foster thinking and self-reflection, not withdrawal into defensive, collective attitudes often resistant and harmful to others. The new masculine logos is not authoritarian but dialogical, open to discussion, able to understand an alternate point of view, receptive to multiple perspectives without losing sight of one's core beliefs. The masculine logos is a reformed logos—no longer prioritizing authority or dogmatic rationality—by giving full attention to feminine perspectives, shared ethical concerns and ideas, receptive and responsive to the beliefs of others.

I regard integrity as a dynamic state open to change and development but stable and enduring in the face of other beliefs or value systems. To have integrity means to know what one believes and why those beliefs matter, without trying to claim the superiority of those beliefs nor using them as a means to demonstrate the weaknesses of other ways of thinking or acting. Critical subjectivity is quite different from the criticism of others who think or believe differently. I frequently note the absence of such subjectivity in those who are the most critical of others. Critical subjectivity proceeds through a careful analysis of one's own beliefs and attitudes not only in terms of the formative origins of such beliefs but also, more importantly, on the impact of those beliefs on the hearts and minds of others. Critical subjectivity is a qualitative attitude, one that seeks to understand the internal life of thought and belief in relationship to core values based on a cooperative ethos of feminized mutual concerns. Such concerns do not exclude others as the circle of influence and affect creates a context for possible discovery in and through others who may think very differently and hold diverse values.

I understand the limits of my own thinking and beliefs; I know there is fallibility in my views and writing, but I nevertheless seek to express those views in a context of shared discovery. The masculine logos of my intent is to learn, to hear others, to share, and to transform insights to better comprehend what is only partially understood in a present context. I deeply believe in the views of Wisdom expressed in this work, but I also know there are other ways and other discourses equally valuable and worthy of reflection; among those discourses feminine ideas and values have acted as a stimulus to hone my subjectivity to a sharper degree of relative self-awareness. I am grateful to the women in my life and their spiritual influence on reshaping my views, and I fully honor the Divine Feminine as source and base for the many internal transformations I have undergone.

The new masculine logos is word-abled, that is, it flows forth from a source of inspiration that takes verbal form as a hieros logos, sacred words, a teaching whose source is from the deep well of the soul seeking Wisdom. And Wisdom teaches receptivity to the spontaneity and flow of that speaking, not through the brute logic of opposites, but instead through the complex labyrinth of soul's becoming, through the logos of poetic insight, story, narrative, dialogue, and metaphoric expressions. This logos is not strictly rational nor is it simply poetic, rather it forms a coherent narrative unburdened by any compelling logic of necessary or inflexible truths serving an ideological code. As a narrative about Wisdom, there is much that is metaphoric, symbolic, and poetic but also much that is rational and analytic, based on virtue-driven ethics whose purpose is open to continued transformation and shared discovery.

The core metaphor of discovery as a metaphysical practice requires a willingness to seek deeper insight beyond the currently known, while also valuing appropriate behavior and quality in all our relationships. The "sacred" character of such writing arises through the sincerity and intent of purpose, to better communicate genuine Wisdom (however limited) as a way to encourage the development of such Wisdom in others—who must then further the path in their own terms. The new masculine logos not only speaks from the heart but also *hears the words of others* and values them deeply; without hearing the words of others we are far too limited by our own beliefs and thought-worlds. Sacred speech has a corollary in *sacred hearing*, the ability to hear the sacred resonant in the words of others.

Wisdom for the new masculine logos is not about words but actual lived experience assimilated into well-integrated understanding and then, when possible, communicated in various media—words, poetry, music, art, science, gesture, performance, ritual, social actions, and in many other ways. Such Wisdom does not prioritize language over experience nor ideas over lived truths; it is a Wisdom that can be communicated with a glance or nod; there is no limit on its variable expressions. Words are only one means and easily misappropriated by an inattentive listener, just as music fails to communicate to those less sensitive to its nuances. There is no perfect medium for expressing this Wisdom; every media has its limits and boundaries; some may excel in one genre and others in another genre. Silence is also an expressive medium for Wisdom, as the poem "Thunder" records of Wisdom, "I shall be silent among those who are silent"—in silence Wisdom dawns beyond all words, concepts, and mental activities.[1]

Silence is the ground of sentience, the ever-living presence abides therein, unexpressed but fully active. Silence is the handmaiden of Wisdom and serves her as the closest of her helpers; they say Silence preceded Wisdom as a necessary Aeonic precursor for Wisdom's forthcoming. If you seek Wisdom then also seek silence of mind and calmness of spirit; a quiet heart open to the Infinite provides the context for her dawning. In that dawning there is light within light and depth within depths, fullness beyond fathoming and emptiness that lacks nothing. And the twin Aeon of Silence is Clarity, a luminous perception of depth and fullness that reveals the web of possible meanings. With clarity we come to understand the nuances of Spirit, beyond the limits of language.

Wisdom and Love are the twin pillars at the entrance to Sophia's temple and the accolades heard within are poetic voices, hymns seeking to harmonize what is knowable with the yet unknown. Listen carefully and you will hear the sound of your thinking magnified and refined by a thousand others, no less aware than you, no less valuable than the source from which they receive inspirations. True Wisdom is immeasurable and cannot be fully described, only embodied and expressed through whatever gifts Wisdom bestows. Great is her grace and precious are her insights. We honor best through what we become and what we offer as examples of what might be. May we be worthy of remembrance and able to add, even in the slightest way, a gift that enhances the understanding of another. Blessings be, thank you for your kindness and attention.

Notes

PREFACE

1. Sextus the Pythagorean, "Pythagorean Sentences" (#86), in Uždavinys, *The Golden Chain*, 42.
2. Bender, *The New Metaphysicals*.
3. Cheetham, *Green Man, Earth Angel*.

CHAPTER 1. PRAXIS OF INCARNATION (BODY)

1. Kajava, "Hestia Hearth, Goddess, and Cult."
2. Freeman, "Toward a Phenomenology of Mood."
3. Biletzki and Matar, "Ludwig Wittgenstein," sec. 3.4 "Language-games."
4. Irwin, *Reincarnation in America*, 361–80; see also Stevenson, *Children Who Remember Previous Lives*.

CHAPTER 2. PRAXIS OF RELATEDNESS (SOUL)

1. Yogananda, *Autobiography of a Yogi*, 478.
2. Irwin, *The Dream Seekers*, 130–31; see also, Jones, *Sanapia*.
3. Irwin, *The Dream Seekers*.
4. Markale, *The Grail*.
5. Hauck, *The Emerald Tablet*.
6. Greyson, "Implications of Near-Death Experiences," 37–45; Ring, *Heading Toward Omega*.

CHAPTER 3. PRAXIS OF AWARENESS (MIND)

1. Grosso, "The 'Transmission' Model of Mind and Body," 79–113; see also Hameroff and Penrose, "Consciousness in the Universe."
2. Hart, *From Information to Transformation*.
3. See Irwin, *Sophos Ontology*.
4. Emmons, "Is Spirituality an Intelligence?"
5. See Irwin, *Dreams Beyond Time*.
6. Sears, "The Construction, Preliminary Validation, and Correlates of a Dream-Specific Scale for Mystical Experience."
7. Kuiken, Lee, Eng, and Singh, "The Influence of Impactful Dreams on Self-Perceptual Depth and Spiritual Transformation."
8. Irwin, "Supernal Dreaming."
9. Irwin, *Dreams Beyond Time*; see also Deslauriers, "Dreamwork in the Light of Emotional and Spiritual Intelligence"; and Larsen and Verne, "The Transformational Power of Dreaming."
10. Krippner, Bogzaran, and de Carvalho, *Extraordinary Dreams and How to Work with Them*.
11. Puri, *From Amma's Heart*.

PART TWO. THE GREATER MYSTERIES

1. See Robinson, "Thunder," 297–303.

CHAPTER 4. MYSTERY OF SALVATION
(HIEROS LOGOS)

1. Ryan, "Wisdom."
2. Lachman, *The Secret Teachers of the Western World*, 27–56.
3. Irwin, *Reincarnation in America*.
4. Smitsman and Houston, *The Quest of Rose*.
5. Irwin, *The Alchemy of Soul*.
6. Anderson, *The Feminine Face of God*.
7. Corbin, *Jung, Buddhism, and the Incarnation of Sophia*, 81.
8. Irwin, *Sophos Ontology*.
9. Heron, *Participatory Spirituality*.
10. Bender, *The New Metaphysicals*.
11. Hwang and Cargill, *She Rises*.

CHAPTER 5. MYSTERY OF DEEP UNION (HIEROS GAMOS)

1. Kripal, *Authors of the Impossible*, 254.
2. Leloup, *The Gospel of Mary Magdalene*; King, *The Gospel of Mary of Magdala*.
3. Mead, *Pistis Sophia*; see also Irwin, *Awakening to Spirit*, 355–58.
4. Wizemann and Pardue, *Exploring the Biological Contributions to Human Health*.
5. *Corpus Hermeticum*, Book 1; see Salaman, van Oyun, Wharton, and Mahé, *The Way of Hermes*.
6. Wilkinson, *The Complete Gods and Goddesses of Ancient Egypt*, 150–52.
7. Irwin, *Visionary Worlds*.
8. Hadot, *The Veil of Isis*, 264–65, 238–43.
9. Conforti, *Field, Form, and Fate*.
10. Feder, *Fractals*, 11.
11. Peitgen, Jürgens, and Saupe, *Chaos and Fractals*.
12. Radhakrishnan, *The Bhagavad Gītā*, 269–90 (chap. 11).
13. Cited from the *Chrysopoeia* [or gold-making] *of Cleopatra*, attributed to Cleopatra the Alchemist written in the first centuries CE, see Wikipedia (website), s.v. "Chrysopoeia."
14. Laszlo, *Science and the Reenchantment of the Cosmos*, 23–35.
15. Kastrup, "The Universe in Consciousness," 125–55; Hameroff and Penrose, "Consciousness in the Universe," 39–78.
16. Gleiser, *The Island of Knowledge*.
17. Irwin, *Sophos Ontology*.
18. Ferrer, *Participation in the Mystery*.

CHAPTER 6. MYSTERY OF THE WORLD SOUL (PSYCHE KOSMOU)

1. Irwin, "World and Soul: An Alchemy of Conjoined Loves," 17–22, 117.
2. Irwin, "A World Full of Gods," 27–52; see also Irwin, "Panpsychism," 417–28.
3. Schroll, *Transpersonal Ecosophy*.
4. Conforti, *Field, Form, and Fate*, 18–29.
5. Koch, "A 'Complex' Theory of Consciousness."
6. Irwin, *Awakening to Spirit*, 355–58.
7. Wisdom of Solomon 7:22–26, in *The New Oxford Annotated Bible with Apocryphal / Deuterocanonical Books*, 66.

8. Conze, *Buddhist Wisdom Books.*

9. Teilhard de Chardin, *The Future of Man*, 55.

10. Rahman, "Dream, Imagination, and 'Álam al-Mithāl," 167–80.

11. Corbin, "Mundus Imaginalis or the Imaginary and the Imaginal."

12. Arcangel, *Afterlife Encounters*; Greyson, *After.*

13. Holden, Greyson, and James, *The Handbook of Near-Death Experiences*; see also Irwin, *Reincarnation in America*, 361–79.

14. Kripal, *Mutants and Mystics.*

15. Otto, *The Idea of the Holy.*

16. Drolma, *Love on Every Breath.*

CHAPTER 7. MYSTERY OF REBIRTH (METEMPSYCHOSIS)

1. Irwin, *Reincarnation in America.*

2. Suzuki, *Zen Mind, Beginner's Mind.*

3. Maslow, *Toward a Psychology of Being.*

4. Irwin, *Reincarnation in America.*

5. Irwin, "American Reincarnation: A Brief History," 222.

6. Carter, *Science and the Near-Death Experience*, 109–12, also see 104–35 for an overview of research in the area.

7. Samuel and Johnson, *Religion and the Subtle Body in Asia and the West.*

8. Graf and Johnston, *Ritual Texts for the Afterlife.*

9. Samuel and Johnson, *Religion and the Subtle Body.*

10. Irwin, "On Lucid Dreaming."

11. See Judge, *The Ocean of Theosophy.*

12. Irwin, "On Lucid Dreaming."

13. Greyson, *After.*

14. Kripal, *Authors of the Impossible.*

15. Henderson and Oakes, *Wisdom of the Serpent.*

16. Irwin, *Alchemy of Soul.*

CLOSING: THE MASCULINE LOGOS

1. Robinson, "Thunder," 298.

Bibliography

Anderson, Sherry Ruth. *The Feminine Face of God: The Unfolding of the Sacred in Women.* New York: Bantam, 2010. Kindle edition.

Arcangel, Dianne. *Afterlife Encounters: Ordinary People, Extraordinary Experiences.* Charlottesville, VA: Hampton Road Publishing, 2005.

Bender, Courtney. *The New Metaphysicals: Spirituality and the American Religious Imagination.* Chicago: University of Chicago Press, 2010.

Biletzki, Anat, and Anat Matar. "Ludwig Wittgenstein." *Stanford Encyclopedia of Philosophy*, edited by Edward N. Zalta (website). Spring 2020.

Carter, Chris. *Science and the Near-Death Experience.* Rochester, VT: Inner Traditions, 2010.

Cheetham, Tom. *Green Man, Earth Angel: The Prophetic Tradition and the Battle for the Soul of the World.* Albany: State University of New York Press, 2004.

———. *Imaginal Love: The Meanings of Imagination in Henry Corbin and James Hillman.* Washington, DC: Spring Publications, 2015.

Chrysopoeia of Cleopatra the Alchemist. Wikipedia (website), s.v. "Chrysopoeia." Last edited on November 20, 2024.

Conforti, Michael. *Field, Form, and Fate: Patterns in Mind, Nature, and Psyche.* Dallas: Spring Publications, 1999.

Conze, Edward, trans. *Buddhist Wisdom Books: The Diamond Sutra, The Heart Sutra.* New York: Harper & Row Publishers, 1972.

Corbin, Henri. *Jung, Buddhism, and the Incarnation of Sophia.* Rochester, VT: Inner Traditions, 2014.

———. "Mundus Imaginalis or the Imaginary and the Imaginal." In *Swedenborg and Esoteric Islam*, translated by Leonard Fox. West Chester, PA: Swedenborg Foundation, 1995. Originally published in 1964.

Deslauriers, Daniel. "Dreamwork in the Light of Emotional and Spiritual Intelligence." *Journal of Advanced Development* 9 (2000): 105–22.

Drolma, Lama Palden. *Love on Every Breath: Tonglen Meditation for Transforming Pain into Joy*. Navato, CA: New World Library, 2019.

Emmons, Robert A. "Is Spirituality an Intelligence? Motivation, Cognition, and the Psychology of Ultimate Concern." *International Journal for the Psychology of Religion* 10, no. 1 (2000): 3–26.

Emmons, Robert, and Michael McCullough, eds. *The Psychology of Gratitude*. New York: Oxford University Press, 2004.

Feder, Jens. *Fractals*. New York: Springer Science+Business Media, 1988.

Ferrer, Jorge. *Participation in the Mystery: Transpersonal Essays in Psychology, Education, and Religion*. Albany: State University of New York Press, 2017.

———. *Revisioning Transpersonal Theory: A Participatory Vision of Human Spirituality*. Albany: State University of New York Press, 2002.

Ficino, Marsilio. *Book of Life*. Translated by Charles Boer. Dallas: Spring Publications, 1992.

Freeman, Lauren. "Toward a Phenomenology of Mood." *Southern Journal of Philosophy* 52, no. 4 (2014): 445–76.

Gardner, Howard. *Five Minds for the Future*. Boston: Harvard Business School Press, 2007.

Gleiser, Marcelo. *The Island of Knowledge*. New York: Hachette Book Group, 2015.

Graf, Fritz, and Sarah Iles Johnston. *Ritual Texts for the Afterlife: Orpheus and the Bacchic Gold Tablets*. London: Routledge Press, 2007.

Greyson, Bruce. *After: A Doctor Explores What Near-Death Experiences Reveal About Life and Beyond*. New York: St. Martin's Press eBook, 2021.

———. "Implications of Near-Death Experiences for a Post-Materialist Psychology." *Psychology of Religion and Spirituality* 21, no. 1 (2010): 37–45.

Grosso, Michael. "The 'Transmission' Model of Mind and Body: A Brief History." In *Beyond Physicalism: Toward Reconciliation of Science and Spirituality*, edited by Edward F. Kelly, Adam Crabtree, and Paul Marshall. Lanham, MD: Rowman & Littlefield, 2015.

Hadot, Pierre. *The Veil of Isis*. Cambridge, MA: Harvard University Press, 2006.

Hameroff, Stuart, and Roger Penrose. "Consciousness in the Universe: A Review of the 'Orch OR' Theory." *Physics of Life Reviews* 11 (2014): 39–78.

Hart, Tobin. *From Information to Transformation: Education for the Evolution of Consciousness*. New York: Peter Lang Publishing, 2007.

Hauck, Dennis H. *The Emerald Tablet: Alchemy for Personal Transformation*. New York: Arkana / Penguin, 1999.

Henderson, Joseph L., and Maud Oakes. *Wisdom of the Serpent: The Myths of Death, Rebirth and Resurrection.* N.p.: Borodino Books, 2017. Kindle edition.

Heron, John. *Participatory Spirituality: A Farewell to Authoritarian Religion.* Morrisville, NC: Lulu Press, 2006.

Hillman, James. *Re-Visioning Psychology.* New York: Harper & Row, 1977.

Holden, Janice M., Bruce Greyson, and Debbie James, eds. *The Handbook of Near-Death Experiences: Thirty Years of Investigation.* Santa Barbara, CA: Praeger Publishers, 2009.

Hwang, Helen, and Kaalii Cargill, eds. *She Rises: Why Goddess Feminism, Activism, and Spirituality?* Lytle Creek, CA: Mago Books, 2015. Kindle edition.

Irwin, Lee. *The Alchemy of Soul: The Art of Spiritual Transformation.* Issaquah, WA: Lorian Press, 2007.

———. "American Reincarnation: A Brief History." *Religions* 8, no. 10 (2017): 222.

———. *Awakening to Spirit: On Life, Illumination, and Being.* Albany: State University of New York Press, 1999.

———. "The Divine Sophia: Isis, Achamoth, and Ialdabaoth." *Alexandria: Journal of Western Cosmological Traditions* 3 (1995): 51–81.

———. *Dreams Beyond Time: On Sacred Encounter and Spiritual Transformation.* Lanham, MD: Rowman & Littlefield, 2022.

———. *The Dream Seekers: Native American Visionary Traditions of the Great Plains.* Albany: State University of New York Press, 1994.

———. *The Labyrinths of Love: On Psyche, Soul, and Self.* Lanham, MD: Rowman & Littlefield, 2019.

———. "On Lucid Dreaming: Memory, Meaning, and Imagination." In *Lucid Dreaming: New Perspectives on Consciousness in Sleep*, vol. 1, edited by Ryan Hurd and Kelly Bulkeley. Berkeley, CA: Praeger, 2014.

———. "Panpsychism." In *Cambridge Handbook of Western Esotericism*, edited by Glenn Magee. New York: Cambridge University Press, 2016.

———. *Reincarnation in America: An Esoteric History.* Lanham, MD: Rowman & Littlefield, 2017.

———. *Sophos Ontology: On Post Traditional Spirituality.* Lanham, MD: Lexington Press, 2024.

———. "Supernal Dreaming: On Myth and Metaphysics." *Religions* 11, no. 11 (2020): 552.

———. *Visionary Worlds: The Making and Unmaking of Reality.* Albany: State University of New York Press, 1996.

————. "World and Soul: An Alchemy of Conjoined Loves." *Elixir: The Journal of Consciousness, Conscience, and Culture* 2 (2006): 17–22, 117.

————. "A World Full of Gods: Panpsychism and the Paradigms of Esotericism." In *Esotericism, Religion, and Nature*, edited by Arthur Versluis, Lee Irwin, and Melinda Phillips. East Lansing: Michigan State University Press, 2010.

Jones, David. *Sanapia: Comanche Medicine Woman*. New York: Holt, Rinehart, and Winston, 1972.

Judge, William Q. *The Ocean of Theosophy*. Los Angeles: Theosophy Company, 1987.

Jung, Carl G. "Concerning Rebirth." In *Four Archetypes: Mother/Rebirth/Spirit/Trickster*, translated by R. F. C. Hull. Princeton, NJ: Princeton University Press, 1973.

————. *Memories, Dreams, Reflections*. Edited by Aniela Jaffe and translated by Clara and Richard Winston. Rev. ed. New York: Vintage Books, 1989. Originally published in 1961.

Kajava, Mika. "Hestia Hearth, Goddess, and Cult." *Harvard Studies in Classical Philology* 102 (2004): 1–20.

Kastrup, Bernardo. "The Universe in Consciousness." *Journal of Consciousness Studies* 25, nos. 5–6 (2018): 125–55.

King, Karen L. *The Gospel of Mary of Magdala: Jesus and the First Woman Apostle*. Temecula, CA: Polebridge Press, Westar Institute, 2003.

Koch, Christof. "A 'Complex' Theory of Consciousness: Is Complexity the Secret to Sentience, to a Panpsychic View of Consciousness?" *Scientific American*, July 1, 2009.

Kripal, Jeffery. *Authors of the Impossible: The Paranormal and the Sacred*. Chicago: University of Chicago Press, 2010.

————. *Mutants and Mystics: Science Fiction, Superhero Comics, and the Paranormal*. Chicago: University of Chicago Press, 2011.

Krippner, Stanley, Fariba Bogzaran, and Andre Percia de Carvalho. *Extraordinary Dreams and How to Work with Them*. Albany: State University of New York Press, 2002.

Kuiken, Don, Ming-Ni Lee, Tracy Eng, and Terry Singh. "The Influence of Impactful Dreams on Self-Perceptual Depth and Spiritual Transformation." *Dreaming* 16, no. 4 (2006): 258–79.

Lachman, Gary. *The Secret Teachers of the Western World*. New York: Jeremy P. Tarcher, 2015.

Larson, and Tom Verner. *The Transformational Power of Dreaming: Discovering the Wishes of the Soul*. Rochester, VT: Inner Traditions, 2017.

Laszlo, Ervin. *Science and the Reenchantment of the Cosmos: The Rise of the Integral Vision of Reality.* Rochester, VT: Inner Traditions, 2006.

Leloup, Jean-Yves. *The Gospel of Mary Magdalene.* Rochester, VT: Inner Traditions, 2002.

Markale, Jean. *The Grail: The Celtic Origins of the Sacred Icon.* Rochester, VT: Inner Traditions, 1999.

Maslow, Abraham H. *Toward a Psychology of Being.* New York: Van Nostrand Reinhold, 1968.

McCraty, Rollin, Mike Atkinson, Dana Tomasino, and Raymond Trevor Bradley. "The Coherent Heart, Heart–Brain Interactions, Psychophysiological Coherence, and the Emergence of System-Wide Order." *Integral Review: A Transdisciplinary and Transcultural Journal for New Thought, Research, and Praxis* 5, no. 2 (2009): 1–115.

Mead, George R. S. *Pistis Sophia: The Gnostic Tradition of Mary Magdalene, Jesus, and His Disciples.* New York: Dover Publications, 2005. Originally published in 1921.

Metzger, Bruce, and Roland Murphy, eds. *The New Oxford Annotated Bible with Apocryphal / Deuterocanonical Books.* New York: Oxford University Press, 1991.

Miller, John P. *Education and the Soul.* Albany: State University of New York Press, 2000.

Netherton, Morris. *Past Lives Therapy: Past Life Regression.* Special Edition. N.p.: Past Life Therapy Center, 2013. Kindle edition.

Newen, Albert, and Leon De Bruin, eds. *The Oxford Handbook of 4E Cognitions.* Oxford: Oxford University Press, 2018.

Otto, Rudolph. *The Idea of the Holy: An Inquiry into the Non-Rational Factor in the Idea of the Divine and Its Relation to the Rational.* New York: Oxford University Press, 1969. Originally published in 1923.

Peitgen, Heinz-Otto, Hartmut Jürgens, and Dietmar Saupe. *Chaos and Fractals: New Frontiers of Science.* New York: Springer-Verlag, 2004.

Phillips, Stephen H. *Yoga, Karma, and Rebirth: A Brief History and Philosophy.* New York: Columbia University Press, 2009.

Puri, Swami Amritaswarupananda. *From Amma's Heart: Conversations with Sri Mata Amritanandamayi Devi.* Kerala, India: Amrita Books, 2010.

Radhakrishnan, S. *The Bhagavad Gītā.* New York: Harper Torchbooks, 1973.

Rahman, Fazlur. "Dream, Imagination, and ʿĀlam al-Mithāl." *Islamic Studies* 3, no. 2 (1964): 167–80.

Ratcliffe, Matthew. "Heidegger's Attunement and the Neuropsychology of Emotion." *Phenomenology and the Cognitive Sciences* 1 (2002): 287–312.

Ring, Kenneth. *Heading Toward Omega: In Search of the Meaning of Near-Death Experience*. N.p.: Amazon Digital Publishing, 2011. Kindle edition.

Robinson, James S., ed., "Thunder: Perfect Mind." In *The Nag Hammadi Library*. San Francisco: HarperSanFrancisco, 1990.

Rubik, Beverly, David Muehsam, Richard Hammerschlag, and Shamini Jain. "Biofield Science and Healing: History, Terminology, and Concepts." *Global Advances in Health and Medicine* 4 (2015): 8–14.

Ruether, Rosemary. *Goddesses and the Divine Feminine: A Western Religious History*. Berkeley: University of California Press, 2005.

Ryan, Sharon. "Wisdom." *Stanford Encyclopedia of Philosophy*, edited by Edward N. Zalta (website). 2018.

Salaman, Clement, Dorine van Oyun, William W. Wharton, and Jean-Pierre Mahé, eds. and trans. *The Way of Hermes*. Rochester, VT: Inner Traditions, 2004.

Samuel, Geoffrey, and Jay Johnson, eds. *Religion and the Subtle Body in Asia and the West: Between Mind and the Body*. New York: Routledge, 2013.

Schaup, Susanne. *Sophia: Aspects of the Divine Feminine Past and Present*. York Beach, ME: Nicholas-Hays, 1997.

Schipflinger, Thomas. *Sophia-Maria: A Holistic Vision of Creation*. York Beach, ME: Samuel Weiser, 1998.

Schroll, Mark A., ed. *Transpersonal Ecosophy: Theory, Methods, and Clinical Assessments*. Llanrhaeadr-ym-Mochnant, Wales: Psychoid Books, 2016.

Scott, Walter, trans. and ed. *Hermetica*. 4 vols. Boston: Shambhala Press, 1985.

Sears, Robert. "The Construction, Preliminary Validation, and Correlates of a Dream-Specific Scale for Mystical Experience." *Journal for the Scientific Study of Religion* 54, no. 1 (2015): 134–55.

Smitsman, Anneloes, and Jean Houston. *The Quest of Rose: The Cosmic Keys of Our Future Becoming*. Hudson, Canada: Oxygen Publishing, 2021.

Spangler, David. *Introduction to Incarnational Spirituality*. Everett, WA: Lorian Press, 2011.

Stanghellini, Giovanni. "Clinical Phenomenology: A Method for Care?" *Philosophy, Psychiatry, & Psychology* 18, no. 1 (2011): 25–29.

Stenner, Paul. "A.N. Whitehead and Subjectivity." *Subjectivity* 22 (2008): 90–109.

Stern, Jesse. *Edgar Cayce's Mysteries of Reincarnation: Intimates Through Time*. New York: New American Library, 1993.

Stevenson, Ian. *Children Who Remember Previous Lives: A Question of Reincarnation*. Charlottesville: University Press of Virginia, 1987.

Suzuki, Shunryu. *Zen Mind, Beginner's Mind*. Boston: Weatherhill Press, 2006.

Teilhard de Chardin, Pierre. *The Future of Man*. New York: Harper Torchbooks, 1963.

———. *The Phenomenon of Man*. Translated by Bernard Wall. New York: Harper & Row Publishers, 1959.

Uždavinys, Algis, ed. *The Golden Chain: An Anthology of Pythagorean and Platonic Philosophy*. Bloomington, IN: World Wisdom, 2004.

Wade, Jenny. *Transcendent Sex: When Lovemaking Opens the Veil*. New York: Gallery Books, 2004.

Wambach, Helen. *Reliving Past Lives: The Evidence Under Hypnosis*. New York: Barnes and Noble, 2000. Originally published in 1978.

Welter, Albert. "Mahakasyapa's Smile. Silent Transmission and the Kung-an (Koan) Tradition." In *The Koan: Texts and Contexts in Zen Buddhism*, edited by Steven Heine and Dale S. Wright. Oxford, UK: Oxford University Press, 2000.

Whitehead, Alfred N. *Process and Reality*. Corrected ed. New York: Free Press, 1985. Originally published in 1928.

Wilkinson, Richard. *The Complete Gods and Goddesses of Ancient Egypt*. New York: Thames & Hudson, 2003.

Wizemann, T. M., and M. L. Pardue, eds. *Exploring the Biological Contributions to Human Health: Does Sex Matter?* Institute of Medicine (US) Committee on Understanding the Biology of Sex and Gender Differences. Washington, DC: National Academies Press, 2001.

Yogananda, Paramahamsa. *Autobiography of a Yogi*. Los Angeles: Self-Realization Fellowship, 1979. Originally published in 1946.

Index